# AMBIGUOUS RELATIONS

# AMBIGUOUS

DANIEL
BRADBURD

# RELATIONS

KIN,
CLASS,
AND
CONFLICT
AMONG
KOMACHI
PASTORALISTS

SMITHSONIAN INSTITUTION PRESS

WASHINGTON AND LONDON

Copyright © 1990 by
Smithsonian Institution
All rights reserved

Edited by Susan Warga
Designed by Lisa Buck Vann

Library of Congress Cataloging-in-
Publication Data
Bradburd, Daniel.
Ambiguous relations :
kin, class, and conflict among Komachi
pastoralists / Daniel Bradburd.
p. cm. — (Smithsonian series in ethnographic inquiry)
Includes bibliographical references.
ISBN 0–87474–306–0
1. Komachi (Iranian people)
2. Shepherds—Iran—Kirmān (Province)
3. Kirmān (Iran : Province)—Social conditions.
4. Social classes—Iran—Kirmān (Province)
I. Title. II. Series.
DS269.K65B73 1990
305.8'91505582—dc20 89–39784

British Library Cataloguing-in-Publication
Data available

Manufactured in the United States of America

97 96 95 94 93 92 91 90   5 4 3 2 1

♾ The paper used in this publication meets
the minimum requirements of the American National Standard for Permanence of
Paper for Printed Library Materials
Z39.48-1984.

To Nat and Kate,

and to the memory of Benny

# CONTENTS

# PREFACE

As with many anthropological projects, this work has ended rather differently from how it began. I went to Iran in 1973 to examine in detail the decision making during migration that Barth described in his monograph on the Basseri. Before my wife and I left for Iran—a leaving delayed by President Nixon's impoundment of funds that included NIMH fellowship money—Bill Beeman, who had just returned from doing fieldwork in Iran, warned us that political considerations might make it difficult to study the Basseri, and he urged us to consider working with the then-unstudied tribes in the Kerman region of south-central Iran.

After we were in Iran, and when we had finally received our research permits from the Iranian government, we decided to go to Kerman. I still planned to study migration, but the more time we spent with pastoralists around Kerman, the less inviting a study of migration became. As we settled in with the Komachi and decided that they would be the people we would stay with, I became more and more interested in their marriage negotiations, the place of shepherds in the society, and the apparently unstable nature of the region's pastoral communities.

When we left the Komachi in 1975, I had spent most of my time examining the first two issues. I planned to return to the area in short order so I could undertake a regional study of pastoral communities, their histories, and the flow of population through them. Of course, when we left Mohammed Reza Pahlavi was still shah. I have not yet returned to Iran, and the plans for my regional study have been long relegated to a dusty shelf. Trying to make a virtue of necessity, I focused my work on questions of kinship, marriage, and the relationship between hired shepherds and their employers. To adequately understand the last, I found I had to put the relationship in its economic context. As I studied the region's economic history, I came to see its importance for understanding the Komachi. My drift in this direction was facilitated by several factors. First, though I had started my graduate career in anthropological linguistics, I was deeply interested in the application of Marxist frameworks to anthropology. I had read Marx carefully, and had spent much of the time just before fieldwork studying structural Marxism. Indeed, my dissertation had a decided Marxist slant. One cannot read Marx and not learn the importance of economic history. Second, as much as I liked it, structural Marxism was not a universal favorite among my teachers at the City University of New York Graduate Center, and I was gently persuaded to consider other views of Marx's work. I finished graduate school with a background in and a bias toward a materialist approach to anthropology, a healthy regard for political economy, and little doubt that good anthropology was not divorced from history. Third, I received strong encouragement to study Kerman's—and Iran's—history from Professor Nikki Keddie of the history program at the University of California, Los Angeles. Nikki was staying at the American Institute for Iranian Studies in Tehran while my wife and I waited, and waited, for our research permits. While she was far too polite to say so, I always suspected that Nikki was rather dismayed by our lack of detailed historical knowledge; in any event, we were given an excellent unofficial tutorial on Iran's history from a most generous scholar. The point stuck; when I returned to the United States, I began seriously studying Kerman's economic history. After I finished my dissertation, I also began reading political economy extensively, particularly studies of the transition to capitalism. E. P. Thompson's 1978 book *The Poverty of Theory* helped me rethink my relationship to structural aspects of Marxism, and my work took a turn toward the position reflected in this work: a concern with practice and human agency as well as structures and determinants.

So, in the end, I have written a book about kinship and class, structure and practice, and history. I have wandered far from the study of migration, but I feel that my understanding of the Komachi, of anthropology, and of the nature of human society has been enriched in the process.

# ACKNOWLEDGMENTS

Few sections of this book have been as worrisome as these acknowledgments. I have not kept notes—unlike fieldwork—on my intellectual life, and so many people have helped me that I greatly fear leaving out someone who contributed to this work. The following people and institutions, however, deserve special thanks.

First, the Komachi themselves. With remarkable good humor and unfailing hospitality, they accepted into their midst two very inquisitive strangers who were presented to them, in truth imposed upon them, by agents of an Iranian state they could never trust fully. The revolution that has prevented our return to them has not only obstructed some paths of anthroplogical inquiry, but has deprived us of relationships we came to value deeply. Our time with the Komachi was truly a time for learning, and as the years pass I have come to see that I learned much more about life from them than I realized at the time.

I also owe my thanks to a number of people who, because they were in Iran at the same time we were and were generous and kindhearted, helped us. Bruce and Gretchen Mero provided us with a place to stay in Kerman City. Hallet Douville did the same in Bandar Abbas. Carolyn Awalt let us stay with her in Tehran, reducing the burden we put on the American Institute and on our pocketbooks. During our brief returns to Tehran, Connie Cronin and many other people, including volunteers in the U.S. Peace Corps, lent us the mystery stories that occasionally let us escape our tent without leaving it. We thank them all.

I owe my thanks as well to a number of institutions. The American Institute for Iranian Studies and its resident directors, Jerry and Jane Clinton and then David and Orick Peterson, helped get us ready to set off for the field, gave us invaluable assistance in our dealings with the Iranian government, and provided a comfortable, welcoming haven when we had to return to Tehran. I must also thank the United States government. My fieldwork was initially supported by a grant from the National Science Foundation (GS–39663), after funds for my NIMH grant were impounded. When that money was released, I also received a stipend from the National Institute of Mental Health (1FO1MH57286–01). Later, a National Endowment for the Humanities Fellowship for College Teachers gave me the time and money to visit the India Office Records Library and the Public Records Office in London to examine British trade reports and consular diaries containing historical data on Kerman's economy. I am grateful to those institutions for allowing me access to their records. I also received a CUNY institutional grant.

Along the way, I have also been helped by many friends, colleagues, and teachers. The list almost reads like a who's who of pastoral studies. In particular, I would like to thank Dan Bates, who not only began my serious education on pastoralists and the Middle East and stood by me through the writing of my dissertation, but also—with characteristic generosity—gave me his economic data on the Yörük so I could undertake a detailed comparative study of pastoral economics. Philip Salzman has read much of my work and has provided very useful comments on it. I have found our discussions fruitful and thought-provoking. Brian Spooner read an earlier manuscript version of this book, and his comments too were most helpful. Brian was also both generous and helpful to my wife and me while we were in Iran, and I thank him for that assistance as well. Bill Irons provided useful comments on some aspects of my work and gave us helpful advice before we set off for the field. Mary Martin was gracious to us in Iran and has been helpful to me here. Richard Tapper, Len Helfgott, Lois Beck, Aparna Rao, and Michael Casimir have all read aspects of this work in different forms, and their critical comments on it have been trenchant and helpful. Discussions with Jan Bauer have helped keep me up on the most current work on Iran. As I noted above, Nikki Keddie has been more than generous in her help to me. Dale Eickelman also read an early draft of this work and provided very helpful and encouraging comments on it; I appreciate both his help and his encouragement. To Abe Rosman I owe a special debt of thanks. Long, long ago, when I was an undergraduate, he made anthropology seem so interesting that I could not help being attracted to it. In the intervening years, he has read my work, encouraged me, prodded me, and generally shepherded me as I have bumbled along in my career. I cannot thank him enough, both for his intellectual guidance and for showing, over and over again, that anthropological concerns with humanity need not be abstract.

More generally, I have reaped the benefits of friendships with people whose only interest in the Middle East or pastoralists was that they knew me. David Glassman and Alan Acock gave me help and guidance in crunching many of the numbers that turn up later in this work. They certainly made my life easier. My good friend Michael Brown, now of the politics board at the University of California, Santa Cruz, has been an important source of support and encouragement. He has also been an enormously useful and patient sounding board for my theoretical concerns.

As is always the case, none of the people mentioned above deserves any blame for deficiencies in this work; their help has made it better, and any fault is solely mine.

Finally, I would like to thank my wife and children. I thank the latter largely for being themselves, for being children, for forcing my attention away from my work, and for helping me realize where the real power of kinship affiliation lies and how contingent life is. Having them has, in its way, brought me a deeper understanding of the Komachi. I cannot thank my wife, Ann Sheedy Bradburd, too much. Her contribution to this work is immeasurable. When a graduate student in anthropology she came with me to Iran, though she felt little innate attraction to the Middle East. In the field we worked together. Having her there to talk over, to argue over, what we had seen and heard greatly improved my understanding of the Komachi and helped make my fieldwork much more productive. Although she has turned from anthropology to accounting, she remains the most honest and effective critic of my work. Whatever credit this work deserves is hers as well as mine.

# INTRODUCTION

*Focus*

When we left southern Iran in 1975 after nearly two years of fieldwork among the Komachi nomads, my wife and I carried away not only notebooks, photographs, censuses, and genealogies, but also overwhelming impressions of Komachi life. These impressions were formed from experiencing Komachi daily life and comprised our responses both to particular, highly charged events whose force left an indelible mark on our consciousness and to the cumulative effect of seeing or hearing some things so frequently and so constantly that we could not help feeling that they were central elements of Komachi life.

For example, the sharpest conflicts we saw among the Komachi arose from competition over arranging marriages. Marriage negotiations engaged not just those Komachi immediately involved in making marriages and the anthropologists studying their efforts. For others the negotiations were a kind of theater, a soap opera observed, followed, analyzed, and commented upon by virtually everyone else in the Komachi community, some members of neighboring pastoral communities, and members of the settled community with close knowledge of Komachi affairs. Marriage negotiations were major social events, generating a concern and excitement that marked their significance and made them hard to ignore. But it was not only the formation of new kinship affiliations through marriage that marked kinship as significant. During periods of actual or potential conflict, neutral parties made appeals to common kinship as a means of creating accord. And all discussions of the formation, maintenance, and structure of the community were couched in terms of kinship, often beginning and ending with the litany "We are all kin, we are all one, there are no strangers here." For the Komachi, to be a member of the community was to share kinship affiliation with the other members. Kinship made an impression on us because it was a key symbol for the Komachi of being Komachi.

A second aspect of Komachi life to which we found our attention ineluctably drawn was the use of hired shepherds among the Komachi. Our reading prior to fieldwork had led us to expect to find hired shepherds; indeed, we had expected to examine their role in the labor process. We had little reason to expect that hired shepherds would be central to the production process, that the relationship of shepherd to employer would be exploitative and conflict-ridden, or that it would be reflective of structured social inequality. However, from virtually the moment we began living in a Komachi camp, we started to notice that some men went out each day with the animals, brought them in for milking, herded them as they were being milked, and left camp again with the herds, while other men virtually never went out with the animals but spent their time in camp, visiting other stay-at-homes in other camps, or traveling throughout the region on "business." Moreover, it did not take us long to see that the men who herded the animals, the hired shepherds, worked for and followed the orders of the men who did not go out with the herds. We also came to see that the wives and daughters of hired shepherds helped the wives and daughters of employers milk animals and prepare dairy products. Similarly, it became obvious to us that most hired shepherds and their families lived in small ragged tents, while the men who employed them lived in large ones. An economic census we conducted later revealed the magnitude of the differences in wealth that lay behind the readily apparent differences. Genealogies and family histories showed that shepherd and employer households reproduced shepherd and employer households. Examination of the relations of production showed why, and revealed the division of the society into two classes with striking similarities to the bourgeoisie and proletariat of capitalism.

At the same time, the flow of events—some striking, such as the negotiation of shepherding contracts in June 1975, and some cumulative and mundane, such as the constant flow of comments and small conflicts over the work of hired shepherds and the "helpfulness" of their kin—constantly called the relationship between shepherd and employer to our attention. We could not help noticing the way in which the use of hired shepherds and the nature of their relationship with their employers influenced other aspects of Komachi life, such as the division of labor by gender, the structure of camps, patterns of residence, and so on. In short, once we became aware of the role of hired shepherds in Komachi production, we became ever more appreciative of the importance the widespread use of hired shepherds had in shaping Komachi daily life and determining the structure and history of the Komachi social formation.

Because we came to feel that the centrality of the notion of kinship and the constellation of features associated with the use of hired shepherds were among the defining characteristics of Komachi-ness and were therefore necessarily key foci in any adequate account of the Komachi, they lie at the heart of this book. In the text that follows, I examine in detail the relationship of shepherd and employer. I set out the relations of production that led to the structured reproduction of economic differentiation, and show how they conjoined with the developmental cycle of households and the reproductive potential of sheep and goats to yield the socially reproduced classes of employers and hired shepherds. By examining the long-term economic history of the pastoralists' ties to the world market, I attempt to explain how and why those relations of production arose. Equally important, I attempt to show what it meant in practice to be a shepherd or an employer by translating the structural features of class into the practical terms of differences in diet, infant mortality, marriage prospects, quality and quantity of kin ties, and personal autonomy. I also attempt to show how the division of the society into classes shaped everyday social relationships among men, among women, and between men and women. In particular, I attempt to show how much of the tension and antagonism apparent in camp life was, in fact, class conflict.[1] In short, I examine the political economy of the Komachi social formation, paying particular attention to the nature, origins, and implications of the class division between employers and hired shepherds.[2]

Recognizing the tensions between hired shepherds and employers as class conflict makes Komachi notions of kinship appear paradoxical. How could people claim to be a community of kin even as the more fortunate members of the community exploited the less fortunate? Indeed, what did it mean in circumstances like those to say, "We are all kin"? Thus, one aspect of my discussion of Komachi kinship attempts to explore the articulation of kin and class by showing how the claim of unity was based on a set of tremendously broad and inclusive principles of kinship affiliation. By showing as well that the Komachi also employed a parallel set of principles that resolved the world of common kin into far smaller epicenters of effective, practical linkage, and by exploring the meaning of these two systems of affiliation, I show how Komachi kinship could join people across class lines even as it consolidated the divisions between them. Here too, I explore not only the multiple structures of kinship, showing how differences in class led to marked differences in such patterns of kinship affiliation as cousin marriages, or numbers of kin, but also the practice of forming kinship affiliation, showing how economic and political considerations influenced— within the "rules"—who married whom, how arranging a particular marriage affected future relationships among a constellation of households, and how these new ties and antagonisms, in turn, structured social relationships.

In examining this practical side of kinship affiliation, I demonstrate as well the ways in which antagonisms between hired shepherds and employers and in particular the means used to reduce those antagonisms promoted divisions among the employers themselves. By focusing on this linkage of kin and class and by following out the practical implications of these relationships, the book moves beyond a static description of Komachi society to a consideration of the internal dynamics of the Komachi social system. In so doing, the book also addresses a fundamental problem in social science: the relation of structure, practice, and history. Let me elaborate briefly.

When my wife and I asked the Komachi about their past, we were told that the community was formed through the union of three small lineages coming from widely separated areas of Iran, and that the linking of these groups began at about the turn of the century. Our systematically collected genealogies, however, showed that over one-third of the tribe's members had entered the tribe even more recently and that the vast preponderance of these immigrants were members of poor shepherd households. In effect, the community had grown through the accretion of poor hired shepherds. Tracing the roots of these hired shepherds, it became clear that at least some came from non-Komachi communities that no longer existed. Further exploration of the question made it clear that the Komachi were not unique. The social systems of the Komachi and many other tribes in Kerman had short developmental cycles and were unstable and ephemeral. That is, in cycles of rather less than 150 years, pastoral communities in Kerman emerged as named social units, grew through accretion and agglomeration, and then fragmented and dispersed as new groups formed in their wakes. Thus, the history of the Komachi and groups like them in Kerman was the history of social groups that did not hold together, that were not coherent, and that did not last, at least in the long run.

Understanding the instability of the Komachi social formation is central to understanding its nature and is thus a focus of this work. Instability, however, and class and kinship are not separate concerns. Among the Komachi antagonisms of class, conflict between hired shepherds and employers, and in particular conflict between the wives of hired shepherds and the wives of employers, led to hired shepherds moving from employer to employer. Further, attempts to palliate conflict between shepherd and employer, including claims of common kinship and the fairly frequent movement of hired shepherds from employer to employer, generated both greater antagonisms between shepherd and employer and substantial conflict among employers. Through a detailed analysis of the actual relations of employers to one another and to hired shepherds, I show how the use of hired shepherds among the Komachi was ultimately corrosive of the social order. I show as well how kinship affiliation, the primary force that countered the centrifugal tendencies of Komachi social relations, reinforced the atomism arising from class relations through both the practical realities of forming kinship ties through marriage and the unfolding of the structural logic of the formal kinship system itself.

My decision to focus on class, kinship, and the linkage between the two not only defines the ethnographic center of the text but also leads directly to the major theoretical concerns that underlie the work. One of these concerns is to show how people's interests and actions—in the case of the Komachi, as hired shepherds, employers, potential marriage partners, close kin, economic partners, and rivals—are structured and structuring, and how they generate the history of a social formation. My other concern is to account for the nature of a social formation: here I discuss the Komachi social formation, with special reference to the dominant place of hired shepherds in Komachi life. I deal with this latter concern by attempting to set out the significant contextual elements that have promoted the type of shepherd-employer relation, the types of kinship affiliation, and, ultimately, the kind of instability I found among the Komachi. The history of the long-term, direct integration of the region's pastoralists into the world market is a central element of the context of Komachi shepherd-employer relations. I trace the virtually continuous involvement of the region's pastoralists in the production of commodities or raw materials for export trade, beginning in the late seventeenth century with the British and Dutch East India companies' exports of cashmere for the manufacture of felt hats and following it through the centuries as the market shifted to cashmere for paisley shawls, raw wool, and finally wool carpets.

Given this focus, it seems important to note at the very outset of this work that I do not see integration into the world market as *the* determining force in Komachi history. My purpose is not to show that the Komachi were part of the world market system nor even how they were integrated into that system, but how and why they were the way they were, to show what it was to be Komachi, and (to the extent possible) explain why they were that way. Toward this end, the framework I use deliberately stresses the complexity of the Komachi situation, the multiplicity of the structures that impinged on them, and thus, in its way, the uniqueness of the Komachi. Of course, the Komachi (and most populations in Iran) can be seen as exemplifying the process of the development of underdevelopment. But I think it is more useful and interesting to describe the practical and theoretical implications of dealing with a multiplicity of structures than to see the Komachi as simply another case of underdevelopment or even a particular kind of underdevelopment. While it is obvious that the Komachi and populations like them have been shaped by their integration into the world market system and by the pressures of that system, the significant theoretical point that emerges through the examination of the Komachi is that their social formation arose through the conjunction of many structures, of which the world market system was but one.

Given the instability of the Komachi social order and the obvious multiplicity of the structures that have played roles in its formation, the Komachi seem to me to be a particularly extreme case, and therefore a particularly good example, of the kind of social entity Eric Wolf suggests we should envision when we think of societies as human aggregates that "emerge as changing alignments of social groups, segments and classes, without either fixed boundaries or stable internal constitutions" and cultures as "a series of processes that construct, reconstruct, and dismantle cultural materials in response to identifiable determinants" (1982:387; see also Wolf 1982:18). This work may therefore be looked upon as an attempt to examine effectively precisely this kind of open, unstable, and changing social system. As a result, this text stresses both descriptively and theoretically the complexity of the Komachi social order. Similarly, my examination of kinship, class, and the linkage between the two foregrounds rather than diminishes the ambiguity of Komachi social life and of the categories that were used to objectify the people who lived it. This stress on complexity and ambiguity arises because I have found it impossible to give an effective account of Komachi society without it. It is important to emphasize that Komachi social life was clearly shaped not by a single structure but by a conjunction of structures, a multiplicity of historically determined forces.[3] This text attempts to identify that array of forces as far as is possible, and to explore the ways they are conjoined.

Put another way, it is because the Komachi social order was complex that my explanation of it is complex. By that I mean simply that I have found that understanding the Komachi requires drawing together many different kinds of data and explanation; it requires a willingness to assume that what happened in Komachi life was not simply determined but overdetermined. Understanding the Komachi requires "thick explanation," by which I mean the careful explication of many complex interrelationships considered as interrelationships, not linearized or forced into a hierarchy of explanatory power.

I approach the Komachi determined to see how the details of their lives, how what they did as people, shaped their history and the history of their society. If we recognize the complexity of human society—if we accept that an understanding of groups such as the Komachi will not come through the reduction of complexity and will not come by asserting the priority of one aspect of the human condition over the other—it will be apparent that understanding comes from the careful, indeed painstaking, examination of people's lives and the multiple forces and contexts that shape them. The ultimate argument of this text is that to do adequate ethnography we must accept fully the implications of complexity for our theoretical stances.

## Theoretical Foundations

No text, no matter how empirically grounded, is without theoretical foundations. As these foundations obviously shape this work, it is important to set out the frameworks and assumptions that lurk beneath its surface.

At the deepest levels, the theoretical framework of the text is a historical materialism very close to Engels's vision of it in his 1890 letter to Joseph Bloch.

According to the materialist conception of history, the *ultimately determining element* in history is the *production and reproduction of real life.* More than this neither Marx nor I have ever asserted . . . . The economic situation is the basis, *but the various elements of the superstructure:* political forms of the class struggle and its results . . . juridical forms, and then even the reflexes of all these actual struggles in the brains of the participants, political, juristic, philosophical theories, religious views . . . *also exercise their influence on the course of historical struggles and in many cases preponderate in determining their form. There is an interaction of all these elements* in which, amid all the endless host of accidents . . . the economic movement finally asserts itself as necessary. Otherwise the application of the theory to any period of history that one chose would be easier than the solution of a simple equation of the first degree.

We make our history ourselves, but, in the first place under very definite assumptions and conditions. Among these the economic ones are ultimately decisive. But the political ones, etc., and even the traditions which haunt human minds also play a part . . . .

In the second place, however, *history is made in such a way that the final result always arises from conflicts between many individual wills, of which each again has been made what it is by a host of particular conditions of life. Thus there are innumerable intersections of forces . . . which* give rise to one resultant—the historical event. (Engels in Tucker 1978:760, emphasis added)

I assume first that the Komachi were what they were ultimately because of their economic activity: they were nomadic pastoralists linked to the world market precisely because they herded goats and sheep. That is, in order to raise goats and sheep successfully in Kerman's climate the Komachi had to move long distances with their herds, and such movement largely precluded production of the agricultural commodities that they consumed. It is worth noting as well that the salience of Komachi nomadism and pastoralism does not simply rise from theoretical assumption, from the fact that it was determined by their system of production; nomadism and pastoralism were also the central defining characteristic that the Komachi applied to themselves. To really be Komachi, one had to be a nomadic pastoralist.

But as the emphasized portions of Engels's text suggest, other factors are involved in shaping history, and in some cases they even predominate. Thus, as I intimated earlier, my second assumption is that social formations such as that of the Komachi arise from the conjunction of many and varied structures. I will argue below that in the case of the Komachi one can see clearly the impact on the nature and history of the social formation of structures that might be considered superstructural, most notably aspects of Islamic jurisprudence. Given this, the theoretical frameworks that I draw on to examine the factors "determining" the nature of the Komachi social system are those that assume an active interaction among and integration or articulation of these structures. These frameworks include a political economy that assumes both that social systems are open and complex and that the values and desires (the cultures) of peoples drawn into the world market shape the outcome of their histories as significantly as does the force of the market itself; I therefore find the works of Wolf (1982) and Smith (1984) more congenial than the more sweeping systemic views of Wallerstein (1974). Because I see the Komachi system as a conjunction of structures, my theoretical base also includes notions drawn from those who are more primarily concerned with structures than with markets, notably Sahlins, Giddens, and to a degree Bourdieu.[4] It seems obvious that understanding how complex systems such as that of the Komachi work is contingent upon understanding the conditions that make one or another of several conjoined structures dominant in shaping practice in a given situation.

With this in mind it I turn to Engels's third point: "History also always arises from the conflicts between many individual wills." To the degree that this book examines conflicts between members of shepherd and employer households over labor and conflicts between members of different employer households over shepherds and potential spouses, it is a study of the conflict of individual wills. To explicate effectively what lies behind those individual wills I have drawn heavily on the notions of practice theory. In particular, I have attempted to link a detailed description of people's daily lives with an effective discussion of the larger contexts in which those lives are lived. In doing this I have attempted to clarify as fully as possible the elements or contexts that comprise the particular conditions under which people live, including both "the winds of history" writ large or small and the structures that comprise their culture. I have attempted to show how these contextual elements, including people's understandings of the events in which they are participants and the cultural knowledge they use to achieve that understanding, shape what they do. And I have tried to show how what people do—their practice—affects structure, and is therefore part of the ongoing dialectic of an ever-changing history.[5]

In sum, this study of the Komachi is grounded in the theoretical insights of Thompson (1978), Wolf (1982), Sahlins (1976, 1981, 1985), Bourdieu (1977), and Giddens (1984), all of whom present forceful and perceptive discussions of the interrelationship of structure, practice, and history. What follows is a deliberate attempt to blend elements of this work and therefore is not, strictly speaking, an attempt to create new theory. My deliberate avoidance of theory creation arises in large part from my strong feeling that, for now, we will move forward our anthropological understanding of complex processes such as the relation of structure, practice, and history more through detailed empirical studies than through attempts at broad theory construction. We have to see how things work in particular cases.

Toward that end, the text proceeds as follows. Chapter 1 examines the environment in which the Komachi dwelt, focusing on the local physical and social environment in which the Komachi were found. Chapter 2 explores the larger social environment in which the Komachi lived, examining the impact of the oil boom of the mid-1970s on rural Iran in general and on the Komachi in particular. Chapter 3 examines the history of the Kerman Province, broadening our understanding of the context in which tribes such as the Komachi developed. These three chapters comprise Part I. Part II, comprising Chapters 4, 5, and 6, contains a detailed examination of Komachi economic life, focusing on the causes and the implications of a wealth differential within the tribe. In particular, I pay close attention to the ways in which cultural and systemic pressures for economic differentiation are manifest in the reproduction of two classes, employers and hired shepherds, and to how the relations between and among members of the two classes emerge in practice. Part III, Chapters 7 and 8, examines the structure and practice of Komachi kinship: the nature and distribution of different kinds of kinship affiliation within the tribe; the ways in which significant ties are forged, leading to particular patterns of kinship affiliation; and the articulation of patterns and claims of kinship affiliation with the rcla tionships between and among the two classes described in the preceding chapters. Part IV is a summary and conclusion comprising Chapter 9, in which I reexamine the Komachi social order, showing how the various aspects of Komachi life join together to generate the instability that characterizes it and how structure and practice come together in its particular, peculiar history, and Chapter 10, in which I briefly explore the implications for anthropology of assuming that most societies are, like the Komachi, unstable and unbounded.

# PART I

# HISTORICAL AND ENVIRONMENTAL FORCES THAT SHAPED KOMACHI LIFE

# 1

## THE KOMACHI
## AND THE
## KERMAN REGION
## OF IRAN

*The Komachi*

Migrating with their herds from lowlands on the coastal plain of the
Persian Gulf to narrow valleys high in the mountains south of Kerman
City, Komachi nomads, like many Southwest Asian nomadic pastoralists, appeared to live timeless "traditional" lives. They dwelt in black
goat-hair tents, herded goats and sheep, and piled their household goods
high on complaining camels for migration each spring. This "traditional" quality of Komachi life was, of course, an illusion. A closer look
would show that motorcycles had replaced horses, that for the fall migration trucks had replaced camels, and that the Komachi produced commodities that were exchanged in a market for other commodities manufactured the world over. An even closer look at the Komachi would
reveal that their untraditional aspect was not a recent phenomenon.

3

The Komachi I lived with were the end product of a very long period of integration into the world market system. And yet, if the Komachi were not untouched and unchanged, neither were they just members of an undifferentiated rural proletariat, a simple segment of the international division of labor. Komachi nomads owned their animals, the dominant means of production; the black tents they inhabited and their migrations were part of a life shaped by the exigencies of herding goats and sheep in a dry and demanding climate. Moreover, they lived a life in which their claims of being kin to one another still played a vital role in ordering social and economic relationships. In short, the Komachi had a social order that, like most others in the world today, reflected the impact of world capitalism on a particular people *with their own history and culture,* of which the forces of capitalism were but a part. Understanding the Komachi therefore requires a detailed examination of the contexts in which they were embedded, of their history, and of the forces that impinged upon them. Toward that end, I will present in this chapter a brief description of the Komachi, and then in the three following chapters set out these contexts before turning to a more detailed discussion of Komachi life.

Unlike many of the other Persian nomadic pastoral communities studied by anthropologists, the Komachi were virtually unknown outside their local region and absolutely unknown outside the borders of Iran. Neither famous nor infamous, the Komachi were a group of people whose main visible activity was one shared by all human populations: simple social reproduction. To accomplish this, the Komachi raised goats and sheep and then exchanged their animals' products for the commodities people consumed.

The term *nomadic pastoralists* often evokes an image of proud, brave, independent, and sometimes warlike people. For some groups, perhaps, that image may be justified; for the Komachi themselves and for the anthropologist who lived among them, however, there was little romance. The Komachi made no claims of great deeds or great ancestors; far from it. In addition to the rather prosaic story of the group's origin through the intermarriage of three smaller groups, the Komachi told tales well suited to an inconspicuous people. When we asked how they came to their current homeland, some people told us that their common ancestor had fled from the area around Sirjan, which is south and west of the Komachi summer quarters. Arriving near the Komachi homeland, he got a job as a shepherd, working for a wealthy landlord.

After some time there, he—or his son—killed one of the landlord's sheep and fled again to the mountains where the Komachi currently dwell. His descendants became key Komachi. Other people with other ancestors told similar stories.

When we asked how the Komachi got their name, we were told that years ago, the Farman Farma, governor of Kerman Province, came to Lalehzar (a mountain village west of the Komachi homeland) on a hunting trip. All the people in the area came and gave him gifts to show their respect. The ancestors of the present-day Komachi, apparently humble people even then, gave as their gift a *komaj*, the rude, unleavened shepherd's bread made of barley meal that is baked directly in the ashes of a campfire. The Farman Farma apparently was stunned by the gift, and asked mockingly, "Who are these breadites?", in Persian, "Who are these *komaj-i!*" The derisive name stuck. In truth, the Komachi were humble folk; they saw themselves as victims rather than aggressors, and they tended to be cautious rather than venturesome in their dealings with the outside world. If the dominant image of pastoralists is one of bold, swaggering, colorful people, then the Komachi fit that image poorly. While their pastoralism and their nomadism were terribly important to the Komachi—it was a defining feature of their self-image—and while they saw themselves as a community defined by common kinship, the Komachi did not claim to be, and they did not act as though they were, descendents of an ancestor such as Ghengiz Khan. The Komachi were more migratory peasants than marauders; they were what Philip Salzman has called economic, rather than political, pastoralists.

There were good reasons for the Komachi to have the character that they did. Perhaps the most important was that they, and other groups like them in Kerman, were so small. Counted as inclusively as possible, the Komachi never quite numbered 120 households, and the group's population never exceeded 550. In part, of course, the group's small size can be explained by its instability: groups that quickly break up do not grow to be large. But that is a point I will explore later. Here it is worth exploring a few implications of the group's small size. As I have noted, it made the group politically and economically unimportant. Because of this, the Komachi were not politically active; their strategy for dealing with the outside world was to be inconspicuous, make the best alliances they could with those more powerful than they, and hope that what they were doing for their own benefit remained unnoticed—or at least unchallenged—amidst the actions of larger, more important groups. This is, to be sure, a very conservative strategy; it also appears to have been an effective one. From the 1930s through the 1970s, at least, the Komachi prospered while larger, more powerful pastoral communities elsewhere in Iran suffered. And since a report on the Kerman region written in 1851 shows that even then the tribes in the province were all small (Abbott 1983:153), I suspect that the Komachi strategy was one that pastoralists in the region had long followed.

As well, the group's small size did not allow us—or the Komachi— to foster any illusions that they were somehow a group significantly set apart from the larger Iranian context. It quickly became clear to us that their culture could not in any sense be called their own, but was a variant of the larger regional and national culture. The Komachi spoke a dialect of standard Persian that was virtually identical with that of settled groups in the Kerman region. While aspects of their vocabulary were elaborated, one could not speak of a Komachi dialect, let alone a Komachi language. Similarly, many of their customs were those of the region: their marriage and circumcision ceremonies, which were the most conspicuous and developed rituals, were virtually identical with those of neighboring pastoral communities and were as well very similar to those of local settled peoples. The Komachi knew this, and they made it clear to us that this was the case. The local customs themselves were variations of larger Persian, if not broader Islamic, cultural patterns. As I have documented elsewhere, Komachi marriage and circumcision celebrations, for example, shared many common features with those of the Basseri as described by Barth (Bradburd 1984a), and, as we will see below, what one might call the "rules" of Komachi marriage were hardly exclusively Komachi rules. The basic categories of permitted and prohibited marriage partners were Koranic, and preferences for close kin marriage paralleled the general thrust of marriage rules reported for virtually every group in the Middle East. At best, what distinguished the Komachi was a single variation: a prohibition on multiple marriages between sibling sets. This variation was significant, but only in the context of the larger shared understandings of who one could or could not, should or should not marry.

Perhaps most important, the Komachi were devout Shi'ite Muslims. By that I do not mean that they all said all their obligatory prayers, gave *zakat* (alms for the poor), or fasted through Ramadan. What I mean is that they accepted as given the precepts and ideas of Islam that were presented to them. They all knew that they should fulfill the Five Pillars of Islam, and they recognized that in not doing so they were not filling their obligations completely. But all Komachi, even the most cynical, fully accepted the validity of the sacred history of Shi'ite Islam. They saw themselves as members of the Shi'ite confession: they were people for whom the martyrdoms of Ali and Hossein were immediate and powerful emotional realities, people for whom the notion of blasphemy was still powerful, people for whom the notion of someone being anything other than a member of the community of Islam was hard to imagine. Their whole sense of being was fundamentally grounded in their being Shi'ite. As such they were by definition part of a larger, similar community. Unlike the Basseri (as described by Barth), Komachi religious belief was not something separate from their lives, something that one might discuss in an appendix: it was a central fact of their existence, one which suffused virtually every aspect of their being. If to be a Komachi one had to be a pastoralist, to be a person one had to be Shi'ite.

There are other aspects of the Komachi that bear noting as well. Like most pastoralists, the actual residential group was far smaller than the tribe as a whole. All migrating Komachi lived in residential groups or camps that they called *ehshams*—literally, retinues. Camps were small: they ranged in size from three to roughly a dozen households. For most Komachi men, and certainly for most Komachi women, the camp was the effective daily social universe. Thus, most of Komachi life was lived in very close proximity to very few people. Moreover, most of daily life occurred within or in front of the large black goat-hair tent that each Komachi nuclear family owned. Since animals were milked near the tent and lambs and kids were kept around it, and since family possessions had to be packed and unpacked in full view of neighbors during the course of migration, all Komachi knew one another, and most Komachi knew far more about one another than we do about other members of our society. Much of Komachi life was public, and few things could be kept secret for very long. I do not think that sharing their lives with others bothered the Komachi a great deal, and I know that social isolation, *tanhoegi*, was considered an evil to be avoided at virtually any cost.

I stress the public nature of Komachi life for the following reason. In much of the discussion that follows, I will track significant conflicts in Komachi life. It was indeed the case that they fought numerous and sometimes interminable verbal battles. There was real anger and real conflict. At the same time, the Komachi were immensely social: people longed to see other people, to hear news of other camps, to visit. Other people, friends or rivals, were terribly important to the Komachi. Without television or movies and with little to read, the Komachi lived in a truly social universe, and the other people in that universe were all significant in one way or another. Perhaps the strongest image I have of the Komachi—one that overshadows images of magnificent desert vistas, clear mountain air, the bleating of sheep and goats and the gargling roar of camels, the excitement of migration, and the variety of peoples' skills, which ranged from making leaf-thin bread to replacing the piston rings on a motorcycle—is of people sitting together in groups, talking. Men talked about the prices of sheep, goats, wheat, and pumps; women talked with other women about marriages; people asked visitors who was sick and who was well. What I remember most is people talking about themselves and their lives.

Life among the Komachi was also marked by the circumstances in which they lived. Animals were central to Komachi life. Rhythms of Komachi life were controlled by the shift of seasons and the life cycles of goats and sheep. However, while goats and sheep were important to the Komachi, no Komachi identified with their animals the way the Nuer identified with their cattle. Animals were important to the Komachi as wealth that could be converted easily into cash, and thus as the means of living a reasonable life; as capital, that is, as the means of producing more wealth; and as the basis of an occupational definition of self. The Komachi relation to their animals was ultimately a practical one. Animals were a kind of capital that provided the Komachi a better life than they could hope to live if they converted their animals to any other form of capital. As a result, pastoralism was an excellent way of life. Movement from place to place, the avoidance of climatic extremes, and the ability to leave dirt and insects behind were ancillary benefits.

In sum, the Komachi were a small population of nomadic pastoralists, one of many similar groups that herded goats and sheep in the mountains and valleys of southern Kerman Province, traded in the market, lived in tents, and migrated as the seasons changed. They were a people for whom kinship was important; they dealt with people they knew and were uncomfortable with strangers and the larger outside world. Attempting to make their way as best they could in a complex world, they were a people whose tents were traditional but whose lives were not.

## Contexts

Virtually all ethnographies set out some historical and/or ecological background before introducing the people around whom the text centers. I follow that pattern here. However, as the Komachi were citizens of a larger society undergoing rapid economic and social change, and because some key aspects of Komachi social organization, including the shepherd-employer relations that lie at the heart of Komachi pastoral production, were clearly the end products of long-term historical processes about which there are some useful records, my discussion of the historical context is extensive. Nonetheless, the Komachi do eventually reappear.

In setting out some of the contexts necessary for understanding the Komachi, I have chosen not to present capsule descriptions of the two most important contexts for Komachi life: Islam and the world market system. Both were so pervasive in their influence and so significant in their impact that I believe it more useful to discuss their impact in situ than to attempt summaries that could only be inadequate. The remaining contexts that form the backdrop to my discussion of the Komachi are: (1) the physical and social environments of Kerman Province, in which the Komachi dwelt and which formed the immediate context within which their history was lived; (2) the immediate historical context—the Iran of the mid-1970s oil boom—that the Komachi experienced while I was living with them; and (3) an outline of the historical forces that impinged on tribes such as the Komachi in Kerman Province from the seventeenth century until the mid-1970s and that helped shape their historical development.

Let us now turn to these contexts.

## KERMAN

Iran's interior is a vast, high plateau, bounded on the north and the west by the Alborz and Zagros ranges. Major Iranian cities generally are located along the interior flanks of the mountain ranges rather than on the plateau proper, for much of the center of the plateau is occupied by two great deserts, the Dasht-e Lut and the Dasht-e Kavir, whose size and harsh conditions have always made them formidable barriers to transportation and communication. Kerman Province lies toward the southern and eastern end of the plateau, and the great deserts lie across the direct routes to such major cities as Tehran, Isfahan, Shiraz, and Mashad. Kerman, therefore, historically has been a far outpost of Persian life. By 1975, Kerman City was linked to Tehran by a paved highway. A railroad link between the two cities was under construction but remained incomplete in 1975.[1] By the time of my fieldwork one could fly between Kerman and Tehran in a few hours, though in days past the journey took twelve days by fast posthorse; caravans needed thirty-two days to make the trip (J. Rabino, quoted in Noshirvani 1981:568). Thus Kerman is far from the economic and political centers of Iran. Standing as it does toward the unprotected eastern end of the plateau, Kerman City and the lands about it were historically the eastern marches of Persian culture and political control.

Throughout the nineteenth and twentieth centuries population growth in the region appears to have lagged behind the nation as a whole,[2] and while Kerman City shared in the general economic growth of the 1970s oil boom, it remained the center of a peripheral region. Though a major copper mine and smelter were under construction at Sar Cheshmeh in the north of the province, agricultural goods (particularly pistachio nuts) and carpets remained Kerman's primary products. While the mine brought jobs to the region as a whole and increased the political and economic importance of the province, the mine itself was some distance from Kerman City; its major effect on the local population was to increase the salary for common laborers and to bring some quite high-salaried employees to the region. Along with increasing numbers of well-paid government functionaries, merchants dealing in Western luxury goods, and individuals controlling import substitution in the region, the mine's upper-echelon employees formed the new regional elite. While this new elite injected substantial new revenue into the region and increased demand for numerous commodities, including meat, Kerman remained the largely sleepy capital of a rural, agricultural province located far from the centers of national power and economic development.

The Komachi thus lived at the margins of Persian society. As nomadic pastoralists, they practiced an economic strategy that was becoming progressively more peripheral to Iran's developing economy.

Kerman, their homeland, lay at the geographic, cultural, and economic periphery of Iran, and indeed, as the Komachi lived near the southern and eastern borders of the province, one might characterize them as living on the margins of the margin of Persian society.

## THE KOMACHI AND THE REGION

From May to October most Komachi were in their mountainous summer quarters, the *sarhad*, while October through March saw them in their *garmsir*, winter quarters on the coastal plain. Only by moving between these extremes on their annual round were the Komachi able to maximize access to adequate pasture for their animals. A brief discussion of the Komachi annual round will set the stage for a more detailed examination of their homeland and their relationship to it.

*An Annual Round.* While the Komachi year had no real beginning or end, starting our discussion of the annual cycle in November as lambs and kids were being born and following it through to the next November will give us both a general feel for the relationship between the Komachi and their region and a skeleton outline of Komachi production that provides a useful basis for later elaboration.

In November, as the Komachi arrived in their winter quarters, kids and lambs were being born. Shepherds brought the young animals into camp shortly after their births. There they were given to their owner's wife, who was told which adult animal was the mother of the kid or lamb. Kids and lambs were not kept with the flock of lactating females but were united with them briefly each day so that they could feed. Because young animals were separated from their mothers at birth and remained separated from them throughout the day, much of November and December's labor centered around feeding the young animals. Each ewe or nanny had to be matched with her offspring for the feeding, at least initially—hence the careful identification of mother and young. Care was taken that the kid or lamb was not rejected by its mother and that it sucked until satisfied.

By February, when young animals required less intensive care, the focus of Komachi activity shifted to dairy production. Young animals, which since November had received all their mothers' milk, were now allowed to nurse only after their mothers had been milked, the milk being processed into products for human consumption. From morning to night women were busy milking animals, churning butter, and preparing other dairy products. Most milk was first made into yogurt, then into butter, and then *roghan, kashk,* and *tarf.* Respectively, these were a clarified butter that was used for cooking, a dried buttermilk that when reconstituted with water was a staple of the Komachi diet, and a sour dairy by-product that the Komachi used as a flavoring and sold in small quantities. *Kashk* and especially *roghan* were highly valued in the settled community, and the Komachi derived a very substantial return from their sale.

Rainfall was a critical factor in the success of Komachi dairy production. If the early rains came, then pastures became green; if the late rains came, then pastures remained green, and milk production was high. If the rains failed, the pastures dried up and so did the milk supply, reducing both the duration of milk production and the quantity of daily production.

Rainfall and quality of pasture also determined the onset of the next major phase of the Komachi year, spring migration. If pasture remained rich, the Komachi lengthened their stay in winter quarters. If the grass was dry, they began their move without delay. Either way, between mid-March and early April the Komachi began their journey northward to summer pasture. Spring migration was long and hard: over 200 miles, and uphill almost all the way. Not only did the Komachi care for their animals and prepare dairy products during migration, but they also had to deal with the extra tasks of packing and unpacking camels, pitching and breaking camp, and walking, walking, walking. Spring migration was difficult, and whatever excitement the Komachi felt about moving on—and they were excited about seeing new pastures and old friends—was mitigated by the burden of the event. Komachi migration was not their central ritual (cf. Barth 1961, R. Tapper 1979a; see also Bradburd 1984a for a fuller discussion of this point), so it was with more than a little relief that, roughly a month after their journey began, the Komachi reached their summer quarters. There activity slowed down: migration was done, some young animals were large enough to be herded with the older stock, and milk production and the preparation of dairy products began to slacken. After late June or early July, when the animals were sheared, there was a true break in productive activity. Women ceased working on dairy products and began weaving tents, pack bags, and *qelims.* Men concentrated their efforts on selling animals and wool.

By mid- to late August, pasture in summer quarters had been exhausted. Hired shepherds accompanied the flocks back to winter quarters. Except for the hired shepherds, most Komachi remained in summer quarters until late October. Late summer was thus the season for marriage negotiations, religious celebrations, weddings, and circumcisions. It was the time when the members of the tribe said that they were *bi kar*, without work; this was a time for intense—and sometimes tense—social interaction, excitement, and rest from work.

In early October the social whirl ended and work began again. Preparations had to be made for migration to winter quarters; supplies were purchased, accounts with merchants in the bazaar were settled, and business in summer quarters was completed. Then, in late October, large trucks were rented and packed sky-high with the Komachi and their belongings. A two-day drive got the Komachi to their winter quarters, where their flocks were waiting for them. Lambs and kids were just being born; another year-long cycle was beginning.

As the outline of their annual round suggests, Komachi divided their territory into two parts: summer quarters, the *sarhad*, and winter quarters, the *garmsir*. The two areas had the following physical and social characteristics.

*The Sarhad.* The eastern extension of the great Zagros mountain range (which runs almost due east to west, about 60 miles south of Kerman City) contains a long, narrow valley that begins at the foot of 14,400-foot-high Kuh-e Hezar and continues on past the base of Kuh-e Shah, another 14,000-foot peak, before it grades into the Persian interior plateau near the town of Baft. Watered by mountain streams, the eastern end of the valley floor, which ranges from 8,000 to 9,000 feet above sea level, was occupied by a series of small agricultural villages, including Giborj, Sarze, and Shirinak, whose nontribal peasants cultivated wheat, barley, potatoes, chickpeas and other pulses, sugar beets, and turnips, as well as small plots of herbs.[3] Water for the crops came from *jubes*, irrigation ditches that drew from streams, and from *qanats*, underground water channels.

Though most plowing was done by tractor, little capital was expended on agriculture in the valley and most remaining work was done by hand or with primitive animal-drawn implements. Wheat and barley often were planted on steep, unterraced hillsides that were heavily irrigated one year and left to lie fallow the next (resulting in severe erosion, nearly irreversible given local resources and conditions). Around the villages the slopes were so completely stripped of larger vegetation that only small shrubs remained. These shrubs—*darman*, a kind of sage (*Artemesia*), *esfan* (also called *dashti*), wild rue, and wild licorice—are all diagnostic of degraded land (Pabot 1967). Demand for fuel for cooking and heating in winter was so great that these small shrubs were usually all that was available for those uses. As they burn fiercely but quickly, vast amounts of them were consumed. Huge piles of this "firewood" were common sights both in nomad camps and around the villages, and for the nomads collection of the brushwood was a daily task. As a result of the demand for fuel, most land near villages had been stripped of even this meager ground cover. *Qanats* in the valley were small and so poorly maintained that people spoke both of the recent diminution of water supplied by *qanats* still flowing and of the total stoppage of some others. Throughout the valley system as a whole, there seemed to be little concern for the maintenance or conservation of resources, and one felt that the valley—a marginal agricultural area—was in a kind of gentle decline. Given the *sarhad*'s limited resources, settling into the local agricultural sector was not and probably never had been a reasonable alternative for the region's pastoralists (cf. Barth 1961).

One drivable dirt track ran from east to west along the valley floor. At the extreme west of the valley, far outside Komachi territory, the dirt track intersected the graveled road that ran from Kerman City to Baft. Komachi rarely traveled in this direction; their major route to Kerman took them through the town of Qaryeit-al-Arab, which they reached by crossing a nearly 10,000-foot-high mountain pass on another rough but drivable dirt track. Qaryeit-al-Arab had several shops that sold small quantities of tea, rice, cloth, vegetables, and other things local or Komachi households might require. There were also a gendarmerie, two banks, a clinic, an agency selling 20-liter cans of gasoline, and twice-daily (at least according to the schedule) bus service to and from Kerman. With the pass open, the trip from the Komachi *sarhad* to Kerman City could take as little as four to five hours. Few of the province's pastoralists lived nearer to the city than the Komachi.

During the summer the *sarhad* can be a most pleasant place. Daytime high temperatures average 85°F while nighttime temperatures fall to the mid-sixties. Summer skies are almost always clear; weeks can go by without a cloud appearing in the sky, and from May to October there is often no measurable rain. By late October, daytime temperatures drop to a high of 65° and the nighttime lows fall below freezing. At nearly 9,000 feet, winters are cold. While there are no significant meteorological data for the *sarhad* itself, Kerman City, the nearest meteorological station with a long run of data, has an average winter high temperature of 55° and an average low of 30°. As Kerman is just over 5,000 feet above sea level, we can safely assume that the *sarhad* is far colder. Villagers told us that winters were "terribly cold," and said that snow was often waist-high. Again, there are no accurate figures for precipitation in the *sarhad*, but Kerman averages about 8 inches of rainfall a year, with most of that falling between December and March. Precipitation is almost certainly greater in the mountains; the *sarhad* probably receives about 16 inches of precipitation, with the surrounding peaks— which can keep a snow cap through late June—receiving somewhat more. The runoff of melting snow and ice on these mountains is, of course, the source for the streams, *qanats*, and irrigation ditches that water the valley in spring and summer.

Seasonal variation made the *sarhad* a pleasant place for pastoralists or anthropologists to spend the summer, but the winter's harsh climate made the year-round maintenance of large herds nearly impossible. Sheltering, watering, feeding, and caring for more than a few animals over the winter was so costly and so arduous that no one attempted it. As a result, there was room in summer for the herds of nomads such as the Komachi (see Barth 1960, 1961 and Spooner 1973 for discussions of the relation between pastoralists and the environment they exploit). Winter's hardships, however, had to be escaped, and so, like other Southwest Asian pastoralists, the Komachi migrated roughly 200 miles to warmer winter quarters.

*The Garmsir.* Komachi winter quarters centered about the town of Manujan in the extreme southeastern corner of Kerman Province (Figure 1). Manujan is about 70 miles due east of Bandar Abbas—the region's nearest major city—and is about 55 miles as the crow flies from the shore of the Persian Gulf. Manujan lies in the center of a large, hill-rimmed, saucer-shaped plain. The hills are about 1,000 feet high, and Manujan itself is about 350 feet above sea level. Traditionally, *garmsir* settlements like Manujan, Rudan, and Jaghin were adjacent to date gardens watered from wells, small streams, and *qanats*. Quite literally, these settlements and gardens were oases.

For many years, the *garmsir* was less hospitable for the Komachi

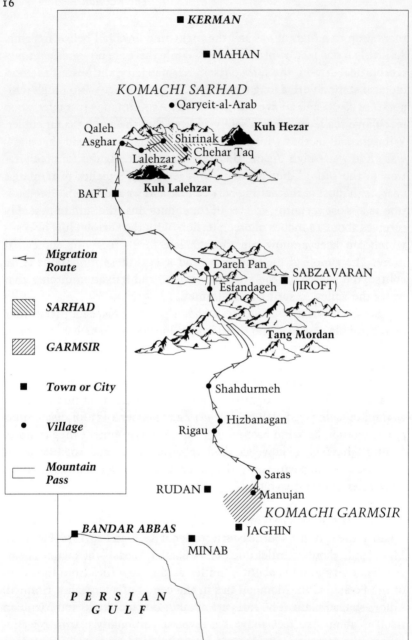

Figure 1.
Map of Komachi migration route, Sarhad, and Garmsir.

than the *sarhad* was. Well beyond the effective control of the Persian government, brigandage and banditry were common. With the countryside not secure, villages were centered around small fortresses from which local strongmen—part chiefs, part thieves, and part petty warlords—controlled the countryside. Malaria was also endemic. During the 1960s and 1970s the *garmsir* changed radically. Bandar Abbas became a major naval port, and chromite mines were developed in the region. By 1975 the *garmsir* had been completely pacified, malaria had been largely eradicated, and new graveled and paved roads had brought the region closer to the rest of Iran. Improved communication brought changes in the region's economy. While dates were still harvested, new crops such as oranges, lemons, grapefruit, cucumbers, tomatoes, and melons, which were grown for markets in Tehran and other northern cities, had begun to dominate agricultural production. Irrigation water for these crops came from large diesel pumps rather than *qanats* or small wells, and much new land was brought under cultivation. Still, much land was neither irrigated nor planted. Flat, dry, and otherwise unused, it was good winter pasture. Camel thorn, acacia, lotus, tamarisk, and other smaller plants and grasses provided grazing for Komachi livestock. Indeed, because the area had been so recently inhospitable and dangerous, there was much more open land in the Komachi *garmsir* than in their *sarhad*—and the *garmsir* pasture was better pasture as well.

Weather conditions in the *garmsir* reverse those in the *sarhad*. Where the *sarhad* is comfortable in summer and difficult in winter, the *garmsir* is comfortable in winter and brutal in summer. Through December, January, and February, the average low temperature for Bandar Abbas (the nearest weather station) is 51°F while the average high for the period is about 75°; in contrast, the absolute low for Bandar Abbas is about 43°F. Days are balmy, nights comfortable and cool, and Komachi flocks were almost never threatened by severe cold. Rainfall was a far greater worry to the Komachi. Average annual precipitation (almost all rain) in Bandar Abbas is about 6 inches, more than two-thirds of which normally falls from November through February. Adequate seasonal rain is vital for pastoralists such as the Komachi. Ideally there is early rain in November and December to start the annual grasses; then if the year is good there are relatively heavy rains in January (3.5 inches on average) that ensure adequate pasture for the rest of the winter. Late rains or a dry January greatly limit available pasture. In good

years, then, winters in the Komachi *garmsir* have moderate temperatures and enough rainfall to support ewes and nannies during peak milk
production. By March, as the average monthly rainfall drops to less than
.5 inch, the temperature rises and vegetation begins to dry rapidly.
Spring is just a pale imitation of summer. From May to September, average total precipitation in the *garmsir* is less than .0008 inches. At the
same time, the average low temperature for the region is about 85°F and
the average daily high temperature is over 99°F. Indeed, the mean temperature for July, the hottest month, is 95°F.

Just as the extreme cold of the *sarhad* winter made year-round
maintenance of a flock difficult, the extreme heat and aridity of the
*garmsir* summer made year-round herding impractical. Thus the
Komachi started migrating back to their *sarhad* well before the on-
slaught of summer's heat.

*The Migration Route.* The Komachi moved about 210 miles (as the crow
flies) each spring and fall. Komachi spring migration—which was done
with herds and camels—involved about twenty moves and took about
thirty days. Fall migration, which took place after the herds had left,
was only a two-day truck trip; therefore I will describe spring rather
than fall migration. Starting from winter quarters in Manujan, the Komachi moved north and west to No Duz, whence they set out nearly
due north (see Figure 1). In its initial stages, the migration route took
them through valleys similar to those surrounding Jaghin and Manujan.
Settlements in these valleys clustered about *qanats* and wells. Each village had its mud fort and its gardens of dates and citrus. Outlying settlements in these valleys were located near deep-bore wells, and there the
major crops were grains such as millet and market produce for the
north, including tomatoes, cucumbers, and melons. As the Komachi
moved northward, the valleys they passed through rose like an enormously elongated flight of stairs. Manujan is only 350 feet above sea
level, but before the Komachi entered the highlands proper, the valleys
were about 3,600 feet above sea level. The valleys were linked by the
generally dry channel of the Rud-e Dozdan, the "River of Thieves." Lak,
Lurak, Sulemani, and other tribes had their winter quarters in these valleys, and the pastures had been grazed all winter. As a result, the Komachi did not linger. Roughly one-third of the way through their journey, the Komachi passed through the Tang-e Mordan (the "Defile of
Death"), which is a long, narrow defile, rising over 1,000 feet in a space

of about 2.5 miles. Near the top of the defile is the village of Zamarkand. Protected by mountains from the extreme cold of the plateau, Zamarkand was the last date and citrus oasis the Komachi passed on their migration route.

After Zamarkand, the Komachi migration route took them over a substantial mountain pass and on into the valley of Esfandagheh. There, in a broad plain, a number of villages were laid out along irrigation ditches rising from *qanats* watered by the nearly 10,000-foot-high mountains around the valley. Esfandagheh was roughly the geographic midpoint of the Komachi migration; it was also the beginning of their *sarhad*. Esfandagheh was for a number of reasons the most important stop on the Komachi migration route. The valley was large and had some good pasture; the Komachi could stay there to recuperate from their exertions and to prepare for the final climb to the high valleys. There were stores in which the Komachi could buy and sell small quantities of goods and supplies, and there was a government clinic that the nomads patronized quite heavily; the valley was also home to a shrine. The Esfandagheh valley and the mountain ranges that surround it were also the *garmsirs* and the *sarhads* for several tribes. The largest of these tribes was the Lori; there was also a small, marginal group of Lur who claimed to be kin to the more powerful and well-known Mammasani Lur of Fars Province. Neither the Lori nor the Lur migrated as the Komachi did. Instead, they spent their winters on the relatively sheltered southern slopes of the Esfandagheh valley, while summer found them on the high slopes to the north. Given their pattern of migration, the Lori and the Lur never really entered the hot coastal plain, and so certain products of great value to nomads—dates and date products for food, and the black goat hair from which they wove their tents—were not readily available to them.[4] Before they left their winter quarters near Manujan, the Komachi purchased black goat hair from the settled communities and tribespeople there. As they passed through Esfandagheh, the Komachi traded some of this hair and some dates and date jam to the Lur and Lori. In return for goat hair and dates, the Komachi got dairy products (which they sold with their own) and some cash. Both the Komachi and the Lori found the relationship useful. The Lori got material they needed with little effort, and the Komachi made a small profit on the transactions. With all the buying, selling, trading, and visiting that went on, the stop in Esfandagheh was a hectic one, but when they left, the Komachi were ready for the remainder of their migration.

From Esfandagheh, the Komachi began their climb into the high mountains of the *sarhad*. With tired camels and tired flocks, they climbed over the mountain rim, and after several days' march stopped again at a spot with rich pasture, the river banks at Dar-e Pan. At Dar-e Pan there was plenty of water, pasture was generally plentiful, and there was very rich browsing for the camels, which were by now lean and cranky. After Dar-e Pan, the Komachi still had to climb a 10,000-foot mountain pass, so Dar-e Pan was a breather before the final push to the *sarhad*. This last stage was a series of four or five hard marches, which the Komachi, with their summer quarters nearly at hand, took at a rush. In the fall, their animals having left earlier, the Komachi returned to winter quarters by truck, which was a two day trip.

## SOCIAL CONTEXT

The great differences in the physical environments of the *garmsir* and the *sarhad* were paralleled by equally different social landscapes. The Komachi, along with the settled populations in the *sarhad*, were ethnically, culturally, and linguistically Persian; they had aquiline and often quite fine features, straight dark hair, and light (though heavily tanned) skin. Among rural populations, men wore dark *shalvar* (pants that were rather like cotton pajama bottoms), long-sleeved collarless tunics that fell to mid-thigh, vests, and Western-style suit coats; most men wore hats, fedoras or balaclava helmets if they were "modern," broad-brimmed felt bowlers if they were more traditional. Women wore long, brightly colored dresses over their *shalvar*, which were generally black for older women and in bright geometric patterns for young women. All women wore flowing light-colored shawl-like head coverings but did not wear veils; only in towns or on formal public occasions did women wear *chadors* (the head-to-toe coverings that have become so familiar in post-revolution times).

By contrast, natives of the *garmsir*, with far greater affinities to the Arabs of the Gulf and the Baluchi to the east, looked, spoke, dressed, and acted differently from the Komachi. While the details of the differences between the Komachi and the residents of the *garmsir* need not be spelled out, they were marked enough for the Komachi to call the people there *garmsiri*. In making this generic reference to the *garmsiri*'s home region, Komachi were clearly marking what they perceived to be (and what really was) a cultural boundary, for Komachi spoke of residents of summer quarters as peasants, merchants, butchers, tribespeople, etc., marking differences that were occupational rather than cultural.

Not surprisingly, interactions between the Komachi and their neighbors in summer and winter quarters were quite different. Komachi claimed to have lived in the valley between Kuh-e Hezar and Lalezar since the "beginning of ancient times." Their actual period of residence had a somewhat less imposing-sounding duration, but it seems likely that they had lived in the region for at least seven generations. During this time, they created numerous alliances with the area's settled population. Most Komachi had long-standing trading relationships with merchants in the Kerman bazaar; these merchants were also patrons and sources of loans. In the days before land reform, most of the pasture and fields of the *sarhad* were owned or controlled by absentee landlords, and these men too were patrons to the Komachi.

The ways in which pastoralists gain access to pasture almost invariably entail significant relationships with members of the settled world, and the nature of these relationships have great impact on pastoralists' lives (see, for example, Bates 1971 and Beck 1980, 1986 for discussions of how variations in these relationships have led to far-reaching changes among particular tribal groups). Relationships concerning pasture— true social relations of production—are among the most important relations pastoralists have with the settled world. Among the Komachi, access to pasture in the past was mediated through the relationships of poorer nomads to wealthier ones, with actual control of the pastures as resources lying with external authorities (either the state or traditional landowners). Throughout recent Komachi history heads of camp negotiated with these authorities for the use of pasture. The question of who the Komachi negotiated with and what the conditions of their negotiations were is somewhat complex, and it is clear that the changes outlined below had substantial impact on particular aspects of their relationships with local settled populations.[5]

Following the land reform legislation of the 1960s and the early 1970s, all lands outside the irrigated extents of villages reverted to the direct control of the central government. Theoretically, access to this land was regulated through the issuance of permits (*parvanes*) stipulating which pasture a permit holder could use and the number of animals that could be grazed on the land under permit. (See Dillon 1976, Hooglund 1982, Lambton 1953, Beck 1980 and 1986, Keddie 1972 and

1978, and Katouzian 1981 for discussions of land reform in Iran.) In some parts of Iran (notably Fars Province, to the west of Kerman) the introduction of permits and the enforcement of their provisions had profound effects on access to pasture (Beck 1986) and tribal political economy. In Kerman, however, implementation of the permit system was spotty and enforcement of the permits' provisions was extremely casual. Among the Komachi only a few wealthier members of the tribe had petitioned for and received permits to graze their traditional pastures. In theory this meant that wealthy members of the tribe were the only tribespeople with legal access to pasture. In practice, however, things were quite different. All members of the tribe were able to graze all their animals (which were held in quite unequal numbers, as I discuss below) on pastures controlled, both traditionally and through permit, by the head of their camp. Conversations with Komachi who had grazing permits revealed that they had sought them as insurance against the very real possibility that they might be denied access to pasture under any one of the number of schemes the government was said to be considering.

Komachi use of permits was revealing. In large part the permit system was designed to regulate the number of animals having access to any pasture. Because most pastures in Komachi territory, and indeed most pastures in Iran as a whole, were overgrazed and degraded, and because the overt aim of the program was the regeneration of pasture, the permits limited grazing to animal populations well below the land's carrying capacity. As a result, all permits limited the pastures under their control to only small herds—on average 150–250 animals. Had the permits been enforced, not even the wealthy Komachi permit holders would have been able to graze their entire holdings on the pastures to which they held usufructory title. Simply put, no one would have had adequate access to pasture. With at least tacit acquiesence by the region's authorities, then, permits were ignored.

Government permits were, however, a recent phenomenon in Kerman. Traditionally, pasture had been controlled by the owners of the *qanats* (see note 5). In Komachi summer quarters—their "homeland"—most of the villages were owned by absentee landowners, who dwelt at the closest in the town of Qaryeit-al-Arab. Komachi gained access to these pastures by paying tribute to these landowners. This tribute, in lieu of rent, appears to have been on the order of several adult animals and several kilograms of dairy produce per camp per year. In return for these "gifts," the Komachi received relatively secure guarantees of access to much—but not all—of the pasture beyond the villages' irrigation ditches, as well as the right to water animals from the irrigation ditches. Although I was unable to collect a complete account of just who received what from whom, it seems that most Komachi dealings about pasture, short of the actual presentations, took place with the *katkhoda* (the appointed headman and landowner's representative) of a village. Komachi "gifts" were conveyed by the various heads of camp to the landowners in return for access to particular portions of pasture near particular villages. Heads of camp then collected some portion of the payment from the poorer members of their camp, thus distributing the cost of access and simultaneously apportioning usufruct. By 1974–5, most landlords had divested themselves (or had had themselves divested) of land in the villages near the nomads, and regular "gifts" no longer flowed. Moreover, some wealthier Komachi had come to possess small shares of water and garden rights in the villages. These guaranteed them both some access to pasture (although this was in theory regulated by the government) and water from the *qanats* that served the valley.

Access to pasture in winter quarters followed a similar general pattern, but the realities of access in that unsettled region were more complex. In the early 1950s the Komachi moved their winter quarters to the very border of Kerman Province. At that time, the area was beyond effective government control and sparsely populated. The Komachi attached themselves to local strongmen who could more or less guarantee them protection. As government influence spread and the region was pacified, many Komachi moved further into the unsettled hinterlands. There the Komachi gave no gifts and had no permits. Komachi who lived nearer to the settlements (largely the wealthiest Komachi, who had substantial herds of sheep as well as goats) also had no permits; however, they gave gifts to prominent local landowners in return for water from the motorized pumps that irrigated fields of cucumbers, tomatoes, and watermelons. Again, some wealthy Komachi bought shares in pumps and thus gained access to water. During the 1970s all land in the *garmsir* beyond the irrigated gardens and fields technically belonged to the government, as was the case in the *sarhad*. Unlike *sarhad* land, however, *garmsir* land was open for development and could be granted to someone who would improve it by buying a pump. Thus all *garmsir* pasture was to some degree insecure. Komachi attempts to gain permits for grazing in the region met with no success.

To summarize, for most of their recent history the Komachi had relatively free access to the usufruct of relatively infertile pastures. At the same time, because the Komachi never owned or had entirely secure access to the pasture on which their survival as pastoralists depended, they were always dependents or clients of those members of the settled community who had the power to help assure continued access to that vital resource. Mobile though they were, the Komachi were held to the settled world by powerful ties to its merchants, landowners, and local functionaries.

In summer quarters, Komachi relations with the local settled community were intimate. The late headman, or *katkhoda*, of the village of Shirinak married a tribal woman, and four of his five children came to migrate with the Komachi. His remaining child—his youngest son, the current *katkhoda*—maintained very close economic relations with his tribal kin. Komachi had no kin ties to a second local *katkhoda*, but they traded with him extensively and considered him as both a friend and an advisor. A number of local peasants worked for those Komachi who owned land in the valley. These peasants and others attended weddings and circumcisions (at which they gave small gifts), and were vital participants in *rozehs* (religious meetings). Some *sarhad* peasants married tribal women and became Komachi, forging active linkages between the tribe and the villagers around them. With the exception of the *katkhoda*'s daughters, no reverse marriages occurred, and the Komachi did not marry and settle.

Komachi relations with their neighbors in summer quarters were very comfortable. They had friends, acquaintances, patrons, and some kin there; they knew the area and its people well, and were clearly part of the social landscape. The *sarhad* was their true home: free from danger, empty of strangers. Relations across the cultural barrier between the Komachi and their *garmsir* neighbors were, for several reasons, less comfortable than relations between the Komachi and the culturally similar, settled population of summer quarters. First, the Komachi were relative newcomers to their specific *garmsir*. Until the early 1950s, they spent their winters in Jiroft, near the town of Sabsavaran. When Jiroft "became too crowded" the Komachi moved to Manujan about 120 miles away. Second, the *garmsir* region was itself a true frontier, lacking the stability and the established markets and towns of the *sarhad*. Third, the cultural boundary between the populations made any flow of members between the two peoples difficult. Fourth, as a frontier, the *garmsir* was a region undergoing rapid development and change. Wealthy and important men were consolidating wealth and power based on new circumstances, for example the introduction of large-scale irrigation agriculture and the rapid development of Bandar Abbas (the nearest large city) as a major port. Under these conditions their own best interests were not clearly defined, and it was difficult for the Komachi to establish stable relationships as clients; indeed, in a period in which the nature of clientage itself was changing, the Komachi also lacked longstanding ties to fall back on.

Rather than having the friends, kin, and known patrons they had in summer quarters, in their winter quarters the Komachi were somewhat adrift. They constantly sought mutually profitable relationships with *garmsiri*—especially with pump operators or small-scale landowners—but Komachi relationships with the settled community in the *garmsir* remained vastly inferior to their *sarhad* relationships. So, for example, when a group of Komachi took a woman to a doctor in Bandar Abbas, they were forced to spend their nights sleeping in that portion of the bus station that acted as a modern caravanserai for poor travelers. On their return, much of the travelers' tale dwelt on the discomforts of the bus station and on an invidious comparison of Bandar Abbas and Kerman. Beyond stressing what a filthy and unpleasant place Bandar Abbas was, the dominant theme of the tale contrasted Bandar Abbas with Kerman, a familiar and friendly place where they would always be received as guests. It was one of the ironies of Komachi life that the area in which they were most comfortable, the *sarhad*, was a land of degraded pasture and inadequate rangeland, while the place that was relatively rich was one in which they were strangers.

# 2

# IRAN, 1974–75:

# OIL, GROWTH,

# DISLOCATION,

# AND THE KOMACHI

As a complex society undergoes rapid social change, some segments of the population are likely to benefit while others suffer. Indeed, some segments are likely to suffer *because* others benefit. This was certainly the case in the Iran of the early 1970s. Rapid economic change, the enormous influx of new oil revenue following the October 1973 Arab-Israeli war and the ensuing OPEC agreement, the institution of dramatic development plans based on that new revenue, and the completion of the land reform program created unique opportunities for some Iranians while others found their lives becoming ever more difficult and dislocated.

In general, the transformations that took place in Iran favored the urban elite and the emerging urban middle class. The traditional middle class of the bazaar and most rural populations seem to have suffered both relatively and absolutely. Nomadic pastoralists frequently suffered severe dislocation during this period. However, the distribution of damage and benefit was uneven, both across segments and within them, and in the case of the Komachi it is quite clear that others' losses were Komachi gains. As a result, the Komachi I worked with were living in unparalleled economic comfort. The conditions that generated this economic success, of course, were part of the context that made the Komachi what they were.

Oil and the revenues that it generated in the early to mid-1970s profoundly affected Iranian life, and the Komachi benefited from these changes. That they did, while others in the rural sector suffered, came about from the fortuitous conjunction of the following factors: (1) greater oil income (both before and after the dramatic surges of 1973 and 1974) and thus greater national wealth dramatically increased Iranian consumers' demands for red meat; (2) demand for meat also far exceeded the available supply, and as a result prices for meat and for animals on the hoof skyrocketed; (3) because the internal distribution system in Iran funneled imports to Tehran, and because Kerman was so far from the capital, the Komachi and their pastoral neighbors had one isolated but large and growing urban market, that of Kerman City, virtually to themselves; (4) at the same time, because government policies held the cost of other agricultural commodities, notably wheat— the staple of the Komachi diet—at artificially low levels, the normal balance of exchange between the value of the commodities the Komachi produced and those that they consumed dramatically shifted in the favor of the Komachi; and (5) the geographical location of the Komachi in a peripheral area of Iran shielded them both from government policies directed at control of (or elimination of) pastoralists and the regulation of rangelands and from external labor market demands that increased tribal wages, thus leaving the Komachi unaffected by both problems and opportunities that affected pastoralists in several other regions of Iran. Let us consider these points in somewhat greater detail.

In 1965 Iranian oil revenues totaled $513 million. By 1973 Iranian oil revenues had increased to $5.6 billion a year. After the OPEC price rise of December 23 1973, revenues for 1974 and 1975 jumped again to $18.5 and $18.8 billion respectively (Halliday 1979:143). While much of this revenue was squandered on armaments, military adventurism, and the like, there was nonetheless a great increase in national wealth, which was paralleled by increased urban consumption. For example, per capita expenditures rose from $232 in 1965 to $522 in 1975.[1] One area to which this outlay was directed was the consumption of red meat. Meat consumption increased at a rate of approximately 12.5 percent per year in the late 1960s and early 1970s (Graham 1979:116; Halliday 1979:127). Although demand for meat was rising, output did not keep up. The size of the gap is not entirely clear. Graham (1979:116) suggests production increased at about 9 percent per annum, while Katouzian argues that there was a "systematically negative rate of productivity growth" (1978:355). Amouzgar notes that from "1960 to 1976 [livestock] registered an annual growth rate of only 3.2 percent, with production of mutton virtually stagnating for some time" (1977:35). Given Iran's population increase in that period, Amouzgar's figure is far closer to Katouzian's than to Graham's. Whatever the specific figure, it is quite clear that there was a significant increase in overall demand for red meat and that this demand far outstripped actual domestic production. There were two immediate responses to this problem: first, meat imports increased substantially (Black-Michaud 1976); and second, the price of meat increased dramatically. Just how dramatically meat prices increased is somewhat difficult to ascertain. For example, the price of lambs in Luristan rose 150 percent between 1970 and 1975 (Black-Michaud 1976); prices for prime stock (kids, lambs, and wethers) increased 86.5 percent from 1970 to 1976 in Fars (Loeffler 1976); and national prices for live animals rose 61 percent from 1970–71 to 1973–74 (Iran Statistical Centre 1970–71, 1973–74). My own figures for Kerman show increases of over 300 percent for the period 1970–75.

Thus if meat prices in Iran at least doubled between 1970 and 1975 (that is, increased at an annual rate of roughly 16 percent), and quite probably increased by as much as 150 percent, meat producers in Kerman saw the price of their product rise at a far faster rate. It was quite clear to the Komachi, and to me, that the Komachi were benefiting from these price increases. At the same time, the values of pastoral products other than meat did not increase as rapidly, and in the case of fiber products may have fallen.

Pastoralists do not generally produce the non-livestock-related commodities that they consume, and so we must ask whether this increase in the price of meat actually benefited the Komachi or whether they stood still, or perhaps lost ground, against general inflation. In fact, the Komachi benefited even more than simple figures for meat prices might suggest, for while the price of meat in Kerman was tripling the prices of other commodities rose less rapidly. Most important, wheat—

the staple of the Komachi diet—was kept at an artificially low price by a government program of imports and subsidies. This had a disastrous effect on agriculture in Iran as a whole; nonetheless, from the purely parochial point of view of the Komachi, this program greatly increased their economic well-being. The price of grain in rural areas in Iran rose perhaps 100 to 150 percent between 1970 and 1975 (Salmanzadeh 1980; R. Tapper 1979a; Black-Michaud 1976); it is clear that the differential rise in prices of meat and grain favored the Komachi and other meat producers. Taking aggregate cost-of-living figures for Iran as a whole for the period 1970–75, we find that the cost-of-living index increased by 50 percent (Parvin and Zamani 1979) at a time when the prices the Komachi received for their animals increased nearly 300 percent. Granted that the figures for the nation as a whole are almost certainly unrealistically low, it still seems quite likely that the Komachi had far more purchasing power in 1975 than at the outset of the decade. The base of their disproportionate gain was, of course, the dramatic increase in demand for meat. Nationwide, this is reflected in official statistics indicating a 25 percent increase in the overall price index for food from 1969–70 through 1973–74 against a 52 percent increase in wholesale meat prices during the same period (Iran Statistical Centre 1973–74:440, 449).

The fact that the Komachi dwelt in a peripheral province also had a profoundly positive impact on their situation. Because the primary— and politically most important—demands for meat came from Tehran and other major cities, little imported meat (either from other provinces or from foreign suppliers, most notably New Zealand and Australia) found its way into Kerman Province. As a result, the Komachi and their neighbors had a captive market in Kerman, one in which price increases reflected increases in local demand that greatly outstripped the elasticity of local production. This did not hold for the price of wheat, for local bakers were supplied with imported wheat at subsidized prices.[2] I should note here other benefits that the Komachi gained from their peripheral location. The relative isolation of the province removed the Komachi from the efficient administrative control of the central government at the same time that their migration brought them near Kerman City, enabling them to market their produce effectively. Pastoralists in other parts of the country not only had to contend with competition from imported meat, but also were hindered by government policies aimed at the direct settlement of nomads and strict control of access to rangeland. At the time that I did my research the Komachi had yet to have these burdens imposed upon them. Thus they were (with other Kermani tribes) the major suppliers of meat to the local market, and no one interfered with their attempts to maximize production. Meanwhile, government attempts to control pastoralists in other regions of Iran appear to have had a generally negative effect on meat production and hence, from the Komachi point of view, a positive effect on meat pricing (see Katouzian 1978 for a discussion of this point).

In discussing these benefits to the Komachi, it is important to realize that though all Komachi, poor and rich, benefited from national economic conditions, wealthy Komachi made far greater gains than did their poorer counterparts. While some of this differential arises from the tribal political economy itself, some aspects of the differential were promoted by circumstantial factors—again, particularly the general isolation of the province and its attendant isolation from significant labor markets. The province lagged behind the rest of Iran in its rate of modernization or development, and did not experience the enormous surge in nonagricultural employment that characterized many of the more developed provinces. Thus, while Black-Michaud (1976, 1986), Loeffler (1976), and Beck (1980) all note that poor tribespeople among the Lur, Boir Ahmad, and Qashqa'i moved from the tribal to the settled sector to take advantage of the high wages available there, poor Komachi remained trapped within the tribal economy. Poor tribespeople in other regions were able either to claim a higher salary from outside sources or to use the threat of migration to gain a higher salary within the tribe, but poor Komachi had little opportunity to press for higher wages within the tribe. Though the cost of labor went up in other regions— sometimes to a point where herding became unprofitable—there were far smaller absolute increases in the cost of labor among the Komachi, even though the price of animals may well have escalated faster there than in the other regions. Simply put, wealthy Komachi benefited from radically increased prices coupled with stable costs. Poorer Komachi benefited from increased prices, but they were unable to make the generally increased cost of labor in Iran as a whole work to their immediate benefit. The result was, of course, greater economic differentiation.

In sum, because they lived in an isolated region of Iran that experienced growth in consumer demand for their primary product, meat, that could not be readily met from other sources, and because they were protected by their isolation from government regulation of their activities at the same time that they benefited from government policies regulating the price of grain, the Komachi were living under conditions of unprecedented economic prosperity in 1974 and 1975. While this prosperity favored wealthy tribespeople over poor ones, it was still the case that all but the poorest tribespeople felt that their standard of living had increased.

I stress for two reasons the fact that the Komachi were successful: first, much of the literature on tribes emphasizes the degree to which they have been damaged by government expansion, and it should be pointed out that conditions of growth and change in developing countries do not have the same impact on all peoples within them, even if they have the same basic adaptation; and second, even in those flush times there was still considerable conflict within the tribe, much of it ostensibly arising from economic factors. As I will posit a model of Komachi society in which friction and tension play an important role in tribal history, the reader should keep in mind that the events I describe took place amidst the best conditions the Komachi had ever experienced; I assume that economic contraction and straitened circumstances would exacerbate rather than ameliorate the points of conflict that I will discuss below.

# 3

# A BRIEF
# HISTORY OF
# KERMAN PROVINCE
# AS IT RELATES
# TO THE KOMACHI

As we have seen, during the mid-1970s the Komachi were intimately linked to external markets. They produced meat, wool, and dairy products, purchased most of what they used or consumed in daily life, and maintained long-term credit relations with butchers and merchants in the Kerman City bazaar. Relations with external markets played a dominant role in the Komachi economic order. Of course, as Wallerstein, Wolf, and others have pointed out, the world market has come to play a dominant role in the economic and social orders of most societies. In many places, however, the larger world market has only recently encroached directly upon "traditional" societies, leaving anthropologists to describe local systems reeling under the impact of rapid change. The Komachi too experienced rapid change, but not from recent direct contact with the world market.

Pastoralists in Kerman have been in direct contact with the world

33

market for at least three hundred years; Kermani pastoral societies and their economies were shaped by that ongoing relationship with the market. In particular, the historic relationship to the market seems a prime determinant of the central, striking aspect of Komachi economic life: the use of impoverished shepherds, who were hired on annual contracts that kept them poor. There are a number of features of life in Kerman that influenced the region's political economy and hence pastoralists' relations with the market. For example, the extreme aridity of the region limited its agricultural potential and made agriculture a highly capital–intensive venture controlled by the urban elite (see Lambton 1953 for an elaboration of this point); concomitantly, economic and political power was centralized in Kerman City, the trade and manufacturing center, rather than in the hinterland.

As well, export trade in animal fibers and animal fiber products played an unusually important role in Kerman's regional economy from the seventeenth century to the early 1970s. As a result, since the seventeenth century pastoral production had been geared toward export trade, which linked pastoralists to the world market. Although the export trade was broadly continuous from the seventeenth century onward, it was also cyclical, leading to substantial variation in demand for pastoral commodities and the prices they returned; hence pressures on pastoralists' domestic economy arose periodically.

As a result of the above, pastoralists developed long-term relationships of dependency with urban merchants, who occupied nodal positions in the exchange of commodities produced and consumed by the region's rural populations, including pastoralists. These merchants also controlled the flow of credit, so they had great power over local small producers even as they themselves were largely captives of forces in the world market.

The factors enumerated above are clearly reflected in the following narrative history of Kerman's economic linkage to the West from the seventeenth century through the late twentieth century.[1]

## Cashmere, Shawls, Carpets, and Wool

Direct European contact with Kerman began in the thirteenth century, when Marco Polo passed through the region on his famous trip to China.[2] Polo found Kerman a center of manufacture whose products included "embroideries of silk and gold, in a variety of colours and patterns . . . designed for the curtains, coverlets, and cushions of the sleeping places of the rich" (Polo 1926:42–43). In the ensuing years the region's importance declined, and Kerman and its hinterland became the ever more isolated eastern march of Persian culture.[3]

After Marco Polo, Kerman came to the attention of the West during the seventeenth century, when European trade with Asia brought enterprises like the British and Dutch East India companies to the region. John Fryer, who lived in Persia from 1672 to 1681, described Persia's trade as limited: "The English Company's trade is but small here, only carrying off somme few drugs, carmania wool, goats, dates, and horses" (Fryer 1912:164). Fryer, however, also saw possibilities for increased trade with Persia:

To these blessings for Pleasure, neccesity, and Physick, are added others for Profit: Gums, the most Rich, distil everywhere: *From Carmania, Goats Wool* (as much prized as Jason's Golden Fleece) *with which our Hatters know well how to falsify their Bevers: and the Natives how more honestly to weave both Cloth and Carpets very fine, which they sell at dear Rates.* The flocks and coarser Wool of their Sheep stand them in some stead, they kneading it into Felts, for seamless Coats for the ordinary sort of People, for their common wearing; and their Skins with the Wool on, are both an Ornament and a Safeguard agains the roughest Weather; But Lamb-skins with their crisped wool are of more Credit . . . and are not disdained to be worn by the chiefest Gentry; of whose leather they make good merchandise, it being esteemed better than the Turkish, their Tanners being expert at dressing, not only these and Kid, but other hides of larger size, which therefore are bought up with Greediness by all Foreignors for their real excellency.

Goats and Camels . . . bequeath their hair to their Weavers, of which they make water'd Camlets.

But above all, the wool-bearing cotton shrub renders by its wealthy down those riches which are deeper digged for. (Fryer 1915:8, emphasis added)

Fryer's list shows that beyond cotton, pastoral products were among Persia's major resources. Moreover, Carmania (that is Kerman) wool was particularly valuable. Carmania wool is, in fact, the downlike underhair of the Kashmir goat— *kork* in Persian, cashmere to us. As three hundred years later cashmere remained an important product for Komachi pastoralists, one can see at a glance the continuity of pastoralists' relation to the market.

Actually, pastoralists appear to have been major producers of cashmere well before the development of international trade. Polo, we recall, found the region a center for embroideries, and as early as the tenth
century Arab geographers described the region as a center for the spe-
cialized production of woven "Kashmir" shawls (Barthold 1984:139ff).
Later, Tavernier, who traveled in Persia some thirty years before Fryer,
noted that

> when I was in Isfahan in the year 1647 a *Guare* shew'd me a sample of [cash-
> mere wool], and informed me that the greatest part of the Wool came from
> the Province of Kerman, which is in the ancient Carmania, *and that the
> best wool is to be met with in the mountains.* . . .
>
> Now you must take notice that they never dye this [Carmania] wool, it
> being naturally of a clear brown or a dark ash colour, and that there is very
> little of it white, which is much dearer than the others, as well for that
> it is scarce, as because the Mufti's and Moullah's and other persons belong-
> ing to the law, never wear any Girdles or Vails . . . but white. (Tavernier
> in Fryer 1909:40, emphasis added.)

Thus early in the seventeenth century Kerman was already known for
cashmere procured "in the mountains"—the homeland of the region's
pastoralists. The arrival of the British and Dutch East India companies
and the beginning of export trade did not mark the beginning of commercial dealings in cashmere in the Kerman region but rather transformed the earlier domestic luxury trade into export trade.

By the 1670s the British East India Company was exporting cashmere from Kerman to manufacture counterfeit beaver hats. British
trade was not directed at procuring woven goods—the traditional
product—but raw material.[4] Toward that end, the British East India
Company established factories and posted agents in Kerman, and considerable quantities of cashmere were exported from Kerman. The
Dutch also established a factory at Bandar Abbas and engaged in upland
trade (Floor 1984, 1986).

The magnitude of the cashmere trade in Kerman and its impact on
the region's pastoralists can be gauged by the amount of cashmere exported by the British. The peak year for cashmere exports was 1736,
when the British exported roughly 138,600 pounds of cashmere (Dillon
1976:224). Goats in the Kerman area yielded an average of 10.5 ounces
of *kork* per year, so production for British exports alone in 1736 would

have required a base herd of 208,000 goats.[5] Given French and Dutch exports and production for Iranian use as well, it is quite likely that this base herd figure is extremely conservative. It seems certain that by the early years of the eighteenth century, Kerman's cashmere export trade drew the region's pastoralists into the orbit of the world market system.

Fashions change, and neither felt hats nor the British or Dutch East India companies remained significant forces in Kerman after the 1760s. Still, the region and its nomads remained bound to the world market as exports of Kermani woven shawls replaced the collapsed raw cashmere trade. These woven shawls were high-fashion items, part of an international luxury trade. Kerman's shawls competed with somewhat more expensive shawls from Kashmir, where the trade had originated. By 1790 demand for Kermani shawls was significant; by the 1820s shawls produced in Kashmir (on whose industry we have more complete data) were being designed specifically for the European market (Dillon 1976:266); and by the second quarter of the nineteenth century Kermani shawls competed against those from Kashmir (Dillon 1976:270).

While it is difficult to judge the exact extent of the Kerman shawl trade, it seems that roughly five-thousand shawls were exported from Kerman each year.[6] More to the point, Keith Abbott, one of the most careful observers of Persian trade in the nineteenth century, noted that "the production of Shawls etc. appears to consume nearly all the Goats Wool in the Country." He also noted that "almost all districts [of Kerman] produce this Article [cashmere] but principally the mountainous parts" (Abbott 1983:110).

Although trade began to decline as the century aged, shawls were manufactured in and exported from Kerman until the end of the nineteenth century.[7] Nomads, who produced much of the region's cashmere, remained bound into export trade—as well as production for national consumption—through the end of the nineteenth century.[8] Thus, we have reasonable evidence for a waxing and waning of Kerman's cashmere exports over the course of the nineteenth century; we have evidence that near midcentury, at the trade's peak, production of shawls used all the cashmere available in the region; and we have evidence of the linkage of pastoralists to this trade.

As the shawl trade disappeared, Kermani pastoralists' ties to the world market did not cease but rather intensified. In the broadest terms, the impetus for this intensification came from changes in Persia's overall economy between the middle of the nineteenth century and the early part of the twentieth century, particularly a dramatic increase in the need for cash. This need for cash arose from the conjunction of several forces. First, during this period there was a significant increase in European imports such as cotton goods, tea, sugar, guns, and ammunition (Issawi 1971:135–36). Second, while Persia remained on a silver standard, elsewhere gold became the sole international currency standard. As the value of silver fell in the late nineteenth century, so did the value of Persian currency, and the increased imports cost even more than they otherwise might (see Avery and Simmons 1974). Third, some traditional Persian exports, notably silk, failed. Finally, the nascent modernizing state needed increased revenues. Consequently agricultural production shifted from subsistence to cash crops (such as cotton and opium), and exports of Persian carpets increased dramatically (Issawi 1971:135–36).

Patterns of trade in Kerman seem to have duplicated those of Iran as a whole. In the mid-nineteenth century Abbott noted that "in return for what the country receives, Kirman sends to Yezd and other towns in Persia, its *shawls* and other *woollens, goats* and *sheeps wool,* opium, lead, . . ." (1851:85: emphasis added). By 1894, however, opium had become Kerman's leading export by value, and by 1910–11 carpet exports clearly dominated Kerman's trade, their value exceeding £170,000 (Government of Great Britain 1912:3318).

In sum, Kerman's shawl trade was first replaced by the export of opium and cotton, then by carpet exports. While the relation of carpets to pastoralists is obvious, it is useful to examine briefly the impact of opium production on the Iranian economy so that the full effect of these shifts in production can be judged.

With the notable exception of carpet and shawl production, Kerman's economy centered about agriculture and pastoralism since the thirteenth century. The province's major crops were wheat and barley, both of which were largely consumed within its borders. In this regard, Kerman was similar to the rest of Iran, where in the early 1860s 80 to 85 percent of the population appears to have been engaged in agricultural production, with perhaps as much as 90 percent of the population dwelling in the countryside (Gilbar 1979:185). Most production had been for internal consumption, but as noted above, the late nineteenth century brought a dramatic increase in the country's need for hard currency.

In the south of Iran this need for cash led to large-scale opium cultivation. Exports increased from 1,560 chests of opium in 1868 to nearly 13,000 chests in the late 1890s (Gilbar 1978:313ff.). Because opium was easy to grow and brought the grower over three times the cash return of wheat or barley, it was frequently planted as a replacement for those crops. As a result, "during the last forty years of the 19th century and the early 20th century the total annual production of wheat and barley in Persia decreased to a considerable extent both in absolute and relative terms [a process that was] *especially* marked in the southern and central provinces" (Gilbar 1978:315).

The decline in the production of wheat and barley, the staple subsistence crops, led to a two- to threefold increase in the price of wheat and bread, severe dislocations in the distribution of food, and ultimately bread riots. Pastoralists who did not produce grain but who consumed it (including most tribes in Kerman) experienced great pressure on their domestic economies as skyrocketing wheat prices dramatically increased their cost of living (Gilbar 1978:319).

It is difficult at this remove, of course, to create a perfectly clear picture of the economic condition of Kerman's nomads during the late nineteenth century. However, drawing together the information we possess, it seems likely that this was a period of some economic stress for the pastoralists. First, as we have seen, there was a decline in the shawl trade, which clearly would have damaged the market for cashmere wool. Second, the increased trade in opium and the consequent increase in wheat and barley prices must have put pressure on the pastoral economy. Third, while ultimately there was a dramatic increase in the demand for pastoral products—this time, wool for carpets—there was a significant gap between the time of the decline in shawl production and the time of the rise in carpet production in Kerman.

To some extent, this gap between periods of extensive trade was bridged by growing exports of raw wool and the development of the export carpet trade in other regions of Iran. That Kermani pastoralists participated in the trade of raw wool is clear. British observers in the 1870s noted both the high quality of Kermani pastoralists' wool and its export:

[Near Rayin in Kerman Province] the road soon quitted the little plain of Tahrud, which is only an expansion of the bed of the river, and with a little more water would be a lake. . . . On the way we passed a small camp of wandering Baluchis. . . . Immense numbers of sheep were being driven up to their summer pastures. They are much smaller than the sheep of western Persia, and mostly white, the rarest of colours elsewhere. Their wool is perhaps equal to any in the world, large quantities being exported to India for mixing with the down of the Kashmir goat, or perhaps for using alone, in the manufacture of the coarser kind of shawl. (Goldsmid et al. 1876:78)

And as we have seen, Abbott listed wool as one of Kerman's major exports. Still, careful examination of export figures shows that as late as 1894 the total value of pastoral products exported from Kerman (wool, cashmere, carpets, and shawls) barely exceeded £20,000 while by 1911 carpet exports alone reached £170,000.[9] It seems quite likely that Kermani pastoralists experienced significant economic pressure during the late nineteenth century and that this pressure was a predictable outcome of the pastoralists' role as producers of materials for which demand varied with the vagaries of European fashion.

## Kerman in the Twentieth Century: Carpets and Capitalists

The early twentieth century saw the beginning of a major boom in the export of Persian carpets, and Kerman experienced a rapid increase in production of carpets for export. In 1900 there were roughly 1,000 looms in Kerman; by 1966 there were 11,000, and by 1970 nearly 15,000 (Dillon 1976; Stöber 1978:234). As I am not concerned with carpet production per se but rather with the impact of carpet production on the region's pastoralists, the number of carpets produced is most significant here as a measure of wool consumption. In 1966, for example, approximately 346,700 square yards of carpet were produced on over 11,000 looms, requiring 1,050 tons of dyed, spun wool (Dillon 1976:341). Carpet production on this scale required the wool from well over one million sheep.[10] Kerman's carpet production grew throughout the twentieth century until 1970, when virtually every wool producer in the region must have been drawn into the market. Moreover, the shift from shawl to carpet trade in Kerman led to a significant shift in the region's pastoral production. Through the mid- to late nineteenth century demand for cashmere was greater than demand for sheep's wool, and cashmere brought a better price.[11] By the 1970s, wool was a far more valuable "crop" than cashmere. According to the Komachi, the shift in the relative value of wool and cashmere drove many pastoralists to shift from herding goats alone to herding diversified flocks of goats and sheep. Thus shifts in the world market apparently helped determine the structure of herds in Kerman. Specifically, Kermani pastoralists kept large herds that included many adult male animals. Since the market also dictated that they herd sheep as well as goats, each wealthy pastoralist was likely to have a flock of male sheep, one of male goats, and similar flocks of females. Keeping many flocks required a great deal of labor— probably more labor than was needed in many other areas of Iran, where fewer male animals were kept and only one kind of animal was raised (see Bradburd 1989 for a discussion of this point).

While the broad picture of twentieth century carpet production in Kerman is one of steady growth, a more detailed examination of the wool market and pastoralists' relationship to it gives a clearer view of the forces that shaped pastoral economies. For example, though the number of looms in Kerman grew between 1900 and 1970, growth was not linear. The market for pastoral products waxed and waned in the twentieth century as it had in the eighteenth and nineteenth centuries. While pastoral produce was in short supply and prices rose during periods of peak demand,[12] it seems equally certain that when demand was absent prices fell.

What impact did this fluctuation in demand and price have on pastoralists? It seems to have put them on an economic roller coaster. There is reason to believe that when demand for pastoral products was high, pastoralists did indeed benefit. I reach this conclusion in part by reading backward from the circumstances I observed among the Komachi, for during the boom in meat consumption of 1974–75 all Komachi benefited economically as the price of meat increased. Also, while pastoralists suffered during the opium boom of the 19th century, peasants (who were mostly tenant farmers) shared economic gains with their landlords and with merchants (Gilbar 1978). In the twentieth century, then, pastoralists continued to experience cycles of boom and bust, periods of plenty and periods of economic pressure.

To some degree, however, economic pressure was never fully released. Pastoralism is always a chancy venture, and bad years would easily drive most pastoralists into debt to their *tarafs*, the merchant middlemen who extended credit to pastoralists and agriculturalists.[13] As well, for much of the twentieth century pastoralists were locked in competition with capitalist producers. Paul Ward English, in his classic study of the geography of the Kerman basin, argues that Kerman City dominated the economy of its hinterland more than most Iranian cities did (1966:xix). Describing situations in the 1960s, English noted that not only was most agricultural land in the region owned by members of the urban elite (1966:66), but that much of the carpet production was centered in or controlled from the city as well (1966:84, 92). Indeed, although the urban elite apparently had less direct control of pastoral production than of agricultural or carpet production, they were nonetheless directly involved in the production of animal fibers: "The urban elite also retain control of production factors in herding. Most of the sheep and goats grazed in nearby mountain pastures are owned by carpet merchants, wool dealers, and landowners of Kerman City" (1966:91). In effect, English describes a vertically integrated carpet industry in which carpet merchants controlled all the means of production: animals, wool, wool processing plants, carpet factories, and labor. Ownership of animals would, of course, give merchants a powerful lever with which they could influence the general market price for wool.

By the time I arrived in Kerman, the vertically integrated carpet industry English describes no longer existed. With the growth of Iran's oil economy, other areas provided far greater potential return on investment than the manufacture and export of carpets. Members of the urban elite turned to other investments: real estate, imports of expensive Western goods, and import substitution manufacturing. At the same time, urban workers who could claim inflated wages in construction and other modern industries abandoned weaving even in such a backwater as Kerman City.[14] As a result, members of the urban elite transferred their interests elsewhere and sold their carpet holdings to smaller entrepreneurs, who were often members of the rural elite. At the same time, carpet production moved ever farther into the hinterland as carpet workshops were established in smaller and smaller villages. Finally, as I noted earlier, with the transformation in Kerman's economy a booming meat market emerged. Thus by 1975 the greatest share of Komachi wealth came from meat, not wool or cashmere, and Kerman's pastoralists had finally escaped total dependence on a luxury export market. This, however, was a most recent phenomenon. Moreover, while this introduced the Komachi to another group of urban retail dealers, the local butchers, neither the new meat market nor the changes in carpet production broke traditional Komachi relations with the bazaar. Traditional merchant *tarafs* still made the market in wool. And while the new entrepreneurs might, and sometimes did, buy some wool directly from pastoralists, they needed access to larger and more secure wool supplies than their own relatively limited capital could assure. So while new capital took control over production of carpets per se, the flow of raw materials remained in the hands of traditional merchants. From the perspective of the pastoralists, remarkably little had changed in the nature of their economic relationship with the market. In the past, pastoralists dealt with *tarafs*, or more commonly their agents, and in the mid-1970s they still dealt with *tarafs* (or their local agents), who still controlled the local market in pastoral and agricultural commodities.

I do not mean to suggest by the above that there were no economic changes in Iran or in Kerman during the twentieth century; there were many. The first carpet merchants were Persians from Tabriz; they were replaced by the British and Germans; they were replaced in turn by local merchants, some of whom became members of the local and even national elite; and they, as we have seen, were replaced by members of the rural elite. During the reign of Reza Shah (1925–41) government monopolies were established on a number of consumer goods, including sugar, tea, wheat, and matches. While the impact of these monopolies on rural Iran remains, to my knowledge, unexplored, my own research suggests that it further concentrated economic power in the hands of those who, among other things, could deal effectively with the bureaucracy that developed. Under Mohammed Reza Shah (Reza Shah's son), land reform altered property relations in the countryside, and attempts at wholesale Westernization, modernization, and development based on oil income rapidly transformed many sectors of the Iranian economy. (For more detailed discussions of these transformations see Banani 1961, Bharier 1971, Graham 1979, Halliday 1979, Hooglund 1982, Keddie 1972 and 1978, and Paydarfar 1974. Discussions of the impact of these changes on pastoralists may be found in Beck 1980 and 1986, Black-Michaud 1986, and Bradburd 1983.) It is clear that all of these changes had an impact on the Komachi and tribes like them. Nonetheless, I would stand by the view articulated by Dillon (1976): the fundamental relationship in Kerman between town and countryside, primary producer and market, was established as a result of the early trade in cashmere, and that as late as 1975, Komachi relationships to the market still reflected those structures. Let us examine the basis for that claim.

## Komachi Market Relations

As we have seen, the Komachi had always been firmly bound by exchange relations to the settled world. Speaking theoretically, they were integrated into a capitalist world market system, a fact of major import in their history. Here I will examine just how the Komachi actually articulated with the market, whom they exchanged with and how. I will also show that the Komachi means of articulating with the market was not unique to them but was part of the general pattern of relations holding between the hinterland and the urban center in Kerman Province. Finally, I will suggest that there is reason to think that the kinds of relations found in the twentieth century had existed for at least 250 years, if not longer.

Unlike the Basseri nomads, whom Barth (1961) described as having individual trading relationships with settled agriculturalists, almost all Komachi exchange involved the purchase and sale of commodities for cash or against prices calculated on the basis of cash. Thus, while some Komachi occasionally exchanged small amounts of pastoral produce directly for other commodities, most Komachi dealt with merchants, butchers, and brokers (generally in or around the Kerman City bazaar) whom the Komachi called *tarafs*. *Taraf* literally means "side," but to the Komachi it implied someone who was a merchant, creditor, and patron.

Komachi said, "*tarafs* are people to whom one is in debt," and there was much truth to that. Most Komachi had debts because their *tarafs* extended them credit, permitting them to purchase commodities they needed against the future delivery of pastoral commodities. Most Komachi remained in debt because pastoralism had so many ups and downs that they often needed substantial loans to get through a bad year. In a way, the willingness of *tarafs* to extend credit permitted many Komachi to continue to live as pastoralists, much as the willingness of banks to make seasonal loans and to carry debts permitted some American farmers to keep farming in difficult economic times. Of course, banks were not acting as charitable institutions, and neither were *tarafs*. *Tarafs* extended credit to the Komachi because they made money on the transaction. However, since Islam formally prohibits usury, and since many of the merchants in the Kerman bazaar were overtly pious, most *tarafs* did not simply make money by charging interest on loans; instead, they made money by buying cheap and selling dear.[15] *Tarafs* accomplished this quite easily, for as the nodal links through which virtually all consumer goods flow, they controlled the market. Let us see how.

All Komachi, and virtually all Kermani pastoralists who followed a similar migratory regime, sold most animals, dairy products, and *kork*, and half the yearly amount of wool in early or midsummer, with the remaining wool and the occasional animal being sold in late spring. Not surprisingly, the flood of material onto the market depressed the prices the pastoralists received. Moreover, as the pastoralists often sold well before delivery, they got less money still. On the other hand, pastoralists needed commodities all year round, and if, like the Komachi, they did almost all their buying and selling in Kerman City even though they migrated several hundred miles from it, their periods of purchasing tended to be limited. Most Komachi bought goods in late September and early October to take with them to the *garmsir* and bought what they would use in the *sarhad* in late April and early May. Particularly at this latter time, wheat was expensive and the tribespeople poor. Their summer produce would pay off those debts and, if they were lucky, pay for their winter needs as well. Most likely there would be a little slippage and a debt to be carried until a future good year. Meanwhile, the merchant who bought pastoral produce cheaply from the Komachi also bought grain seasonally (and cheaply) from local peasants, or even at subsidized rates from the government.

By working on fairly substantial markups based on differences in times of delivery and local availability, *tarafs*, acting as small-scale merchant capitalists, were able to earn quite substantial incomes and extend credit without ever charging overt interest. By extending credit *tarafs* in Kerman engaged in a very common form of economic activity, and, like most similar merchants the world over, they used the credit they extended to virtually quarantee themselves access to the commodities entering the market. With both pastoralists and peasants in debt to them, merchants did not have to worry about much competition in the marketplace. Like beggars, debtors cannot be choosers, and few pastoralists (or peasants, for that matter) had the privilege of shopping around for the best prices at which to buy or sell; the market that producers and consumers faced was hardly free, a reality that the merchants literally capitalized on. Let me add here that while I did not have an opportunity to examine the merchants' side of the business in detail, it is my impression that they were able to carry debts that were quite substantial for the nomads with little burden to themselves, for they moved locally purchased commodities against credit and rarely had to put up large amounts of cash. At least some merchants seemed to reap short-term profits large enough to make out well, even if some of the debt they held ultimately turned out to be bad.

One can see evidence of the importance of *tarafs* in Paul Ward English's descriptions of exchanges, or the lack of them, among residents of large villages in the Kerman basin. Noting that the division of labor between weavers and cultivators was the most significant one in the village, English goes on to point out that though weavers did not cultivate and cultivators did not weave, there was little direct exchange between them or between them and herders. "There is little cooperation or exchange between the two groups. The agriculturalists cannot supply the weavers with food stuffs, since most are sharecroppers and have no surplus. Weavers do not buy wool directly from herders, both groups work under contracts with carpet factories in Kerman" (1966:84). English describes a situation similar to that of the Komachi, in which virtually no direct exchanges linked the region's primary producers to one another; rather, all exchanges took place through nodal links in Kerman City. At the center of this web of exchange lay the wholesale import export merchants, of whom English writes,

the elite . . . wholesale import export merchants (*tajir*) . . . export carpets, wool, dried fruit, and nuts from Kirman and import sugar, rice, tea, cloth, hardware, and machinery. These men live in large houses in the suburbs of Kirman but work in small, sparsely furnished rooms around the caravanseries. These surroundings are deceptive, for the *tajir's* money and influence are spread throughout the city at all levels. Most of his capital is in real estate. . . . Some is in merchandise, however, and the wealthiest of these merchants are creditors for hundreds of retailers, hawkers, and vendors. (1966:74)

English does not note that these men were also the *tarafs*, but they were. These men made the markets: they bought agricultural products and pastoral products; they imported tea, sugar, and the other basic commodities people consumed; they extended credit, and through the extension of credit they controlled the markets in locally produced commodities. English suggests that agriculturalists did not exchange with weavers because they "ha[d] no surplus." It is clear from his own later discussion (1966:90) that this does not mean they had no surplus above the wheat or barley their household consumed. Rather, they had no surplus above their household budget. Indeed, they may not have produced enough to make ends meet.

[The sharecropper] cultivates cereals in a marginal environment, receives 30% of the harvest. . . . He must survive periods of want and depend on the landlord or a moneylender in the bazaar to tide him over these bad years. All loans are raised on the security of next year's harvest. . . . debt keeps the sharecropper at the subsistence level; he works his way from harvest to harvest with little prospect of bettering his position. (1966:90)

In short, for both peasants and pastoralists, merchants controlled rates of exchange, held debts, and dominated the market. English's work provides insight into the mechanism through which the elite dominated the local economy through the 1960s: they owned most of the resources and, through the extension of credit and control of linkages among the commodities produced and consumed by weavers, pastoralists, and cultivators, they controlled the distribution of what they did not own. Peasants and pastoralists were thus dependent upon them.

When land reform ultimately broke the control on land held by large landowners, it did not damage the position of the merchants and may well have intensified their power. With most production in the hands of small producers, merchants did not have to contend with landowners whose economic and political resources matched or exceeded their own. Rather, they dealt only with smallholders who almost inevitably were in debt, who bought and sold exclusively in the local market, and who, lacking the credit formerly extended by landlords (see English 1966:171, note 7), were completely dependent on *tarafs* operating in the bazaar. Thus peasants were no more independent after land reform than before. Neither were pastoralists. Trade still flowed almost exclusively through the bazaar, *tarafs* still extended credit, and the Komachi, like their peasant neighbors, still operated in a market that was far from free.

There is good reason to think that the situation I describe for the mid-1970s and that English describes for the 1960s was anything but new. A fascinating quote from the so-called Gombroon Diary, a record book kept by the British East India Company at Bandar Abbas, suggests that relations like those of 1975 might well have held 250 years earlier as well.

June 16, 1727. Rec'd a letter from Cosroe [the British East Indian
Company's wool buyer in Kerman]. . . . [N]ow he advises us, those merchants who were indebted to him and had promised to make over some
parcells [of cashmere] to him as security were gone into the country, that
since his last he had not been able to make any purchases through the extravagant exchange there was betwixt black and white money, mamoodies
being at 50 percent and each abasee at 6 shahees 6 gaz. Which advantage
the merchants had now taken over him, they bring [buying?] all their wool
up the country with brass money and will sell it him only for white which
with the troubles not being yet over he says they are afraid to bring it down
in any considerable quantities but in a few days he hopes he can buy it at
about 20 shahees per maund. That there had already been brought some
small parcels . . . which he had not yet bought, the merchants desiring him to
stay till the rest came out of the country. . . .

[Cosroe further made allegation that] Cossum he having given notice
to all those from whom the wool is to be bought at first hand so early as
in the month of January that he would give them from 16 to 18 shahees
per maund in white money which had been the occasion of enhancing the
price very considerablly. . . . [Cosroe further noted that] Mahmoud Ally and
Nagd Ally cannot clear their debts in wool but have promised the amount
in wheat in a small time. (British East India Company 1727; not paginated)

The quotation above gives us insight into the structure of the local market at the beginning of the eighteenth century. It shows that merchants
or their agents were going to the hinterland and buying and selling
goods there. It suggests that the buyers of pastoral products and the sell-
ers of wheat were the same people, for they could clear their debts in
either wool or wheat. It suggests that all commodities had a cash price.
In short, it suggests that merchants in the 1720s dealt with the countryside in ways that differed little from those of the 1970s. The linkage
of pastoral producers (and peasants) with the market in Kerman is a
longstanding one.

Given the historical depth of the relationship between merchants
and the countryside, it is no wonder that the ties between the Komachi
and their *tarafs* were complex. *Tarafs* were honored guests at weddings;
they spoke for particular Komachi both within the tribe and outside it;
they extended credit as part of a largely economic transaction, but they
lent money to help their clients buy motorcycles and pay for their
children's education. While one can hardly call people locked in a some-

what antagonistic and certainly asymmetrical relationship friends, *tarafs* were far from strangers. Intimates always mediated the Komachi relationship to the market: there were no strangers there. Thus some of the harshness of external market forces was softened by the mediation of agents who were known and who had some sympathy with the nomad's way of life. Still, as holders of Komachi debt and as manipulators of the market, *tarafs* were clearly in a predatory relationship to the pastoralists. All Komachi, rich and poor, were dominated by relationships that served to extract wealth from the tribal economy; it is important always to bear that in mind, along with the fact that the local merchants and brokers were merely the next-to-last links in a very long national and international chain. If local merchants extracted credit from tribespeople by offering them a lower cash-on-the-barrelhead price for goods than for payment after thirty days, they too were being squeezed by their creditors. The Komachi, like so many other primary producers caught in the web of the world market, could not control the forces that ultimately determined the quality of their lives.

Overall, until the rise of the meat market in the mid-1970s Kerman's pastoralists remained producers of raw materials for fashionable export goods. Their relationship with the market in the twentieth century was an intensified continuation of relations that had begun in the seventeenth century.

## A Brief Historical View of the Population of Kerman Province

In the Introduction I noted that Kermani tribes were ephemeral social entities. The nature, structural causes, and effects of the fluidity are a major focus of this work. Anticipating those discussions, I will conclude this discussion of the contexts in which Kermani tribes were embedded with an examination of changes in the area's population over the last 150 years. This discussion of Kerman's population is important because my argument for the fluidity of tribal composition is contingent on the existence of open territory for new tribes to move into. The following section is, within the limits of the evidence, a demonstration that Kerman was an open area and that the necessary conditions for the processes I describe did hold.

## THE DATA

The first official census of Iran was undertaken in 1956. Virtually all discussions of population prior to that time are therefore unofficial estimates. Much of the published literature on Iran's population prior to the census concerns estimates of the reliability of the estimators and reasons for their reliability (or lack of it). There is maddeningly little solid data. Fortunately, however, there are three studies of Iran's population in the nineteenth and twentieth centuries that tie together much of this disparate information, and in the discussion that follows I have drawn heavily on the work of Issawi (1971), Gilbar (1976), and Bharier (1968, 1971).[16] Using these studies, I have attempted to put together an overview of Iran's population characteristics during the nineteenth and twentieth centuries, which I use as a base for an outline of the likely conditions in Kerman.

## IRAN'S POPULATION: THE NINETEENTH CENTURY

According to Issawi, Iran's population rose from between 5 and 6 million in 1800 to roughly 10 million by 1914 (1971:20). If this is true, then the overall rate of Iran's population growth throughout this period was 0.5 percent per year. Gilbar presents a somewhat different picture of the situation. He argues (1976:128) that the two most reliable reporters of Iran's population in the mid- to late nineteenth century were H. C. Rawlinson and A. Houton-Schindler. The former claimed that Iran's population was roughly 6 million in 1873, and the latter recorded figures of 7.65 million in 1881, 9 million in 1900, and 10 million in 1910 (Gilbar 1976:126–27). Reviewing figures on the population growth rate of this period, Gilbar also concludes that it was almost certainly between 0.5 percent and 1.0 percent per year (Gilbar 1976:131ff.). Combining these two sets of data, Gilbar creates a model of Persian population in the late nineteenth century in which that population rose from between 7.5 and 8.5 million in 1872 to about 10 million in 1900. This leads him to assume that Persia was likely to have had a population of about 9 to 10 million in 1850 (1976:144), a figure that exceeds a projection based on Issawi's figures by 1.5 to 2.5 million persons. Gilbar believes that population growth after 1850 was limited by disease and famine, particularly the great famine of 1867–72 and the concomitant cholera epidemic that struck the southern part of the country (including Kerman). Indeed, Gilbar thinks that Persia's population probably dropped between 1850 and 1872, recovering slowly after that time. Overall, Gilbar believes that there was no substantive increase in the population of Iran from 1850 to 1900 (Gilbar 1976:144). In comments of particular interest to this work, Gilbar also expresses the opinion that the total number of nomads in Iran fell during this period from between 3 and 3.5 million at mid-century to some 2.5 million at the beginning of the twentieth century. He attributes a good portion of this drop in population to differential mortality during the great famine (1976:145).[17]

While one can readily see that there are no absolute figures on Persian population in the nineteenth century, it does seem possible to conclude the following: (1) Persian population as a whole grew quite slowly through the nineteenth century and may not have grown at all from 1850 on; (2) tribal population probably decreased as a whole, as tribespeople were subjected to more adverse conditions than was the settled rural population; and (3) in 1900, the population of Iran was still less than 10 million and was growing at a rate of less than 1 percent a year.

## IRAN'S POPULATION: THE TWENTIETH CENTURY

Virtually all analysts agree that Iran's population was slightly under 10 million in 1900. The first national census in 1956 gave a population of 20.38 million (Bharier 1968); at the second, in 1966, the population was 27 million (Bharier 1971); and according to the third census in 1976 the population of Iran was over 33 million (Graham 1979). These figures show that in the twentieth century there was not only significant growth in Iran's population but also a dramatic increase in the rate of population growth. Bharier (1968, 1971) estimates that between 1900 and 1925—a period of civil war, world war, famine, and disorder—the population growth rate did not exceed 0.75 percent per year (which means the rate remained constant from about 1873 to 1926). From 1926 through 1946, the growth rate is presumed to have been about 1.5 percent per year; the rate seems to have increased to 2.5 percent between 1946 and 1956. Between the first two censuses, the rate increased again to 2.9 percent. This declined slightly to 2.5 percent from 1966 to 1976 (Bharier 1968). Assuming that the estimates prior to the censuses are accurate, Iran's population in 1945 was about 15 million, roughly half again Gilbar's estimate of its population in 1850. During this period there seems to have been no substantial difference in the rate of population growth between rural and urban areas. Thereafter, however, there were radical divergences. From 1945 to 1966 the rural population of Iran grew at a rate of 1.6 percent per year, increasing from 11.7 million in 1945 to 16.5 million in 1966. By contrast, the urban population increased from 4 million to 10.5 million in the same period (Bharier 1972). A good portion of this increase reflects migration to cities, particularly Tehran. Bharier also suggests that the number of nomads dropped from about 2.5 million in 1900 (a figure that agrees with Gilbar's) to about 250,000 in 1966 (1971:58). Although this latter figure clearly is too low, it does reflect a general trend of decrease in nomadic populations throughout the period.[18]

In any event, as with the nineteenth century, we can draw out a general view of population in Iran in the twentieth century. Population increased dramatically; the rate of increase rose dramatically; there was increased urbanization; and there seems to have been a continued national decline in the country's tribal population.

## KERMAN

If national census figures for Iran are sketchy during the nineteenth and twentieth centuries, those for Kerman, an out-of-the-way province, are even more sketchy. Here almost all the information we have comes from British political agents' estimates of their circumstances. In 1867, British consular sources estimated that Kerman Province had a population of 207,000 (Issawi 1971:27). With the province comprising some 73,000 square miles, its average population density was just under three people per square mile. Given our interest in tribes, however, we are less concerned with absolute population figures than with figures for the rural areas of the province. To arrive at these, one must extrapolate from figures for total population and estimates of urban population. At the time that these consular sources estimated the population of the province to be 207,000, they also estimated that Kerman City, the center of the province, had a population of about 30,000 (Issawi 1971:28). This figure seems low, however, for Bharier (1970) estimates its population to have been 60,000 in 1900, and Issawi suggests a population of between 40,000 and 50,000 for the mid-nineteenth century. Bharier's figure, which seems to be drawn from fairly reliable sources (including

Percy Sykes, who was consul in Kerman at the time), is particularly problematic for the other estimate, if we asssume a population of 30,000 in 1867—that is, prior to the famine and cholera epidemic of 1867–72, an event that must have reduced the city's population significantly (see Gilbar 1976:144, 137 and Issawi 1971)—then the population growth rate that would have been needed to bring the population to 60,000 in 1900 was over 2.1 percent per year. This vastly exceeds even the most optimistic estimates of Persian population growth for that period. As a result, a midcentury figure of about 50,000 seems more reasonable. An examination of population figures (rough though they be) for other nonrural centers of the province, such as the smaller cities of Sirjan, Bam, Mahan, Jupar, etc. (see Bharier 1972 and Stöber 1978 for lists of some estimates of these figures), suggests we may assume as well that an additional 25,000 people were not exclusively rural. If this is so, then the rural population of the province would drop to about 125,000, and the rural population density would drop to less than 1.75 people per square mile. While these figures are clearly estimates, there are two reasons to suspect that they are not too far wrong. First, if we accept the 1867 British figure as a base and apply to it the estimated national rates of population growth that I enumerated above, we find a figure that is quite close to that of the 1966 census, which gave Kerman a population of 761,851. A second reason for supposing that this low figure is accurate is the knowledge that Kerman had suffered significant population losses throughout the eighteenth and nineteenth centuries, not to mention earlier. For instance, we know that Kerman suffered heavily during the invasion by Timur (Tamerlane) during the fourteenth century (English 1966:26). While Kerman substantially recovered from these problems during the Safavid period, it suffered greatly as Safavid power began to decline. In 1720 and 1722 Kerman was overrun by Afghan invaders. During Nadir Shah's reign, Kerman served as a supply base for his armies, and in 1737 he drew off the whole of the province's grain reserves and requisitioned most if its baggage animals to provision his army (English 1966). Following this economic disaster, Kerman had only a brief reprieve until 1747, when it was again invaded by the Afghans. More problems followed when in the course of a power struggle between Lotf Ali Kahn Zand and Agha Mohammed Qajar Kerman supported the former. As a result, when Lotf Ali Khan was defeated in 1794, 20,000 of the cities' inhabitants were sold into slavery and another 20,000 men were blinded (English 1966). Then for three months the victorious Qajar troops were allowed to pillage the countryside freely. Even then, the Qajars' rage was apparently not satisfied, since for the next fifty years Kerman was governed by the harshest and most rapacious of the Qajar governors (English 1966). Indeed, it is not hard to believe that Kerman was underpopulated in the nineteenth century; one only wonders that it had any population at all.

The impression of empty space gets further support from other quarters as well. In 1832 the governor of the province felt that there was sufficient room in it to invite the Qashqa'i khans to move to Kerman Province, and provision was made for summer and winter pasture for 100,000 tribal households (Busse 1972:209). While this offer was never accepted—and one wonders if there could have been room for a horde that probably was larger than the extant population of the province at that time—it does suggest that there was significant open rangeland within the region.

## Conclusions

It has not been my intention in this rather dry review of the population history of Kerman Province to arrive at any definitive analysis of its population parameters; rather, what I have attempted to do is clarify the kinds of population pressure that tribes within the province were likely to have faced in the nineteenth and twentieth centuries. While the information presented above clearly is not perfect, it is good enough to support the following general conclusions: (1) Iran's nineteenth-century population was never larger than 10 million and may well have been as low as 7.5 million following the famine and cholera epidemic of 1867–72; (2) there is no reason to assume that Iran's population growth rate was higher than 1 percent per year, and it probably never exceeded 0.75 percent per year until the mid-1920s; and (3) nationwide, both the absolute number of nomads and their percentage of the population dropped during the late nineteenth century, probably due to differential mortality during the famine period and to increased economic pressure as exchange rates for pastoral produce fell with the shift to opium production.

With regard to Kerman Province, it seems reasonable to assume that (1) the population in the mid-nineteenth century was approximately 207,000; (2) its population growth rate was not dramatically different from that of Iran as a whole; (3) the region lost population during the period 1867–1872; and (4) overall, the region's population and population density were quite low until at least the 1940s.

These circumstances seem to translate into a specific set of conditions for pastoralists. Through much of the nineteenth century there must have been a great deal of open rangeland within the province (*vide* the offer to the Qashqa'i). The openness of territory seems likely to have persisted, to a greater or lesser extent, throughout the nineteenth century. In particular, it seems likely that the famine and epidemic of 1867–72 would have led to an increase in free territory. This open territory should have provided ample opportunity for the establishment of new tribes in unpopulated areas. There is certainly no suggestion of restriction of pasture during this period. This evidence accords well with tribal views of their own history. The Komachi believed that the current Komachi tribe was made up of people whose ancestors migrated into the province from other areas of Iran; they were uncertain of dates, but assuming their genealogical evidence is at all correct, these migrations occurred in the nineteenth century. This view of Kerman as the endpoint of migration was supported by other tribal peoples within the province, who told me (during a survey of the region) that they too were descendents of immigrant ancestors (see Sykes 1902 for a discussion of this point). In the twentieth century, it seems likely that the slow rate of population growth precluded any real pressure on resources or limits on availability of pasture (in general; for specific areas this may not hold true) until the post–World War II period. This too accords well with the Komachi view of their history. They did begin use of their current *garmsir* in the early 1950s, and they moved there as a result of pressure in their old territory. Still, it is quite clear that there was open territory, both in summer and winter quarters, as late as the 1950s. However, one should note also that since that time, rapid population growth (within the tribes as well as outside them), coupled with development of pump-based irrigation agriculture in the south, severely restricted the amount of land available to nomads. That, however, was a recent phenomenon, and I believe that the evidence strongly supports the view that throughout the nineteenth century and well into the twentieth century there was more free pasture in Kerman than there were pastoralists to use it. As a result, wherever internal pressures drove tribes apart, there was room for the splinters and remnants to form new tribes. How and why they did so is a problem that I shall deal with later. For the moment, however, we can see that the possibility of the formation of new units clearly existed, and we have also seen that the tribes that were formed in this period lived within an environment in which the hand of the market was far from invisible.

# PART II

# KOMACHI ECONOMIC LIFE

# 4

# AN OVERVIEW
# OF KOMACHI
# ECONOMIC LIFE

The Komachi were pastoralists who lived on the value of the commodities their animals produced. Production and consumption were centered in the nuclear family, and households comprising nuclear families were the fundamental economic units of Komachi society. Each Komachi household owned the animals its members (or its shepherds) cared for and from which they produced the pastoral commodities they consumed and exchanged. This chapter sets out in broad strokes the basic outline of Komachi production and consumption. I describe what the Komachi produced and what they ate, and I outline the division of labor by class and gender. Following chapters will explore aspects of the Komachi economy in greater detail.

## Production

Komachi pastoral production entailed two primary tasks: the actual care of the animals and the manufacture of marketable commodities from the animals. As the sine qua non for the production of any pastoral commodities was the maintenance of the household's animals, the basic task confronting the Komachi was caring for their animals. Goats and sheep had to be fed and watered and protected from predators or harsh weather; female animals had to be bred successfully. To achieve some of these ends, household flocks were combined into larger camp herds. Animals were then redivided on the basis of age, sex, breed, and other criteria into several smaller herds whose composition varied with the annual round. In general, sheep were kept separately from goats, male animals from females, and kids and lambs were kept separately from each other and from larger animals. During the breeding season in early summer, male and female animals were run together in common herds. In late fall, pregnant female animals were separated from the common herd, while those that had not become pregnant were kept with the male stock in the hopes that they would give birth in the spring. As a result, each wealthy Komachi household had several separate flocks, each with its own shepherd.

Komachi raised both Kashmir goats and fat-tailed sheep. These animals produced meat, which the Komachi sold (on the hoof) and occasionally ate, wool and cashmere (*kork*) that the Komachi sold, and a variety of dairy products including milk, which the Komachi converted to yogurt for their own consumption, clarified butter, which they both sold and ate, and a dried whey, *kashk*, which they both sold and consumed as a staple of their diet. Though under the conditions that prevailed in 1974–75 a successful sheep owner could earn far more from his animals than a goat herder, the Komachi herded twice as many goats as sheep. Sheep yielded a greater return because goats produced only small quantities of *kork* once a year, while sheep yielded larger amounts of wool in two shearings. Moreover, the prices of lamb meat and wool were consistently higher than the prices of goat meat and *kork*. Sheep were not as resistant to drought as goats, however, and they were far worse foragers. A bad year—particularly in the winter quarters—was likely to force herd owners to buy fodder for sheep that they did not need to purchase for goats. Thus, though the gross yield per sheep was higher than that per goat, there was also greater risk involved in sheep production. I believe this accounted for the fact that throughout the tribe wealthy nomads owned large numbers of both goats and sheep while poor nomads, in the main, had only goats.[1]

Setting aside for the moment questions of variations in holdings or in annual production, the average annual yield of a Komachi animal was about $14.00 per year;[2] I will use this as a base figure for my later discussions of household earnings and calculations of household viability. The average cost of maintaining an animal for a year, exclusive of labor, was $2.25, and so the average net yield of a Komachi animal was $11.75 per head.

Given an annual maintenance cost per human consumer of $180 (see below) and an average net yield of $11.75, each Komachi consumer had to be supported by roughly 15 animals. As the main body of the Komachi tribe comprised 348 consumers,[3] support of that population at a basic standard of living required a herd of 4,900 animals yielding a total annual product of $57,600. In point of fact, the Komachi owned a total of over 9,300 animals, producing an estimated net annual yield of $110,000. In a good year the 4,300 animals over and beyond the number needed for basic support produced nearly $55,000 more in revenue than the tribespeople needed. Bad years, however, dramatically diminished this yield. In fact, in bad years only the wealthiest families produced a surplus. Thus, as we shall see below, bad years helped create and amplify differences between rich and poor at the same time that they diminished differences between poor and middle-level pastoralists.

## Consumption

Komachi patterns of consumption varied tremendously, and citation of an average annual cost for maintaining a person implies a homogeneity that did not exist. I have therefore chosen to center my general discussion of the Komachi economy about what I call a *basic maintenance cost*, derived by extrapolating from the household budget of a shepherd family that in 1975 had a low but not abject standard of living. A basic diet of bread, tea, *kashk*, and sugar cost the equivalent of about 35¢ per adult per day. With occasional purchases of supplementary and luxury foods (such as rice, spices, oil, fruit, and vegetables) and provision for clothing, shelter, transportation, medicine, fuel, etc., the cost of maintaining an adult consumer was roughly $180 per year.

With the exception of dairy products and meat, virtually everything the Komachi consumed was purchased in the market. In practical

terms, this meant that every Komachi household purchased the following items: wheat for bread; tea; loaf sugar; rice; salt; onion, garlic, and
other spices; black goat hair for tent panels; clothing; blankets; tinning
for copper pots and pans; matches; tobacco; water for animals in winter
quarters; and a proportion of the cost of migrating by truck in the fall.
Quantities of materials consumed varied with household size and to
some degree with household wealth; the quality of the commodities
consumed—and there were significant ranges—varied almost directly
with household wealth.

Like other Southwest Asian pastoralists, the staple of the Komachi
diet was bread. The Komachi ate a lot of bread, about 18 ounces a day
or roughly 400 to 450 pounds of bread per person per year. Komachi
bread was a real whole-grain product. From roughly ground whole-
wheat flour, Komachi women prepared two types of bread: a nearly
paper-thin, unleavened flat bread that was baked in rounds 15 to 18
inches across, and a sourdough loaf that rose perhaps half an inch and
resembled an unadorned pizza when it was completed. As the unleavened rounds could be made in great quantities and kept well, they were
the more common loaf. Both breads were brown, tasty, and as filled
with nutrients as they were with roughage. Komachi breads were
substantial—but then they had to be, for bread was what most Komachi
ate.

Most meals for most Komachi consisted of three or four rounds of
unleavened bread and a bowl of *kashk*, a by-product of Komachi dairying. *Kashk* was made by first turning whole milk into yogurt, churning
the yogurt into butter, then separating the buttermilk from the butter.
The thin liquid was then cooked until it formed a thick paste, which
was rolled into balls and dried in the sun. To prepare *kashk* for eating,
women rubbed several balls together in a bowl of water, in effect recon-
stituting the original buttermilk. Mixed with a little melted clarified
butter and a sprinkling of salt and herbs, *kashk* was an all-purpose liquid food, part soup, part beverage.

Normally, bread and *kashk* were consumed by tearing several of
the unleavened loaves into small pieces and mixing them carefully into
the *kashk*. The remaining pieces of bread were torn into larger pieces
and used as a kind of wrapper for the now-sodden small pieces of bread
drawn from the *kashk*. Bread and *kashk* formed the nucleus of most
Komachi meals and were, as I noted above, the meal that most Komachi
ate day in and day out. The greatest changes in this diet arose from sea-

sonal variations in food. For example, from February through June *kashk* was replaced by fresh yogurt, and in late summer small amounts of homemade cheese were added to some meals.

Along with their bread and *kashk*, the Komachi drank tea and sugar. Tea was the Iranian social beverage *par excellence*, and one could not visit a Persian house or tent without being offered several small glasses. The Komachi participated in this social ritual, but it seemed to me that tea was more than a social beverage for them. Whatever its quality, Komachi tea was always an extremely strong brew, drunk very sweet. Over the course of the day, people would drink enough tea to consume 4 ounces of sugar; the roughly 400 calories the sugar supplied represented one-fifth to one-sixth of most peoples' caloric intake.

Tea and sugar were products the Komachi purchased, as was most wheat for bread. However, while we may assume that pastoralists in the region had consumed bread or some other wheat product as a staple of their diet for a very long time, the same was not true for tea. Tea appears to have become a common beverage in the late nineteenth century. Older Komachi recalled that during their youths in the early years of the twentieth century tea was scarce, a true luxury item, and the Komachi drank herbal infusions. I note this because it is quite clear that the introduction of tea and sugar into the tribal diet and custom (and quite likely the general Persian diet and custom as well) represented a major transformation of consumption patterns; it was certainly a significant step in the integration of these people into the world market.

It will have become apparent to the reader by now that although the Komachi raised animals, meat was not a feature of their own daily diet. This was true of wealthy and poor Komachi alike, although as with other foods, the wealthy did eat more meat more often. I hasten to add that one should not imagine that the Komachi rarely ate meat for reasons of taste. Meat was their most highly valued food; as such, it was also a currency of social exchange, a marker of social worth. But meat came from animals, and in 1974–75 animals were walking money. Even the wealthiest Komachi did not eat meat casually; who ate what kind of meat, when, and how they got it were complex issues of etiquette and obligation as well as matters of taste and wealth.

In general, the Komachi consumed meat in four sets of circumstances. First, if an animal was so ill that it appeared unlikely to survive, it was slaughtered for meat. When this happened, the owners of the animal generally consumed the bulk of meat, distributing small amounts to kin who lived nearby.[4] For most Komachi, meat from sick animals comprised the major portion of the meat that entered their diet. Second, the Komachi consumed the meat of animals killed as sacrifices, *nazri*. In contrast to the meat from animals killed for any other purpose, meat from *nazri* did not quite belong to the owner of the animal; rather, the Komachi saw it as "belonging" to the recipient of the sacrifice—often the Imam Hossein or another important figure in Shi'ite sacred history. This meat was then broadly distributed to members of the camp, close kin, and others who were nearby *in the name of the sacred figure*. In a very real sense, this was meat that was intended for distribution. Virtually every Komachi household killed some animals for *nazri*.[5] Third, the Komachi served and ate large quantities of meat at significant ritual occasions, particularly wedding and circumcision celebrations and *rozehs* (religious events). At all these events, meals featured a main course of stew (*ab gusht*), rice (absent at *rozehs*), and bread. Every guest at the celebration received a large piece of stewed meat as part of his or her portion. As these events always took place in late summer and early autumn, generally one right after another, this was a time of the year when all Komachi, rich and poor, ate large quantities of meat. The last set of circumstances in which the Komachi regularly ate meat arose when they were guests or hosts for significant visits. Since meat was highly valued, one in effect honored a guest by preparing a meat meal for him (or, far less commonly, her). Given the value of meat, and the fact that it was clearly being used to mark the importance of a guest, just who got meat and who did not were facts of some importance; so too was the question of who did or did not provide meat for which guests. As a general rule, the higher the status of the guest, the more important it was to show proper respect by feeding him or her properly. If a guest was important enough—for instance, of high status and not a member of the tribe—then a sheep or goat was killed. Failure to do so would be seen as a grave lapse of hospitality and would diminish the host's reputation. For a guest who was not quite as important meat still had to be served, but killing a sheep or goat would have been thought extravagant. Guests such as these were fed meat from already slaughtered stock if there was any available; if there was no meat in camp, then the host would kill one of the chickens that most Komachi tried to keep both for eggs and for these social occasions. If more than a few guests arrived— for example, to negotiate a marriage contract—the host was, again, expected to kill an animal as a proper sign of respect and hospitality.

In sum, the Komachi lived on bread, tea, and sugar that they purchased in the bazaar. Dairy products, their other staple, came from their herds, as did meat, the most highly valued food.

## Labor and its Divisions

Among the Komachi, access to labor was organized along three axes. There were two primary divisions of labor, one dividing tasks between men and women and a second separating poor men who worked as hired shepherds from the wealthier men who hired them. In addition, there was a crosscutting axis that distinguished labor that was based on contractual obligations—largely shepherding labor—from labor that was given or extracted under the rubric of *komak*, neighborly assistance. As the following discussion shall show, the conjunction of these axes created a situation in which most pastoral production was carried out by poor men selling their labor power to wealthy men, wealthy women producing dairy products from their households' herds, and poor women, who were pressured into giving large amounts of non-compensated "help" to the women of wealthy households. Wealthy men did very little physical work. Thus, though wealthy women, in theory, shared their husbands' high status, and though help was supposed to be a freely given gift, we shall see that in practice the position of wealthy women was strikingly similar to that of poor shepherds, and most help was anything but freely given.

### SHEPHERD AND EMPLOYER

Komachi pastoral production was based on the extensive use of hired shepherds, who worked for an annual compensation with a cash value of roughly $350 to $400. Wage labor—albeit a particular kind—was a dominant feature of the Komachi economic order. Wealthy herd owners could gain access to herding labor from outside their household because other Komachi did not have enough animals to support themselves without supplementary income from employment. There was no regular access to extrafamilial male labor other than through shepherding contracts. Herding labor was provided either by members of the household (largely for less wealthy Komachi) or by hired shepherds.

As a result of the division of labor between shepherds and employers, wealthy members of the tribe (in this discussion, tribesmen who owned over 200 animals) almost never engaged in the actual tasks of herding animals: their shepherds did the work. Cooperative herding that took place among the households of a camp did not just divide kinds of animals among all available male workers. Rather, the care of the total camp herd was entrusted to men who were independent small herdowners caring for their own animals and hired shepherds employed by wealthy herd owners. Just who was watching any given animal at any given time was the result of a series of formal and practical decisions made by both the herders and the owners (though owners held hired shepherds liable, at least emotionally, for the well-being of any animal that was nominally in their charge).

Day-to-day care of most animals was therefore largely entrusted to hired shepherds who saw that the animals were fed, watered, and protected. Shepherds also helped female animals give birth. Only flocks of newborn kids and lambs, which were herded in or near camp by women or children, were not the shepherds' responsibility.

Although a camp's animals were joined together into common flocks for efficient herding, other productive labor was not strictly cooperative. While all ewes that had lambed were herded together, for example, women from each household separated their ewes from the common herd for milking. Similarly, when kids and lambs were to be fed they were brought to their mothers, which were separated from the common herd on a household-by-household basis. Finally, men generally sheared only their own animals, and they always sheared all their own animals before helping anyone else. Thus, though herding labor was cooperative and generally in the hands of hired shepherds, most remaining labor was done on a household-by-household basis. Cooperation was specifically recognized as the members of one household giving assistance, *komak*, to the members of another.

## KOMAK

In theory, *komak*, which literally means help or assistance, was the aid people gave each other at times of need. Thus, when guests appeared at one family's tent, their neighbors would give *komak*: they would help bake bread or help with the cooking. If someone went to town, picking up small things for one's neighbors was *komak*. On a larger scale, help with the preparations for a wedding or circumcision celebration was *komak*, as was the gathering of kin about someone who was ill or injured. *Komak* was in essence the social obligation one had to those with whom one lived. As a social obligation, *komak* was to be given freely; in anthropological terms, *komak* followed the ground rules of general reciprocity.

As Bourdieu (1977) has noted concerning kinship, where differences between formal theory and practice are encountered one of the more interesting subjects of inquiry is how the formal system is manipulated strategically to evaluate, validate, or challenge practice. Among the Komachi, the gap between the theory of *komak* and its practice was wide and fascinating, and I will return to it in some detail later. Here the following features ought to be noted. While some *komak* was given by men to men, most *komak* was transferred between women. By far the greatest amount of *komak* given among the Komachi was that given by poorer women to help their wealthier neighbors milk their animals and process dairy products. Herding labor, which was sold and purchased, thus contrasted quite sharply with female labor, which was taken and supplied under the rubric of *komak*. While women's *komak* was truly noncompensated and was always considered rhetorically as neighborly assistance, it was in fact an essential source of labor for dairy production for wealthy households. Most *komak* therefore entailed a regular flow of noncompensated, time-consuming, and arduous productive labor from poor households to wealthy ones. Not surprisingly, there was often considerable conflict about *komak*. Given that women gave *komak* and men did not, one may see male and female labor as representing different kinds of production relations. *Komak* and contracts were manifestations of the division that existed within the Komachi social formation between what may be characterized as a moral or good faith economy and a political economy.

## WOMEN AND MEN

Within the household there was a clear division of productive labor. Men—whether hired shepherds or not—did all the herding of adult animals, all the shearing, and all the preparation of wool and cashmere for market. Women did all the dairying, from milking through processing of the finished products.

Komachi use of hired shepherds had a profound impact on the nature and quality of men's and women's lives. Because the owners of large herds hired poor men to work for them, wealthy men could avoid virtually all of the actual physical labor required to maintain or produce commodities from such large herds. Except for shearing, which they did, wealthy men were largely a managerial class. Questioned on the subject, wealthy men asserted that they were "working" by traveling from camp to camp, getting information on prices, pasture conditions in other areas, and the like. I followed these men as they visited, talked, ate, and drank tea, and while these men were indeed gathering and exchanging information, I concluded that this was far more a social than economic practice. Poor men worked; rich men did not.[6] By contrast, wealth and labor were inversely related for women. Rich or poor, all Komachi women participated directly and extensively in the actual processes of milking, preparing dairy products, and (with the help of children) caring for young animals. As there were very few economies of scale in Komachi dairy production, it was far more time-consuming to process the dairy products of a large herd than of a small one. Because more work was needed to milk 500 animals than to milk 50, women in wealthy households had far more work than women in poorer households. Women of wealthy households, as noted above, helped meet this burden by calling on the help, *komak*, of poorer women who were their neighbors in the camp, but women of wealthy households still had to spend many hours dairying; they were, with good reason, always labor-hungry. Poor men worked harder than rich men, but rich women worked as least as hard as poor women; I think it quite likely that rich women and their unmarried grown daughters did more work than any other Komachi.

As it has not been stressed in earlier ethnographies of Southwest Asian pastoralists, I wish to make clear one point about women's labor. Komachi pastoral production absorbed enormous quantities of women's labor. To a substantial degree, women's labor was the form of labor that was scarcest in the society; it was the major labor bottleneck, and negotiations concerning access to women's labor—marriage contracts and *komak*—were, as we shall see, events of considerable intensity. The vital importance of women's labor is perhaps best revealed by noting that although widows were able to maintain independent households following the deaths of their husbands, men could not live without women to run the household and do the dairying. Households that had no female members could not survive.

In spite of the need for access to female labor, the availability of both male and female extrafamilial labor (through *komak* and shepherding contracts) freed Komachi households to a considerable degree from one of the constraints on household viability frequently mentioned for pastoralists: meeting the labor requirements of their herds from within their own households or through strictly cooperative labor-sharing practices. As a result, the links between labor and wealth that have been suggested for some pastoral societies (Barth 1961, 1964; Bates 1973; Irons 1975) did not directly hold for the Komachi.[7] Further, use of hired rather than simply cooperative labor also greatly increased the flexibility of labor organization, particularly from the perspective of the wealthy herd owner. These advantages should not be considered trivial, and, as we shall see, they were maintained at some social cost. As there were other ways to solve the labor problem—most notably cooperative herding arrangements within camps—Komachi use of hired shepherds cannot be explained as a simple function of household labor requirements. In effect, it remains the problematic of the Komachi economy, and thus we must look at it more closely.

# 5

## SHEPHERDS AND EMPLOYERS: DIVISIONS AND AMBIGUITIES

So far, I have presented a broad overview of Komachi economic life, describing the animals the Komachi herded, the amounts, kinds, and values of the commodities those animals produced, and the nature of the production process. I have also outlined Komachi relations with the market, described some of the commodities the Komachi consumed, and discussed some aspects of the division of labor, stressing particularly the place of shepherds and women in the production process. In this chapter, I focus on the division of labor, particularly the class division between shepherds and employers. The material that follows is an attempt to clarify the structural bases and implications of that class division and to show how it was lived and experienced by the Komachi.

Much of the following discussion centers on relations between Komachi classes, and a good portion of it details conflict between mem-

bers of shepherd households and members of employer households—
conflict that I believe is proto-class conflict, if not class conflict itself.
It therefore seems important to start this chapter with a caveat: things
were not as simple as they may seem. The positions of both shepherds
and employers have their ambiguities, and it is reasonable to ask just
how sharp the division between the two classes was. In fact, the question itself raises ambiguities, for one must consider the division between employers and shepherds from not only the perspective of what
was happening among the Komachi but also from the perspective of
what was happening in the larger society. Even within the limited confines of the Komachi social formation, the vagaries of pastoral production (the differences in yield between good years and bad, the potential
for catastrophic herd loss due to drought and disaster, and changes in
the market) might lead one to ask whether shepherds and employers
were really that different. Looking at the Komachi in the context of the
larger Iranian society of which they were merely an insignificant frag-
ment, one might ask whether any or all of the differences between
Komachi shepherds and employers distinguished them from each other
in the eyes of the outside world.

Later chapters make it clear that despite—or perhaps because of—
the vagaries of pastoral production, the class division between shepherds and employers was quite real. Only a small group of Komachi,
not more than 20 percent of the households, had resources enough to
reproduce themselves as employers. Virtually all shepherd households
lacked both the resources and the structural opportunities to reproduce
themselves as anything but shepherds. In its broad outline, the division
was clear, but of course there were other households whose position was
less clear. In good times, these households employed hired labor; some
individuals from these households may never have worked for another
household or taken a herd to the *garmsir*, either as children or as adults.
But many such households were not secure in their status, and we will
soon see that it was easier to drift down in class than to move up. Moreover, my wife and I lived among the Komachi in a time of nearly unprecedented affluence. I suspect that without a booming meat market many
of the independent young households would not have been able to stay
independent. I am certain that without the meat boom wealthy households would have kept more adult animals for wool and cashmere; they
would have had even larger and more complex herds, and they would
therefore have needed more shepherds to care for their flocks. I think

it likely that if we had done fieldwork ten, twenty, or thirty years earlier, the internal class divisions of Komachi society would have been greater and more clearly marked.

In the context of the larger society, Komachi class differences became less distinct. While members of the local settled community—bazaar merchants, butchers, and *tarafs*—distinguished between rich and poor Komachi, in the larger context all Komachi were the same: they were all unsophisticated, economically dependent pastoralists. All Komachi were small producers of raw materials, and all needed credit; no Komachi produced enough of anything to influence significantly the market price of any commodity.

While the division between rich and poor Komachi loomed large within the limited confines of Komachi society, one must remember that Komachi society was but the tiniest piece of a much larger Iranian society. Within that complex and highly stratified society, no Komachi occupied a position of power or significant status. No Komachi owned a Mercedes-Benz, traveled to Europe, or sent his or her children to school in Europe. No Komachi had ever gone on the pilgrimage to Mecca. To the outside world, all Komachi were the same. If, as I shall argue, wealthy Komachi exploited poor ones, we must remember that wealthy Komachi were in turn exploited and oppressed by members of an external society who commanded resources and power that made the differences between rich and poor Komachi trivial by contrast. In short, one must never forget that in dealing with any Komachi, whether the richest or the poorest, one was dealing with a person who was among the least powerful, least wealthy, and least important members of the larger Iranian society. All Komachi, "rich" and "poor," were members of the Iranian rural poor, and had this lesson powerfully brought home to them in their encounters with the outside world. So if in the context of Komachi society employers seemed powerful and oppressive, we must recall that overall they were powerless, vulnerable, and exploited, and they knew it.

## Wealth

Class divisions imply differences in wealth, and this certainly was true of the Komachi. For the Komachi, wealth generally meant animals; speaking of wealthy men, Komachi were just as likely to say that they were *maldar*, owners of animals, as they were to call them *puldar*, possessors of money.[1]

In spring 1975, all Komachi households in the main body of the tribe owned 9,335 animals, a mean holding of 128 animals. However, wealth was anything but evenly distributed throughout the society, as can be seen in Table 1. (Census data on 73 individual households can be found in the Appendix.)

**Table 1.** Average Herd Size and Inheritance for Types of Komachi Households, 1974–75

| Type of Household | Average Herd | Average Inheritance (in animals per household) |
|---|---|---|
| Households currently employing shepherds | 269 | 121 |
| Households in which the head (or son) never had been a shepherd | 204 | 105 |
| Households in which the head formerly had been a shepherd | 99 | 57 |
| Independent households, not currently employing shepherds and in which the head (or son) had never been a shepherd | 78 | 61 |
| Households in which the head (or son) had ever been a shepherd | 74.5 | 47 |
| Households in which the head (or son) was currently a shepherd | 62 | 43 |

This uneven distribution manifested itself in many ways. For example, the wealthiest Komachi household owned 840 animals, more than forty times as many as the several poor households that owned only 20. The 16 households in the top quartile of the tribe[2] owned 59 percent of all the animals, while the 15 households in the bottom quartile of wealth owned only 6 percent. And the holders of the only significant political positions in the tribe (heads of camps) owned just over 40 percent of all the tribe's animals; their mean holding was 302 head per household while the remaining households owned on average 85 head.[3]

Most wealth in Komachi society lay in the hands of a relatively small number of tribesmen, and despite the claims of equality among pastoralists that are often found in the anthropological literature (an idea that the Komachi would have found strange, at the least), the Komachi were decidedly not egalitarian. Understanding how such differences in wealth arose and were maintained is central to understanding the Komachi. Toward that end, I shall first discuss some general aspects of pastoral production that appear to shape the distribution of wealth in pastoral societies. With that as a base, I then shall examine the distribution of wealth and its relationship to the division of labor among the Komachi.

## PASTORAL WEALTH: SOME THOUGHTS AND PROBLEMS

While integration into the world market has had, in general, an impact on pastoralists that parallels its impact on settled peoples, there are aspects of pastoral production per se that give pastoral societies a distinctive character. Mobility is clearly one of these aspects, but a second important aspect is the fact that animals, the dominant means of production in pastoral societies, are a form of wealth which can increase naturally. This potential for increase and the factors that influence and limit it profoundly shape the general character of pastoral societies as well as particular societies. Let us examine some of these factors.

As I have noted, herds can increase naturally; they can also suffer natural losses. The balance between the two will determine, roughly speaking, the rate of herd growth. Examination of available data suggest that among Southwest Asian sheep and goat herders, the long-term rate of growth will average somewhere between 5 and 10 percent per year (see Bradburd 1982). Differences in growth rates seem determined in large part by richness of pasture. As I noted above, Kerman is among the less-favored regions of Iran. Not surprisingly, therefore, the average rate of herd increase among the Komachi, about 4.6 percent per year, was lower than the rate among pastoralists living in more-favored areas of Iran or of Southwest Asia. Comparison of the rates of growth for the Komachi and for the Yomut, a group with a much higher rate, illustrates the implications of these differences. Komachi herds, on average, increased at about 4.0 percent per year while herds among the Yomut Turkmen increased at a rate of about 11.5 percent per year (Bradburd 1982; Irons 1975). This means that an average Yomut herd doubled in a bit over six years while the average Komachi herd doubled in 17.5 years. With the average Komachi herd taking nearly 3 times longer to double than the Yomut herd, we can see that while a Yomut with a relatively small inheritance of, say, 40 animals would own over 200 animals fifteen years later, a Komachi with the same inheritance would own fewer than 80. The Yomut would be very comfortably off, the Komachi still poor. Limits on herd growth among the Komachi meant that herd owners who received relatively small inheritances were unlikely to see them grow rapidly enough to shift radically their economic situation. The Komachi do not seem to have been able to grow their way out of debt. This low rate of growth plays a particularly important role in the reproduction of shepherd households.

The fact that herds both increase and decrease also has important implications for differentiation among the Komachi. As I showed in an earlier work, unless cultural practices lead to a redistribution of wealth, the effect of random variation in rates of household herd increase and loss in pastoral societies will be increasing economic differentiation (Bradburd 1982). That is, where the rates of herd growth are volatile— where individual herd owners experience sharp annual gains and losses in their holdings as one year's increase is followed by two years of decline, followed by another year's increase—the cumulative impact on the herd-owning population as a whole is not an equalization of wealth as everyone's gains and losses lead to a roughly equal distribution of wealth, but a growing differentiation of wealth as some herd owners' losses escalate while others' gains multiply. There is therefore movement away from the mean rather than toward it. (See Bradburd 1982 for a discussion of how and why this seems to be the case among pastoralists; see Mansfield 1962 and Scherer 1970 for discussions of Gibrat's Theorem, which predicts this effect as a general outcome of stochastic processes.) The greater the volatility of growth and loss, the greater and more rapid the differentiation will be. Put succinctly, pastoral production in Southwest Asia's variable environment will lead to economic variation unless cultural forces intervene.

Other aspects of Southwest Asian pastoral production also seem to promote the maintenance of economic differentiation. For example, where access to pasture and water is not limited, animals, and in particular breeding stock, constitute a pastoral society's dominant means of production. From a pastoralist's point of view, breeding animals have many marvelous characteristics, but one of the most marvelous is the fact that they reproduce and can therefore increase over time. Thus, a man who owns an adequate herd of animals can pass on to his children breeding herds that can grow to be as large or larger than his own. Given a decent herd to start out with and a little luck, a reasonably successful herd owner should be able to pass on to each of his children herds that will permit them to be as wealthy as he. Moreover, since the animals he passes on come from the natural increase of his herd, he can transmit inheritances without ever receiving additional animals from someone else. Pastoralists thus seem quite different from most peasants, who cannot pass on shares of their agricultural holdings to their children that are the same size as the original. In short, most pastoralists should have less difficulty passing on their economic status to their children than most peasants do.[4]

While data for the Yörük, Yomut, Shahsevan, and Komachi show statistical associations of household size and wealth, I believe it is quite unlikely that pastoralists can successfully increase their herds or the growth rate of their herds by intensifying production. I assert this for the following reasons.

The Yomut association (Spearman's $\rho$ = .66; data from Irons 1975) quite clearly seems based on a household's ability to convert excess male labor into animals through remunerative shepherding contracts. That is, it is not simply the result of a household working harder on its herd, but rather the result of households being able to use their labor to build herds from outside sources. Regarding the Shahsevan ($x^2$ = 32.2, $p < .001$; data from R. Tapper 1979a), Tapper notes that they regularly pool labor, and he sees no basis for assuming that the link of household size and wealth has anything to do with labor (1979:70). Among the Komachi, as we shall see, shepherds do all the work, but the association of household size and wealth is strong for employers and not for shepherds ($r^2$ = .045 for shepherds, $r^2$ = .41 for employers). Thus, in some sense, the strongest case for the linkage is the one made by Bates for the Yörük ($\eta^2$ = .64, $p < .01$ and $r^2$ = .21, $p < .001$; data from Bates 1973). Bates believes that a number of factors play a role in determining a household's wealth, and he points out that—to the degree that a household's wealth seems determined by such variables as labor—a household's economic circumstance is labile, while close association of wealth with inheritance suggests that there are constraints on mobility (1973:169). In surveying these factors for the Yörük, Bates finds their economy responsive to the demands and needs of its units of production. Bates's major support (1973:177ff.) for this contention comes from his examination of the relationships that hold among such variables as household size, wealth, and, most important, ratios of animals to workers and consumers to workers. Looking at these figures by quartile of wealth, Bates notes that (1) as household size increases, wealth increases, and (2) there is also a significant and interesting relationship between the animals-to-workers and the consumers-to-workers ratios.

Indeed, Bates suggests that "examining the relationships of sheep/ worker ratio versus consumer/worker index, . . . it is clear that there is a significant percentage of variation in the sheep/worker index determined in each quartile by the ratio of consumers to workers" (1973:185). Bates does note that there is considerable variation in these relationships from quartile to quartile, but clearly he feels that there is both an overall relationship between these facets of Yörük economic organization and a particular relationship in their third quartile of wealth that cannot be ignored. In short, Bates argues that intensity of production (the animals-to-workers ratio) responds to the consumers- to-workers index, and that therefore households adjust productivity to consumption (1973:188). However, using both Bates's Yörük data and my own Komachi data, I have been able to calculate an average annual rate of herd increase or decrease for most households. Yörük and Komachi rates of herd growth, the figures that should be the most responsive markers of circumstantial factors operating to increase animal wealth, do not correlate very strongly with household size and in the Yörük case are in fact inversely correlated with the numbers of workers in a household. Thus, while I am not quite certain what the association of the consumers-to-workers and animals-to-workers ratios among the Yörük shows, I believe that in these pastoral societies, at least, labor is not simply being converted into wealth. Examination of labor's relationship to wealth in both pastoral and argricultural societies helps clarify this point.

Most discusssions of the relationship between household size and wealth among pastoralists are built around the underlying framework of Chayanov's (1966) work. But the logical and structural linkages between labor and wealth (yield) seem quite different among pastoralists than they do among agriculturalists. One of Chayanov's key assumptions about the relationship of household size to wealth is that intensification of labor bears fruit. Households that have high consumers-to- workers ratios increase their gross family product (their total yield) by greatly expanding their labor expenditures. Additional labor increases production in two ways: it may used to increase the amount of territory under cultivation, so that one finds (as Chayanov did) a correlation between the amount of land under cultivation and the consumers-to- workers ratio of the household, or production may be intensified by accelerating the amont of effort put into a fixed quantity of land. The latter is less efficient, as households choosing this route generally suffer a decline in the actual rate of production (amount of product to unit of labor), though they are still able to increase their absolute production to meet increased needs. We would do well to inquire whether either or both of these forms of intensification are possible for pastoralists, and if they are, whether they are truly analogous to intensification among peasants.

I think there are reasons why this may not be the case. Expansion of pastoral holdings must involve simultaneously both forms of intensification: increasing yield from a given quantity of wealth and putting labor to work on a larger holding. For pastoralists, the association of herd size with household size implies that herd owners have been able to increase their herds' rate of growth by doing more work *and* that as the number of animals increases they have been able to maintain the intensified level of care that has generated (in theory at least) the superior rate of increase. But if more work on each animal produces a greater yield, then what happens as the number of animals increases in response to that labor input? Either the amount of labor expended on each animal—effectively the intensity of labor per animal—must decline, with a concomitant decline in yield, or the household must demand yet more work from a labor force already engaged in intensified production.

In effect, then, intensification of pastoral production embodies two simultaneous and contradictory forms of intensification of production. Systems of pastoral production have a structure that is quite different from agriculture and that seems likely to place severe limits on the degree to which households can intensify production. Anecdotal support for this proposition may be found in Barth's (1961, 1964) famous description of the downward spiral of ever-increasing debt and poverty that trapped Basseri nomads as their herd size dipped below a certain point (an implicit argument against a household's ability to increase herds through work) and in Bate's own data, which show the closest association of wealth and labor in this third quartile of wealth, suggesting that the contradictions entailed by the intensification of pastoral production can be overcome only within the ranges of household size and wealth found in this quartile.

In sum, in the absence of culture-based mechanisms for the redistribution of wealth, one should expect to find economic differentiation among Southwest Asian pastoralists and, except where herd growth rates are particularly high, one should expect to find little upward economic mobility. This certainly is true of the Komachi.

## THE KOMACHI

Among the Komachi, culturally accepted means of allocating resources did not redistribute wealth but rather helped perpetuate—if they did not actually magnify—economic differentiation. Among the Komachi, the "culturally accepted means of allocating resources" was, in general, inheritance. The base of a household's flock was the herd of animals that a young man inherited from his father when he married (his "anticipatory inheritance"), so a man's future economic trajectory was set largely by his father's wealth. A father tried to give his son enough animals to have a comfortable and independent household. The actual number of animals was determined by the size of the father's herd at the time his son married, the number of children that remained in the parental household, and, to some extent, the man's feelings toward his son. If a man lived to see all his children marry, he generally continued to maintain an independent household until his death;[5] then a second division of his estate among all his heirs (including his wife if she was alive) took place. Under either of these circumstances the preponderance of a man's estate passed to his sons rather than his daughters. This was so even though the Komachi formally recognized a daughter's right under Islamic law to one-half the share her brother receives. In practice, I found only one instance in which a man reported that he had received no inheritance (his father had died when he was young, and he had given his share of the inheritance, along with the debts, to his brother), while there were thirty daughters who did not inherit any animals. Daughters who did inherit generally did so only after their father's deaths, and the 16.7 animals they received on average (8.4 if one includes women who received no inheritance) does not compare favorably to the average inheritance of 73 animals reported for men.

Other than inheritance, no significant means of acquiring breeding stock existed. Shepherds received only one female animal per year as a portion of their annual wage (see below); small gifts of animals (*pahnoz*) given to boys at their circumcisions and to bridegrooms did not materially affect herd size one way or the other. Finally, the Komachi did not buy, sell, or lend breeding stock among themselves. Only when they had reached the end of their productive and reproductive careers were female animals sold, and then they were sold outside the tribe. Thus my discussion of wealth among the Komachi focuses largely on how inheritance, levels of animal yield (income), and consumption combined to structure differences in wealth, and what those differences entailed.

As noted above, the 9,300 animals owned by the Komachi produced in a good year a product of about $110,000, leaving a surplus of roughly $50,000 above people's basic subsistence cost. All years are not good, however. In Kerman City, for example, two years out of the eight-year period 1967–74 had rainfall at least 25 percent below average. In Bandar Abbas, the region in which rainfall was most critical to the Komachi, in three years of this eight-year period the annual rainfall dropped to less than half of the average (Iran Statistical Centre 1973–74:17). Bad years affected the Komachi in two ways: they reduced the number of newborn animals, and they increased the amount of fodder and water the Komachi had to purchase. Reduction in the number of newborn animals diminished the number of male animals the Komachi could sell for meat and, since fewer births means fewer dams, it also reduced the number of animals giving milk. The reduction in the number of animals giving milk combined with the fact that drought generally leads to lower milk production per animal means that bad years cause a sharp decline in milk production. At the same time, it is obvious that increased need for fodder and water raises the cost of keeping animals. Calculation of the effect of a bad year is not easy; one cannot simply multiply through the reduction in births and reduce yields accordingly. My guess is that, overall, in a bad year yield was reduced by about 33 to 40 percent.[6] A good year's yield of $110,000 would thus be reduced to between $66,000 and $74,0000.

Even in good years, a number of Komachi households' flocks were so small that they could not maintain a basic minimum standard of living. Given such differences in wealth, the impact of a bad year was far from even: the richest households continued to produce a substantial surplus, while households having as many as 100 animals suffered shortfalls. Households that could not meet their needs from the produce of their own herds had to seek alternative ways of balancing their budgets. Within the Komachi social formation, shepherding contracts were virtually the only source of income sufficient to permit poor households to survive economically. In fact, while some of the surplus produced by wealthy Komachi households was used to maintain their high standard of living, some of it was diverted into wages that helped maintain poor households in the tribe. However, one should not assume that Komachi shepherding contracts were mechanisms that leveled differences in wealth by distributing it more evenly throughout the society (Irons 1975; Dahl 1979); shepherding contracts were not the Komachi form of redistribution.

## Shepherds and Employers: The Economic Relation

Shepherds and their employers were bound to each other in many ways, and there was tremendous ambiguity, contradiction, and conflict within their relationship. I shall discuss qualitative aspects of the relationship in the next chapter. Here I concentrate on quantitative considerations, the purely economic parameters of the relationship.

Komachi herd owners estimated that they needed one shepherd to care for every 200 to 300 animals. Assuming an average net yield per animal of $11.75 in good years and $7.75 in bad years, we find that a flock of 200 animals under the care of a single shepherd would have a net yield of $2,350 in a good year and $1,550 in a bad one. Assuming that the household owning the flock was average and had five consumers, it would have a surplus (above a very basic level of consumption) of some $1,450 in a good year and $650 in a bad year. One can rapidly see that while a household with 200 animals that hired a shepherd for $350 continued to produce a quite reasonable surplus in good years, roughly $1,100, the surplus available to it in bad years, about $300, or $60 per consumer, was negligible. We can see better the implications of these figures by looking in more detail at models of average shepherd and employer households.

### EMPLOYER HOUSEHOLDS

On average newly established employer households received an anticipatory inheritance of 105 animals. The flocks of men who had never been shepherds grew at an average long-term rate of 3.6 percent per year (actual long-term rates ranged from a loss of over 16 percent per year up to a 14 percent annual gain). On average, employers married at the age of twenty-eight and had six living children born about two and a half years apart. And an average employer household hired one shepherd for every 200–300 animals it owned.

Using my earlier figures for net yield per animal and basic cost per consumer, a newly-established employer household with two consumers and a flock of 108, spending $180 per year on shepherding labor, would have a surplus of $730 over labor and basic costs in a good year but only $300 surplus in a bad year. After five years, the number of consumers would have increased to three and the herd to 124 animals, and the good-year surplus would be $750 while the bad-year surplus would drop to $240. After twenty years, this average employer household would have a flock of 211 animals supporting seven consumers and would pay out $360 in wages for labor. The surplus over labor and basic subsistence costs in a good year would thus be $860, while such a household in a bad year would realize a surplus of only $15. Of course, these households did not really live at a basic subsistence level: they consumed rather than saved most of the surplus from good years, as we shall see. Because employer households did not keep to a basic standard of living, bad years left them with shortfalls of hundreds of dollars that had to be made up rather painfully in good years. It was no wonder the Komachi said that "*tarafs* are people to whom one is in debt."

While virtually all Komachi, rich and poor, felt that their lives were better in 1974–75 than they had been before the oil boom, and while Komachi with 350 or more animals enjoyed a very comfortable standard of living, many Komachi—including some households in the top quartile of wealth—felt, with some reason, that their economic well-being was precarious. With the exception of those very few households that owned very large herds, most Komachi employers lived on the margins of affluence. Bad years did them real damage; a series of bad years or a run of bad luck could diminish their herds so much that they ceased to be viable employers. Generally this did not mean that the head of household would immediately go to work as a shepherd or that his sons immediately began working as shepherds. It was more likely that the sons of a household in straitened circumstances would not receive an inheritance sufficient for them to reproduce themselves socially as employers. It is true that new households were able to live independently on a small inherited herd; they had few consumers, and they received from their parents virtually all the material goods they needed to establish themselves. Indeed, early on they could even produce a surplus, and thus the fall of an impoverished employer household might not be immediately apparent. However, as such a new household grew, economic pressure would increase and the likelihood of working as a shepherd would loom ever larger.[7]

## SHEPHERD HOUSEHOLDS

Shepherds' compensation averaged $165–185 in cash plus food and cloth-
ing, and so shepherds in effect received both the cash value of their basic
subsistence and the goods that comprised that subsistence. A bachelor
shepherd thus might appear to have had nearly as much surplus to allocate to his own consumption as did individuals in many employer
households. Of course, there was a catch, indeed a triple catch. First,
although shepherds often had no wives and children for portions of
their working lives, most eventually established families; hence some
of the shepherd's compensation had to go to support his household and
pay for the social reproduction of labor. Thus the shepherd did not always have so much surplus to allocate to a higher standard of living,
though not all shepherds lived lives of abject poverty. Second, unmarried shepherds generally still were tied closely to their natal households
and their income was needed to help those households break even, so
an unmarried shepherd's surplus often was not even his to spend. The
third catch is that shepherds received one female animal as a portion
of their compensation. We may choose to look upon this as a reflection
of noncapitalist relations of production or as the remnant of a type of
contract (absent among the Komachi but present elsewhere in Iran) in
which a shepherd's return was calculated as a share of the value produced by the herd for which he cared. However one wishes to consider
it, the shepherd got only *one* animal, the least recompense in animals
that could be given. The addition of one animal per year to a shepherd's
herd could not transform an inadequate herd into one that could provide sufficient sustenance and allow the formation of a new independent household. Shepherds were shepherds because they had not
enough animals to support themselves solely from the produce of their
herds, and the transfer of one additional animal a year did not alter
these circumstances. Moreover, herd growth determined not only a
household's economic status but also the likely economic statuses of
its offspring; thus the shepherds' wage, which included the transfer of
only one animal, ensured the reproduction of shepherd households.
While the cash supplied by shepherds' wages may have been adequate,
the denial of animals had even harsher implications than one might first
think. But—and this is a point I will take up below—the transfer of even
*one* animal also meant that shepherds owned animals; they did have
herds comprising more than just the animals with which they were

paid. Unlike workers in a capitalist factory, shepherds did own some portion of the means of production, and were not simply a rural proletariat. Their wage was expressive not only of their economic situation but also of the ambiguity of their situation. Let us examine the developmental cycle of a shepherd household in greater depth in order to explore these issues.[8]

An average Komachi shepherd was 33.6 years old when he married for the first time, and already had spent many years working as a hired shepherd.[9] Shepherds' late age of marriage had significant implications. About 70 percent of all men who had been shepherds died before all their children married; others ceased working for hire long before all their children matured. Either of these eventualities reduced potential household income. More important, the early death of the shepherd father shortened the period during which the household's herd increased before being dispersed through inheritantce. Death of the father also generally reduced the inheritance portion of younger siblings.

An average shepherd household was established with an inheritance of 47 animals.[10] In its first years of existence, if years were good the household was likely to have a cash surplus above the cost of basic subsistence whether the husband continued working or not. This surplus of several hundred dollars a year is directly attributable to the very low cost of maintaining a household with only two adult consumers. Were all years good, a shepherd household requiring only the minimum maintenance could live off the herd it inherited, with a constantly declining surplus, from its inception until roughly its fourteenth year of existence. From there on, even in a good year, a typical shepherd family that had inherited 47 animals, had six living children, and had a herd that grew at 4 percent per year would run a constant minor cash deficit. These minor shortages would become acute the moment the first son married, taking with him his 47 animals, which at that point would represent about 30 percent of his parents' holdings. In effect, then, even given the fantasy of consistently good years, a household with an average shepherd's inheritance would begin to be unable to maintain itself on its herd alone after its fourteenth year of existence. A string of bad years would be disastrous; the early surpluses would become losses, and as the number of consumers increased the burden would become unsupportably large. In ordinary circumstances, with one year in four bad, the household would produce surpluses in good years but losses of several hundred dollars in bad years; as a result, it would show an average annual surplus after thirteen years of under $40, and all the while its members would have lived a life empty of all luxury. From that point onward, it would accumulate ever greater debts.

But as I am describing a shepherd household, external income must be figured in. The average Komachi shepherd received an income of $350–400 per year, of which about $160–180 was cash with the remainder being food, clothing, and a single female animal. Assuming that the head of household worked twenty years and that his first child was a son who commenced work at the age of fifteen, the shepherd household would, under our presumed normal conditions, virtually never run a deficit. Often it would have a substantial cash surplus, giving household members considerable disposable income. What shepherd households did not have, however, were breeding herds capable of either supporting the household or supplying inheritances that would enable their sons to establish independent households. Let us see why.

## Inheritance and Herds

On average, Komachi herds have a long-term growth rate of about 4 percent per year. A shepherd household that began its developmental cycle with a breeding herd of 45 animals would therefore own 64 animals after ten years, 95 after twenty years, and 140 at thirty years. The most significant figures are those for households established more than twenty-five years, for these were the households that were beginning to give up animals to sons as they married. Were a shepherd's son to marry at twenty-four, the family's original breeding herd would have increased to 115 head. If the son received the same inheritance that his father had, he would set off with 45 animals, mostly female, and his natal household would be left with a breeding herd of 70 head. Several difficulties would arise at this point. First, the herd of 70 head could be expected to yield a net product of no more than $822. The household would be quite likely, however, to have six consumers (assuming that in addition to the son, one daughter had married) whose consumption costs—setting aside such major costs as the son's wedding and the daughter's trousseau—would be roughly $1,100. Our original head of household, now nearly sixty, would be unlikely to be working, so we can assume that at most there would be two sons working as shepherds. If this were so, then the household would show a surplus of about $400 in a good year and about $150 in a bad one. In effect, it would remain solvent. But what would happen next? Over the next five years the family breeding herd would grow from 70 to 85 animals, and as long as its sons worked the household would remain solvent, good year or not. However, when the second son married, taking with him a herd of 45 animals, the original household would be left with a herd of 40 animals. Assuming that another daughter had married and that no one had died, four consumers would be living off 40 animals. In a good year, the yield of that flock would not exceed $470, but the costs of maintaining a household of four consumers would be $720. Even with the young man earning a salary, the family's surplus in a good year would be minimal, and in a bad year the family would have no chance of breaking even. More important, under the best possible conditions this shepherd household would be able to pass on to its sons only enough animals to ensure that they too would be shepherds. We can readily see that this must be true if we consider the requirements of establishing an independent household. Again, the shepherd household that commenced its existence with a herd of 45 breeding animals would have a herd of 115 animals after 25 years. Were it to establish its son on a minimum trajectory for independence, it would have to supply him with an inheritance of at least 65 breeding females. However, we can quickly see that were the son to inherit 65 animals, the parental herd would now have only 50 females. Not only would this strain the household's economic resources, but it would create tremendous problems for all younger sons. Specifically, if the herd of 50 animals grew at an average rate over five years, the family holdings would increase to 63 head. One cannot take an inheritance of 65 animals from 63! Indeed, as one cannot even take an inheritance of 45 animals from 63 and leave a viable household behind, it is clear that under circumstances such as these shepherd households must reproduce shepherd households.

Of course, one solution to this problem is the late marriage of shepherds. As we have seen, shepherds were on average nearly thirty-four when they married. Under these circumstances, the family herd would number about 175 head when the oldest son married. But the father would not be likely to live to, much less much past, seventy, and after his death there would be real pressure for dissolution of the household. While the oldest son might be able to build a herd that permitted independence, his younger siblings would be unlikely to be able to do so. Indeed, the only clear cases of shepherds rising to independence that

I knew of were unusual ones. In one case, a man remained unmarried until his early forties. Then, having lived a nearly feral existence for twenty-five years, he was able to put together a flock that let him live without working and that seemed large enough to let him supply his children with an inheritance if things went well. In the second case, a man with several sons lived to his late seventies. With his base herd, his sons' income, and the animals they received from their employers, the household was able to put together a flock that let him marry off his oldest sons with herds that seemed large enough to ensure their future independence. These were rare cases, however.

And what of our employer household? As we noted earlier, the average inheritance for an employer was 108 animals. Given an age at marriage of twenty-eight, a young employer would draw his inheritance from his father's flock after his father had been independent for twenty-nine years. Assuming the average rate of growth for employers (3.6 percent), the father's herd would at that point number 290 animals. From this herd he would be able to give his eldest son an inheritance of 108 head. As we have seen, at the outset of the marriage this herd would in a good year easily support the new husband and wife. Meanwhile, the boy's parents would be left with roughly 180 animals and one fewer consumer. Assuming that one of his sisters had also married, which is likely, the parental herd would still adequately support the remaining family members in a good year, though not in a bad one. Given the likely marriage of two additional daughters before the second son married, the parental household would probably have a herd large enough to supply the second son with 108 animals as well. However, the third son could not inherit 108 animals, but could only expect perhaps 80 were he to marry before his father's death. Were all the sons to receive somewhat smaller inheritances, they could probably all gain animals enough so that they would be unlikely to have to work as shepherds.

Of course, the 3.6 percent growth rate for employers was an average long-term rate. Some households' herds grew far more rapidly, some much more slowly. Where herds grew more rapidly, the families' sons were even more likely to be able to establish self-supporting households; where the growth rate was lower, sons were likely to have to begin working as shepherds at some point.

While Komachi employers did fall in class with some frequency, it was the rise of shepherd's sons to employer status that was far more unusual. Of 19 households in which the head had never worked, 5 had sons who worked. Of 15 households in which the head was currently working or had worked, 13 had sons who worked. These numbers, along with the model household figures given above, demonstrate that while wealthy employers usually were able to produce a substantial surplus year in and year out and could expect their herds to grow at a rate that would permit them to pass on their employer status to their sons, there were more than a few employers whose economic life was far more precarious. Some of these men's sons would inevitably experience a growing gap between the demands of their households' consumers and their ability to pass on enough animals to their sons to ensure them positions as employers. As well, the model suggests that while in some circumstances shepherd households might be able to achieve a standard of day-to-day living that was not radically different from that of poorer employers, they did so only at the real social cost of being shepherds, which I will discuss further below. Moreover, they did so under conditions of compensation that virtually precluded their sons ever being anything but shepherds. The intersection of the structures of Komachi herd and household demography with the practice of partible inheritance created a system in which most employer households faced a struggle to maintain their viability without becoming suppliers of labor, while many faced an inevitable absolute fall from which resurrection was at best unlikely.

At this point, it seems reasonable to ask what determined the level of compensation for shepherds. As with many other aspects of Komachi life, the determinants were complex. Komachi shepherding wages tended to be somewhat lower than those of other Persian tribes. To some degree the depressed salaries among the Komachi probably reflected both the isolation and the marginality of the region they inhabited. In particular, given the aridity of Kerman Province, agriculture was quite limited; thus, unlike the Basseri (Barth 1961), there was little incentive for poverty-stricken Komachi to settle. Quite the opposite occurred, in fact: historically the tribe absorbed new members, including impoverished shepherds from other, poorer tribes and from the settled world. I discuss in detail the nature and the implication of this process later; however, it seems likely that this too helped keep shepherds' wages down. Moreover, given economic trajectories, it is likely that Komachi society always included some newly poor households (though members of such households resisted working for as long as they could). Since shepherds did not usually grow out of poverty, the pressure of newly impoverished households may have helped keep salaries low. Finally, through 1975 Kerman lagged far behind many other regions of Iran in economic development. Unlike shepherds in many tribes, who radically transformed their relationships with tribal employers by forcing them to match the much higher salaries paid unskilled labor in the settled sector, Komachi shepherds had no such lever. Beck (1980:346, 350) reports that the salaries of Qashqa'i shepherds increased tenfold from 1971 to 1977 (after doubling from 1966 to 1971), and that the cash salaries that shepherds received from "capitalist stock raisers" increased sixfold over the same period; Loeffler (1976) shows that expenditures for shepherds among the Boir Ahmad increased nearly threefold between 1970 and 1975; and Black-Michaud reports that within the Lur "tyranny," when extratribal labor became available, salaries for shepherds increased nearly 500 percent between 1970 and 1975 (1976:401). In contrast, Komachi salaries increased much more modestly. Given the cash and commodity mix of Komachi salaries, it is difficult to calculate their rate of increase exactly; the cash portion increased roughly fivefold, but the noncash portion remained the same. If we take the commodities as representing a fixed value, then the total compensation increased by about 70 percent. No matter how one calculates the rate of increase, the absolute compensation for the Komachi—at most about $400—remained far below that reported for more developed areas of Iran.

It is important to note that dramatic increases in shepherds' wages in other areas of Iran led to widespread detribalization of the groups involved (Beck 1980, 1986; Black-Michaud 1986). Komachi economic figures can give us some indication of why this occurred. The salaries of shepherds working in areas of Iran that were more developed than Kerman were three to six times higher than those of the Komachi. Were Komachi shepherding salaries to have increased 300 percent, virtually all the tribe's surplus product from a good year would have been diverted into shepherd salaries; were they to have increased 500 percent, then shepherding salaries would have absorbed the entire net yield of employers' flocks. Even assuming an additional meteoric rise in the value of pastoral products, the existing Komachi pastoral economy would have been severely pressured if new employment opportunities in the settled world forced Komachi employers to increase tribal salaries to match. Faced with circumstances like that, Komachi herd owners could have made out well in a good year only if they owned herds of 400 animals or more. Indeed, at the salaries that prevailed among the Lur or Qashqa'i the household of a Komachi herd owner with 300 animals and two hired shepherds would have had virtually no more to live on than a household with 100 animals and no shepherds, and a poor shepherd household with only 50 animals but two working sons would have had a greater disposable income than a household with 400 animals. Under such circumstances, it literally would not pay for most Komachi to remain pastoralists. Herd owners could only remain viable by dramatically increasing the size of their average holding, and probably all that would remain would be a few major herders—really capitalist ranchers—who hired shepherds to care for large flocks. Pastoralism as a form of household production would disappear.[11] In short, under the conditions in Kerman, employers would have found it impossible to pay the kinds of salaries shepherds received in other regions of Iran. Thus, though the Komachi at least heard rumors of high shepherding salaries elsewhere, Komachi employers did not rush to match them.

Still, shepherding salaries did go up during the boom. Part of the reason was surely external: the cost of living rose, and shepherds bargained for higher salaries. Even in the absence of external employment, shepherds could still play one employer off against another. Employers saw themselves locked in competition for shepherds. During the period preceding and following the annual negotiation of shepherding contracts, a dominant topic of the employers' conversation was the perfidy of their fellows. As a matter of fact, employers did not present a common, united front to shepherds (nor, of course, did the reverse obtain). Contracts were not negotiated collectively, and people competed for shepherds, trying to hire them away from their closest friends and allies. And though competition seemed to emphasize far more the quality of the relationship than its economic points, wages did rise during my stay with the tribe.

Did employers need to compete? It is hard to tell. Komachi estimated that they needed one shepherd for each 200–300 animals. During 1974–75 there were about 275 animals per hired shepherd throughout the tribe as a whole, and there were enough independent herders to bring the total number of animals per herder down to about 210. Given that wealthy men owned most of the animals, however, and that poorer independent herders often preferred to cooperate among themselves rather than be dominated in a partnership with a single wealthy herd owner, some slight shortage of shepherds may have existed. In this regard, it is important to note that employers who lost shepherds during annual negotiations were forced to hire shepherds from outside the tribe. Moreover, it is very clear that employers believed there was a shortage of shepherds and that that belief led them to offer somewhat more generous contracts. Employers complained bitterly about having to offer better contracts; such complaints contributed to Komachi class strife.

Whatever the absolute need, the hiring of shepherds was, along with marriage negotiations, one of the major arenas in which wealthy men competed for reputation and political influence. Competition for shepherds breached employer solidarity, frequently creating considerable friction and hostility between them, as I will show below. In the long run, this discord among wealthy Komachi helped drive the Komachi system's structural logic; it was a prime factor in the instability of the tribe and its neighbors. But in the short run such discord among employers had most effect in contract negotiation. No functionalist logic is operating here: conflict between employers hardly seems likely to have arisen because shepherds needed it to negotiate effectively. Rather, as I shall argue below, this competition existed because, for complex historical reasons, the Komachi lacked a coherent tribal political hierarchy and lived in conditions that made mutualism difficult to sustain. Nonetheless, it was competition that made employers woo their shepherds and competition that gave shepherds room to maneuver. In its way, it was the struggle between shepherds and employers, which took place within the context of Kerman's marginal environment, the limits of Komachi pastoralism, and the competition of employers, that set Komachi wages, low as they may have been. Despite low wages, it also seems likely that during the mid-1970s, at least, Komachi shepherds made slight gains in their class struggle. One should bear this in mind as our exploration of the relationship between shepherds and employers continues in the following chapter.

# 6

## SHEPHERDS AND
## EMPLOYERS
## IN PRACTICE

The great differences in wealth among the Komachi created variations in the ways that people lived. Rich employers and poor shepherds differed greatly in the quality of their lives. Wealthier Komachi consumed more and better foods: imported rather than domestic teas, a more granular rather than a denser, more heavily caramelized form of loaf sugar. Wheat bread was the staple of the Komachi diet, but wealthy Komachi also ate rice regularly. Only the wealthy ate rice because it cost three to four times as much as wheat, and because rice was not a substitute for bread but a supplement to it. Ideally prepared with large amounts of clarified butter and raisins (or lentils, caraway seeds, or cumin), rice added variety and calories to lunch and dinner. Wealthy and poor households also differed in meat consumption. I noted that few Komachi ate great amounts of meat, but wealthy Komachi ate far more meat than poor ones. First, as Komachi generally ate meat from sick animals, wealthy households—that is, those with more animals—had more opportunities to eat meat than poor ones. Moreover, as wealthy men visited frequently and had more contact with (relatively) important members of the settled world, they played the roles of host and guest far more frequently than their poorer neighbors. This too gave them greater opportunity to eat more meat. Finally, wealthy Komachi had vegetables and fruit—particularly dates and date products—more frequently than the poor.

Differential consumption had obvious effects. Sahlins, speaking of Polynesian chiefs, quoted Gifford's informants as saying, "Can't you see he is a chief? See how big he is?" (1963:289). Wealthy Komachi too showed signs of their wealth; they were not taller, but were far heavier than others.[1] The shepherds' meager diet may also have had less obvious but far more sinister effects. Komachi census data showed that while on average 1.08 children in each employer family died before maturity, a crude rate of about 15.6 percent of all live births, about 22.3 percent of the children born to shepherd families died in childhood. On average each poorer family lost 1.5 children before maturity. It is clear that many factors converged to create this difference in infant and child mortality, but it seems quite likely that differences in the quality and quantity of the food available to children and mothers in Komachi families must have had some impact on children's health. Put bluntly, differences in the consumption patterns of rich and poor Komachi did not only affect adult Komachi but could be deadly for children of the poor. While differences in diet were most important, other areas of consumption showed differences as well. All Komachi dwelt in black tents made up of several long panels woven from goat hair purchased in winter quarters. With four or five long panels sweeping over a 30- to 40-foot semicircle, the head of camp's tent differed strikingly from the two or three shorter, often ragged, panels of a poorer household. Similarly, most wealthy Komachi had lanterns or pressure lanterns; radios or radio-tape recorders (the rage at the time); knives, forks, and spoons (often produced only for guests); a relatively large number of dishes, glasses, teacups, kettles, and teapots; pressure cookers; carpets to sleep and sit on; large numbers of blankets, sleeping robes, and pillows; and, in more than a few instances, motorcycles to ride as they went off to visit other wealthy men. Poorer households inevitably lacked many of these items, and those they had were fewer in number and poorer in quality than those of their wealthier neighbors.

Who had what was not secret knowledge. Children played a game in which one would shout out, "Who lives in a tent with only one teacup?" or "Who lives in a tent with a pressure lantern?" while his or her playmates would shout out the name of the fortunate or unfortunate party. In similar ways, new purchases were examined, commented on, and evaluated.

All the above items were purchased. So were clothes, tobacco, cigarettes, and opium. Here too standards of consumption were radically different and were marked. Poor men smoked cheap cigarettes made in Iran of Persian tobacco. Wealthy men smoked Winstons and Marlboros that were (allegedly) made in the United States. At weddings and circumcisions, when guests were given cigarettes by the host, there was no general largesse: shepherds got the Iranian cigarettes and wealthier men the Marlboros. If one could not tell the status of a man by his weight, one could tell it by what he smoked. And if that failed, one could certainly discern it from his clothes. Wealthy men affected a kind of Western garb: sports jacket, shirt, fedora, shoes, and occasionally Western pants, though most often traditional *shalvar*. Poorer men wore more traditional clothes: plain black *shalvar*, a long, collarless shirt, a broad-brimmed black felt hat, and generally a traditional heavy felt wrap instead of the Western coats and sweaters worn by wealthier men. Women's clothes did not vary as much in style, but wealthy women changed their clothes more often (as did wealthy men) and their clothing tended to be made of brighter, more expensive fabrics. Differences in wealth thus translated into very clearly marked and remarked differences in consumption that had a profound impact on peoples' lives. These differences were there for everyone to see, know, and feel every day of their lives. Differences such as these helped make and mark the boundary between poor and rich, shepherd and employer. More importantly, differences such as these helped shape peoples' attitudes and understandings of these relationships, of who they were and what it meant to be a shepherd or an employer.

As I turn to an examination of the attitudes and practices that created and perpetuated Komachi class distinctions, I wish to stress in advance that relations between shepherds and employers were complex and fraught with tension. The tension was intrinsic to the quality of the relationship—a relationship which, frankly, I saw as exploitative. The complexity flowed from the multifaceted nature of the relationship that held between shepherds and employers who were simultaneously clients and patrons, neighbors, kinsmen, employees and employers, fellow pastoralists, and much more. As we shall see, its complexity made the relationship of shepherd to employer ambiguous and occasionally paradoxical; this both palliated and exacerbated tensions between employees and employers.

To be a shepherd was to open oneself to criticism; the very nature of the job invited it. Shepherds worked, and work had no great value. Worse, to be a shepherd was to work for someone else, to be at their command, to have surrendered one's autonomy. To nonshepherds this aspect of the shepherding contract, this abandonment of self, made the prospect of being a shepherd unthinkable or, worse, dishonorable. A shepherd's life required many compromises with honor, but perhaps the greatest was that the shepherd had to take commands from his employer's wife if need be. Indeed, not only did shepherds take orders from their employers' wives, they took verbal abuse from them, further compromising their honor. Thus, like the Southeast Asian peasants Scott describes, a shepherd's "living is attained . . . at the cost of a loss of status and autonomy" (1976:5).

Each animal a shepherd cared for was valuable in its own right, with female animals having added value as the family estate's "capital." Alas, animals were relatively perishable capital. In 1973–74 Komachi herd owners lost about 780 of 8,600 animals, roughly 9 percent of their holdings, while in 1974–75, on a slightly smaller base, about 560 animals were lost. Herd owners hated to lose animals under any circumstances, though losses clearly beyond human control—for example, those due to an epidemic that struck everyone's flock, severe drought, or extreme cold—were greeted with grudging fatalism. To be a pastoralist was to live with risk. However, faced with low long-term growth rates for herds and the ever-present specter of real disaster, Komachi herd owners detested the unexplained, random loss of animals. Losses that seemed somehow avoidable galled owners. Most "avoidably lost" animals were in a shepherd's care. And though everyone knew that accidents happened, employers still seemed to feel that their shepherds' negligence caused all losses. As losses accumulated over the course of a contractual year, inevitably the relationship between shepherd and employer became strained. Most often, that strain was expressed in loud harangues by the employer's wife, which everyone, including all the shepherd's neighbors (and, if they were present, kin), heard.

The strain of labor relations was magnified by its conjunction with the requirements of the annual round. Komachi shepherds worked on an annual contract that started on June 21. Contracts were negotiated just before and just after this date. Negotiations took place when the herds had recently arrived in summer quarters, when milking was done, or nearly so, and when male and female animals were being herded together. A shepherd thus began working for an employer in a period of light work. Toward the end of August, shepherds and flocks left for winter quarters; the work became more difficult, but supervision was remote. Balanced against the lack of direct supervision were the realities of going to the *garmsir* in late summer: fiercely hot, still malarial in 1974–75, and formerly politically insecure and dangerous, it was not a pleasant place to be. Moreover, while shepherds toiled in the *garmsir*, the rest of the tribe remained in summer quarters, enjoying the leisure, excitement, entertainment, and feasts of the high points of the social year: weddings, circumcisions, and *rozehs*. Indeed, the simple juxtaposition of a shepherd's life and that of a herd owner in September says almost all that need be said of the qualitative differences in the lives of shepherds and employers.

When employers, their families, and shepherds' families arrived in the *garmsir* in late October, young animals were being born. Employers received at that time a full accounting of losses that occurred between August and October. Concerns arose about the births of young animals, and losses in the perinatal period were often blamed on shepherds, whose job it was to help females give birth and to bring the young animals to camp quickly. Shepherds and employers thus came together again in a time of tension and pressure. Moreover, the pressure and tension never slackened. During the early winter shepherds had to bring female animals into camp so that young animals could nurse; later, shepherds had to control animals during the organized pandemonium of milking. Because female animals had to come to camp, most shepherds' activities during this time took place under direct and rarely benign observation by their employers. Tempers frayed. During spring migration, the relationship between shepherd and employer hit its nadir. On migration, the shepherd's work was most difficult: animals still had to be milked, and all the work of migration, including driving the herds roughly 10 miles a day, had to be done too. By that time, shepherd and employer families had already been locked in struggle for several months, not least over the amount of help the female kin of shepherds gave to employers' households during the processing of dairy products.

It is no wonder that, with everyone tired and on edge, herd owners and shepherds quarreled.

As I turn to even more qualitative assessments of the relationship between shepherds and employers, I must acknowledge again that to me the relationship appeared relentlessly exploitative. Komachi shepherds worked hard at a difficult job, and compared to shepherds in other parts of Iran they were poorly paid, with the nature of their compensation leaving them trapped in their position. Moreover, the economic reality was not the only negative aspect of the relationship, which also was soured by the thousands of small indignities that it entailed. Shepherds were referred to as members of a *tabaghe*, a class, indicating the employers' feelings of difference. More pointedly, employers spoke of shepherds as servants (*noukar*) or slaves (*ghoulam*), and as shepherds prepared and served tea for their employers' guests, butchered animals, and helped clean wheat, this usage and all the indignity it implied came uncomfortably close to the truth of the relationship. Employers played on this. One of the longest sustained jokes I heard was made at the expense of a young, fair-haired shepherd who, people claimed, should accompany my wife and me to the United States to be our servant there, pouring our tea. This was a far different fantasy from the one imagined for the son of a herd owner, who, people said, could be our guest as he studied in the United States.

Shepherds most commonly became the butt of jokes or heard employers' denigrating remarks about other shepherds at mealtime, when unmarried shepherds ate in their employers' tents. The meals themselves had their own indignities. While the employer's family dined around the hearth, often eating luxury foods, the shepherd sat off to one side of the tent, eating the bread and *kashk* that were part of his salary. The ambiguity of the shepherd's position was quite marked here: he sat in the family tent, ate (at least sometimes) when the family ate, and participated to some degree in the conversation, but he was not really part of the family or part of the meal. The scene was Dickensian: employers and guests sat eating meat and rice around the fire while the shepherd had *kashk* and bread in the corner. Employers and their guests discussed other shepherds, often abusively, while the shepherd sat there, and they talked about their prospects in front of a man who had none. I was constantly amazed at the frankness of these conversations; for example, I heard an employer say in front of his shepherds, "It's hard to be a herd owner now. In the old days people were so poor and hungry that they came running to do what we wanted for a few scraps of food; but shepherds now are all rich and lazy." If the shepherd did anything in his employer's tent but eat, he served tea.

Paradoxically, some—though by no means all—of the difficulty between shepherds and employers seemed to arise precisely because the relationship itself was not unambiguously a class relationship. There was class conflict, but the individuals who confronted each other were united in some ways as much as they were divided in others. As I will show when I present a detailed description of shepherding negotiations below, both shepherd and employer recognized that claims of kinship affiliation (and what they implied) played a role in creating their mutual understandings of the shepherd-employer relationship. While such a relationship hardly ever approached the ideal of relations among kin, neither side rejected the legitimacy of such claims. The pattern of the negotiations was such that the shepherd nearly forced the employer to assert their mutual kinship and explicitly recognize common kinship's understood obligations; both the negotiations and their outcome added complexity to the relationship. Claims of kinship were not the same as acts that fulfilled its obligations, of course, but claims of commonality were not just hollow rhetoric or mystifying platitudes that duped the poor shepherd. Rather, claims of mutual kinship or of a relationship were claims that the shepherd could work on. Claims of kinship were part of the understandings called upon and interpreted by *all* shepherds and *all* employers (and hence *all* Komachi) as they struggled to set the bounds of the relationship between them. Forming part of the weaponry deployed in the daily skirmish of Komachi class struggle, claims of kinship helped people hammer out the socially determined allocation of resources that define class relationships in any social formation at any time. Among the Komachi these relationships were as ambiguous as the terms used to describe them. Let me expand upon that point.

Komachi (and standard Persian) for shepherd is *chupan*. To the Komachi, *chupan* denoted someone who was at the moment working as a shepherd. Komachi called employers *arbab*. In standard Persian *arbab* means master or lord and is generally used as the term for the major landowner in an agricultural village, the "land lord." It is quite easy to see why the Komachi extended this term to wealthy herd owners or employers (whom my wife jokingly called "sheep lords"), for the central concept of management or ownership of the means of production remained the same. But to the Komachi *arbab* also meant someone who did little or no actual work. The relationship between the two senses of *arbab* is obvious: landowners were traditionally a class of *rentiers* and on the whole did very little work, so that the central attribute of *arbab* in this scheme was *not working*. Among the Komachi there were two groups of people who did not work: those Komachi who were wealthy employers and hired *chupan* to work for them, and retired shepherds who were no longer actually working but lived off the income of their own small flocks or, more likely, the incomes of their working sons. Wealthy Komachi, at least, called both *arbab*. For example, during contract negotiations a shepherd said, "I don't want to do anything"; his employers recognized that he was saying, "I want to be an *arbab*," and responded, "Well then, work now and save your money, so you can be an *arbab* later." But the shepherd really meant that he wished to be like them, and the promise they held out sounded far better than it really was. By encompassing portions of a life cycle that saw every man who lived long enough ultimately cease working, Komachi use of the term *arbab* did more than play on its range of meanings; it obscured the very real differences between *arbab* and *chupan*, employers and shepherds, by conflating class and category. Since both shepherds and employers eventually could be independent synchronically, the Komachi could employ conceptualized categories of their own class system that substantially mystified the real division between them.[2]

The manner in which employers drew noncompensated labor from their shepherds also highlighted the relationship's ambiguity. These were little demands for labor—for example, asking the shepherd to take grain to a nearby mill, prepare tea, spin wool and goat hair, or butcher (though not slaughter) animals—that, though individually trivial, accumulated into a significant claim on labor. These little demands were seen as something extracontractual; they were quite explicitly balanced against the small services performed for shepherds by employers, such as acting as shepherds' "patrons," speaking for them at their marriage negotiations, acting as their *tarafs*, and lending them money in return for *komak* or other such "favors."

As I have documented elsewhere (Bradburd 1983), Komachi exchanges of "favors" were structured so that employers constantly gained direct material benefit (labor or a return on capital) while the shepherd gained only a far more diffuse form of aid or assistance. But the very existence of a noneconomic relationship—the fact that an employer did try to help an unmarried shepherd get a wife (keeping in mind that such assistance would bring his wife more of the female labor she needed), or that he transported a shepherd's sick child to the doctor— made the perception of the relationship as an unambiguous opposition of class interests difficult for the Komachi; an anthropologist probably would be incorrect in assuming it as well. At the same time, the ambiguous and perhaps contradictory nature of these exchanges seemed to amplify rather than diminish distinctions and antagonisms between herd owner and shepherd; at any rate, they created an issue about which antagonisms were voiced.

Antagonisms arising from contradictory expectations manifested themselves most clearly in the struggle over *komak* that took place between the women of shepherd and employer households. I described earlier the tremendous workload borne by wealthy women. They attempted to alleviate this burden by calling on the help, *komak*, of their kin and neighbors in camp. But the concept of *komak* implied the irregular transfer of neighborly assistance, whereas wealthy households' demands for female labor were hardly ever irregular or neighborly. Wealthy women needed labor, asked for it, and ultimately demanded it from the other women who lived in their camps. As the dairying season went on, all women became tired, and poorer women had little desire to give large amounts of noncompensated help to their wealthier neighbors. Women argued over how much help was given and how much was needed. I often heard the morning quiet rent by an employer's wife crying out that the shepherds' wives were unneighborly and wouldn't give *komak*, and I just as frequently heard the shepherds' wives shout back that they were tired, that they had done a great deal of work, and that the employer's wife was a demanding ingrate. The shouts that filled Komachi camps were the noises of class struggle. Not surprisingly, the discourse often moved beyond the narrow topic of women's labor. Employers' wives castigated shepherds as well as shepherds' wives. When tempers flared, losses of animals were recalled, and blame and aspersions were cast. Shepherds were characterized as careless, lazy, or corrupt. Shepherds' wives responded by calling employers cheap, unsympathetic, and unfair. Attacks and counterattacks were couched in purely personal terms; there was no great class consciousness there, though occasionally wives of other shepherds would join in the fray. Still, the subject of discourse was the struggle over the labor power of the employee and his family.

It is significant that women's work was absolutely noncompensated. A shepherd who was unmarried and had no kin living in camp would get as high a salary as a shepherd who had a wife and several daughters giving *komak*. *Komak* drew noncompensated productive labor from a shepherd's household. Owners of the means of production thus gained access to the labor power of the poor. It is important to remember that although the ideological frameworks were different, the cultural pressures that required neighbors to do things for other camp members were in their way nearly as constraining and just as real as the jural pressures that drove labor dues in feudalism. Like the serf, the shepherd had few overt weapons to employ in his struggle with employers. If the shepherd had a family living in his employer's camp, then the cultural constraints of *komak* forced them to give labor. The family's only way out of this onerous burden was not to live in camp. But the conjuncture of structural forces made this a difficult alternative. First, no matter where their wives, families, or parents dwelt, Komachi shepherds lived in their employer's camp. That was where they were fed and received their instructions, and that was where the animals they herded had to be brought. Any other residential pattern was impossible. Second, all adult Komachi shepherds owned some animals. Shepherds liked to care for these animals themselves as much as possible—who else would give them better care? Thus shepherds were likely to bring their stock with them to their employer's camp. If a shepherd had his stock with him and wished to gain any return from dairy production, he needed his wife, mother, or daughter in camp with him. Practically, this meant that if a shepherd had his stock with him, he would have his female kin in camp, and if they were in camp, they were subject to his employer's wife's demands for *komak*. To live in camp and not give *komak* was almost impossible. If his family did not live in camp, a shepherd had to entrust his animals to someone else's care, which he would be loath to do, or else he had to forgo whatever return he might get on his dairy production. Given this disagreeable choice, most shepherds opted for the financial return, but the pressure helped sour the employee-employer relationship.

When the relationship soured, the employer (or his wife) vented his spleen by publicly denouncing the shepherd. How did the shepherd respond? As we shall see, the primary arena the shepherd had in which to deal with his frustration was the annual contract negotiation, which permitted him to turn the tables on his employer— sometimes within the ritualized frame of negotiations and sometimes outside of it. But shepherds had other weapons as well, and it is worth seeing what they did and did not do.

James Scott, in a marvelous recent work, has drawn our attention to the "weapons of the weak" in class strife (1985). Pointing out that in most times and places the structural conditions of class struggle overwhelmingly favor the rich and powerful, Scott argues that as a result the poor often engage in quiet warfare. One significant form of quiet struggle that Scott identifies in rural Malaysia, theft, was strikingly absent among the Komachi. While in other, larger pastoral communities, shepherds' killing and eating of their employers' animals was such a regular occurrence that it discouraged employers from hiring shepherds (Barth 1961), such killings and accusations were rare among the Komachi. During the eighteen months I was there, I heard only one very vaguely worded accusation (which I will discuss below), and there was virtually no discussion of the problem. As employers freely catalogued other complaints, I am quite certain that the lack of comment indicated a lack of problem. Similarly, even though shepherds were occasionally several hundred miles from their employers, and though animals were certainly a valuable commodity, I heard only one story, and that an old one, of a shepherd running off with and selling his employer's animals. Theft of stock did not seem part of Komachi class warfare. It is my belief that, unlike the situation Scott describes, theft within the community was virtually unknown. There were at least three reasons for this. First, as I noted above, everyone knew what everyone else had, so the appearance of someone's carpet or cooking pot in someone else's tent would evoke nearly instant comment. Second, though all sheep tended to look alike to me, every Komachi knew his own sheep and goats by sight, and sometimes could distinguish others' animals as well, so it would have been virtually impossible to steal an animal and keep it. Third, for reasons that I will outline in my discussion of kinship, the Komachi community was, in fact, a community whose members, regardless of their antagonisms, had too many ties among themselves for theft without flight to be possible.

But if theft was not a possible weapon for shepherds, there were others. The most common one, or at least the most directly visible one, was the claim of illness. As we shall see below in my account of Mahmoud's contract negotiation, illness was one way that shepherds and their wives could resist employers' demands for labor. I do not mean to say that shepherds were malingerers. Anyone who worked out-doors all day following animals up and down mountainsides, often slept on the cold ground of summer quarters with nothing but a felt coat, ate poor food and drank water that was questionable at best, and lived in the malarial winter quarters during the late summer heat was almost certain to be truly sick sometimes, let alone to suffer from occasional aches and pains. What I am claiming is that shepherds used those ill-nesses and aches and pains as weapons in their struggle with their em-ployers. Shepherds complained loudly and constantly about their aches, clearly attributing them to their work, and used those complaints to claim respites from work. Employers and shepherds might argue about what to do about an ache or pain, but a shepherd who said he couldn't walk would stay in camp until he could, and if he didn't press his case too far he was likely to be rehired the next year. Claiming illness thus permitted the shepherd to put a moral burden on his employer and limit demands for labor. In its way, this was a far more effective weapon than theft.

I would like to pause at this point and consider a common thread that linked shepherd-employer and male-female relationships. Among the Komachi, dominance always entailed the control of another's labor power. We have seen that the employer's economic domination of his shepherd enabled him to draw surplus value from the shepherd in a vari-ety of ways. Because Komachi shepherds worked for nugatory recom-pense, Komachi employers could keep substantial herds and could be rich without having to work for their wealth. Wealth was the sine qua non of tribal status. By this I do not mean that there was necessarily a linear relation between wealth and status, but lacking wealth, which was the basis of independent action, one could not achieve high status at all. With wealth one could do the things that brought high status: display hospitality, feed guests well, sponsor *rozehs*, or give large gifts at weddings and circumcisions. A wealthy man's children were, almost by definition, good marriage partners, so a wealthy man could actively and effectively seek good marriages for them, thus simultaneously cre-ating and ratifying his high status. Moreover, wealth gave a man the in-dependence without which high status could not be maintained. Note that it was wealth which was the basis of status, not the reverse. One could deploy one's resources to achieve higher status, but status could not bring wealth. Loss of wealth inevitably, if not immediately, dimin-ished status. Having shepherds not only enabled a man to accumulate wealth without expending great amounts of labor, but also freed him to play the game of building status. Being free of work, an employer had the time to be political. Male domination of women had the same end. While wealthy men did not work, their wives did. In a very substantial fashion, women's work helped create the wealth that built men's statuses. Wealthy men's dominance of their wives led, in most cases, to these women's generally successful attempts to assert their dominance over other men's wives, thereby bringing even more labor under a wealthy man's control.

This line of thought leads to one more brief digression. Clearly, the Komachi were part of a larger Middle Eastern, Islamic world in which, as a whole, women have a secondary status (see Nelson 1974, Altorki 1986, and Beck and Keddie 1978 for various views on this issue). Therefore, one cannot simply claim that Komachi women were subordinate because their husbands needed their labor power. Indeed, among the politically, economically, and culturally dominant classes of the traditional Middle East, male dominance was marked by the restriction of women to the confines of their homes, which precluded women's participation in most production. Persian pastoral women, who traditonally have been neither confined to their tents nor veiled, have been seen as freer in a way than those in cities. Certainly Komachi women participated publicly in discourse that must be considered political. But did this signal their liberation? I am not certain. As Komachi women (and presumably other tribal women) were vital to pastoral production, they had to be free to move beyond their tents. Given the structure of Komachi pastoral production, male dominance was expressed not in keeping women silent and invisible but in controlling their labor power. Dominance did not disappear; it was transformed. For both men and women among the Komachi, because the economic was dominant, dominance was economic.[3] Once we recognize this, another striking point makes sense. As I noted above, shepherds complained bitterly of aches and pains, *and so did women, rich or poor.* Conspicuously, wealthy men did not. If they were acutely ill they, or their families, might complain and worry, but they did not nurse chronic grievances, nor did they have constant concerns with aching wrists, knees, shoulders, backs, or necks. One heard of all these complaints and more from shepherds and women. Poor women often claimed pain as a reason for not giving *komak*. As with shepherds, it was a reason that ultimately had to be accepted. Wealthy women did not as often claim illness as a reason not to work. Indeed, one could argue that most of the time, sick or not, they had to work. Wealthy women did complain, however, and they often ascribed their pain to their labor. I think it more than coincidental that male employers, who controlled the labor power of others, rarely complained about pain or tried to use it as a means of controlling others' access to their labor power, while shepherds and women, whose labor power was under another's control, often complained of pain, either using it as a reason not to work or using the complaint itself as means of reminding their employer or husband that the extraction of labor power did not come without cost.

Returning to my main point: claims of illness and malingering aside, the shepherd caught in an oppressive relationship with his employer found recourse through either renegotiation of his contract or flight to another employer. As employers did compete to hire and rehire shepherds, during contract negotiations each year shepherds were wooed, fed, and entertained as if they were guests. Rather than commanding, the employer beseeched. Shepherds sat in their tents like Achilles, while those who sought their services, those who castigated them in the past, sent emissaries.

While one may see this reversal as ritualized—which it certainly was—it was not without beneficial effect for the shepherd. Consider the case of Ali's shepherd Qadam. Qadam was an older married man who had moved to the Komachi area from a neighboring tribe and had worked four years as a shepherd for Ali. During the first two years, Qadam's wife, Xanom, her brother, and their mother had lived with him in Ali's camp. For 1974–75, however, Qadam's kin returned to their own tribe's territory. They did this in spite of substantial costs, and they did so (as I later learned) in response to the labor demands of Ali's wife, whom they considered overbearing and grasping. Indeed Qadam's wife and Ali's wife truly disliked each other in a manner unusual in the small tribe.

When contract negotiations for 1975–76 began, questions about Qadam centered on whether he could get his wife to live in Ali's camp and thus live a somewhat more normal life for a married man, or whether his wife would get him to move away from Ali's camp. Perhaps the clearest clue to how things would turn out presented itself on June 15, when Xanom and her mother arrived at Ali's. Shortly after her arrival, Qadam and his wife began a loud argument. She urged him to separate his animals from Ali's flock and leave camp, while he was furious at her for telling him publicly what to do. Ali's wife, Sekine, then invited Xanom into her tent for a visit. Xanom refused, but her mother went in. The two fenced verbally for nearly an hour. Ali's wife offered Xanom's mother and brother paid work in Ali's camp, and the woman responded that Qadam had had a job offer from one of the settled Komachi: he could work as a shepherd, and his children would be found employment in a carpet workshop.

When Qadam's mother-in-law left, Ali's wife began a vitriolic public attack on both Qadam and his wife. Qadam wasn't a man because he let his wife boss him around, she said, and Xanom was the worst woman in the tribe, a slut whose children all had different fathers; by not keeping her with him, Qadam had let this happen, and was a cuckold, a man without honor. From here on, events became almost melodramatic. On June 17 Qadam left camp. No one knew where he was going, but he was rumored to have been in one of the Sanjeri brothers' camps, about 9 miles up the valley (the period of shepherd negotiation was a peak period of rumor mongering). Later that same afternoon, Qadam was said to have been seen in Ali's wife's brother's camp, about 700 yards away. A third rumor reported that Ahmad Sanjeri, the oldest, wealthiest, and most important of the dominant Sanjeri brothers, had said that he would not hire Qadam away from Ali. People debated whether this meant that he really would not try to hire Qadam, or if it meant that one of his brothers would hire Qadam in his stead; very few people assumed that the rumor accurately reflected the reality of the situation. Still, Ali wrote a letter to Ahmad asking him not to hire Qadam, claiming that were Qadam to go he would have to sell off his flock and give up herding (despite the fact that he was employing three other shepherds at that time).

With Qadam gone, people's views of him shifted: the lazy good-for-nothing of two weeks before became a valued employee, old but smart and diligent. His potential loss was now a cause for concern. On June 18 Ali received new assurances from Ahmad, so the focus of suspicion shifted to Ali's own brother-in-law. On June 19 Qadam returned, but as another negotiation had entered its critical phase, people largely ignored him. On June 21, another shepherd reported that Qadam had said he wanted to work for Ali but that his wife wanted him to work for the Sanjeris. This led to another round of discussion about her deficiencies and, by way of extension, Qadam's. Thus by June 22, when Qadam's contract negotiations officially began, emotions were running high. One sign of this was Qadam's refusal to come to Ali's tent. Instead, he sat in the tent of Ali's nephew, at the far end of camp. Qadam, like other shepherds who had been maligned, refused to negotiate, and appeared very angry. When Qadam was eventually cajoled into speaking, it was interesting that he did not refer to the scandalous things said about him and his wife, but expressed his anger about an allegation that an un-named shepherd had killed and eaten an animal. Seizing on this affront to his occupational integrity, Qadam sputtered with rage. Ali and his family sought to mollify him by telling him that they knew he was hon-est and an outstanding shepherd, that they had never found any fault with his work, and that he was not accused of anything. As Qadam sat stony-faced through this flattery, an older former shepherd passed by. Looking at Qadam and his entreating employers, the shepherd, noting the striking structural parallels in negotiations for brides and shep-herds, quipped, "So, Qadam is getting married."

Shortly thereafter, Qadam calmed down, the flattery having had its effect. Ali immediately asked him to name his price. "You have the ledger, you write it," said Qadam. After some polite back and forth, Qadam finally requested 1,300 tomans, 24 kilos of sugar, 3 packages of tea, and a sleeping cloth. Ali agreed and wrote out the contract, but just before he was to sign it, Qadam blurted out that, in fact, he had signed a contract with Ahmad Sanjeri and that he had sworn an oath not to work for Ali. Sekine, Ali's wife, assured him that there would be no problem; Ali would fix it with Ahmad and give Qadam an animal to sacrifice for breaking the oath.

Then occurred an exchange that captured the essence of the rela-tionship. Qadam had no sooner put his mark on the paper than he said, "Wait, I wanted a jacket, too."

"No, *baba*, it's too late," Ali replied. "Besides, a jacket is 100 to-mans." He paused and, fingering his own very worn jacket, said "I'll have to get a new jacket soon. When I do, I'll give you this one." The drama appeared over.

On June 24, however, two days after he signed his contract with Ali, Qadam disappeared. Rumor had it that when he had left camp to bathe prior to making his sacrifice, he had been waylaid by his wife and several others who had "kidnapped" him and had taken him to the Sanjeri camps.

"May a donkey stick his cock up her cunt," was Ali's wife's imme-diate and shouted response to the situation.

During the next several days, rumors, letters, and messengers sped back and forth from Ali's camp to Ahmad's, from Ali to the gendarmerie in the nearest town, from Ali to the wealthiest man in Qadam's own tribe, and through networks of kin of all the participants. Ali hoped that Qadam's wealthy fellow tribesman would pressure him to stay with Ali; this seemed to be a forlorn hope, since the man had far closer ties to Ahmad Sanjeri, the other disputant, than to Ali, and indeed nothing happened. It was, as Ali's wife succinctly put it, "a waste of a chicken." Ali's appeal to the gendarmes was equally futile; they ruled that Ahmad's contract was signed first and had precedence. Moreover, in a quiet display of state power that recalled days past when employers threatened to keep the animals of shepherds who left to work for another, the gendarmes later returned to Ali's camp and watched as Qadam reclaimed his animals from the camp's herds.

After Qadam left Ali's employ, Ali's son-in-law rode his motorcycle to the outskirts of Ahmad's camp and yelled futile, if annoying, insults into the air. The affair left a severe chill in the relationship between Ahmad and Ali, the two most important men in the tribe. Ali later hired another shepherd, but he and his family were clearly discomfited by the outcome. Later, when my wife and I visited Ahmad's camp, Xanom—now living with her husband's employer—made a point of coming over to chat with us about the events, reviewing her triumph.

Qadam was a relative newcomer to the Komachi and essentially powerless, while Ali was certainly the wealthiest and arguably the most powerful man in the tribe. But even in this extreme case, the very act of negotiating brought Qadam significant rewards: his employer sought him out, flattered him, and came as close as a Komachi was likely to come (and that is never 100 percent of the way) to apologizing for past problems. Qadam was able to force his employer to acknowledge his value and his honesty, making the wealthiest and most important man in the tribe extend himself and offer Qadam a raise. After all that, Qadam was still able to change employers and embarrass Ali in the process.

Changing employers had its burdens: frequently shepherds were in debt to their former employers, and shepherds and their families had to adapt to the routine of a new camp, and adjust to migrating between different areas. Even so, Qadam's case shows that the shepherd could use contract negotiation as a weapon against his (former) employer. For individuals who felt that they had been put upon (which was almost certainly true), seeing their former employer embarrassed was no small triumph. I know that Qadam's wife derived great pleasure from Ali's discomforts, for she made every effort to make that clear to us whenever we visited the camp of Qadam's new employer.[4]

Exacting praise or even moving on is only a small and transitory victory in the struggle between employer and shepherd, but then shepherds' lives were rarely filled with even small victories. Of course, in a larger sense, movement from employer to employer no more freed the shepherd from an exploitative relationship than claims of common kinship caused a shepherd to be treated as a son. Whether the situation was defused through flattery or movement, the result was temporary and palliative rather than curative. Qadam would soon find his relationship with Ahmad would sour; it had to, for that was the nature of the relationship. A shepherd would find out—if he didn't suspect it as he signed his contract—that June's promises faded in December.

Still, contract negotiation was not simply an arena in which shepherds could express their displeasures. Rather, it was part of a relationship structured in a fashion such that shepherds could not only express their concerns but also move within the tribe or outside it.[5] While in the long run this may not have improved shepherds' lives at all, the possibility of movement did help shape shepherds' relations with employers and also their relationships with other shepherds. Movement or the threat of movement by shepherds also shaped employers' relations with one another, as it promoted competition among them. I shall argue below that both of these aspects of shepherd mobility had a profound effect on the way in which tribes like the Komachi developed—that, in effect, class struggle helped to determine tribal history.

But contract negotiation revealed another side of the story as well. They showed that assertions of solidarity between employer and shepherd could be made, and that even as the practical reality of the relationship generated conflict, frameworks of commonality existed. There *were* bonds other than contracts between employers and shepherds, and if they were engaged in class struggle, they were also linked by ties that made the relationship more ambiguous, sometimes palliated the conflict, and certainly made both groups see themselves not only as employers and employees but members of a tribe. Kinship *as the Komachi conceived it* was clearly the dominant bond, and in the remainder of this book I show how the structures of kinship and class were conjoined in Komachi practice so as to generate tribal history.

# PART III

# KINSHIP

# 7

# ALLIANCE AND
# DIVISION

Examination of the relationship between employers and shepherds showed them to be complex, filled with ambiguities and tensions. Some short-term relief of those tensions occurred when shepherds moved from employer to employer, but that generated conflict among members of the tribal elite. Class division in Komachi society thus seemed to create pressures for the dis-integration of the society. Working against the potentially centrifugal forces of class division was a bond that, in the Komachi view, held the society together: kinship affiliation. The ultimate instability of the Komachi social order might lead one to believe that kinship was an ineffective bond, no more than a vague ideological prop drawn upon in times of tension. However, Komachi claims of common kinship should not be taken lightly. The nearly liturgical incantation, "We are all kin, there are no strangers here, we are all one," that accompanied virtually every negotiation of a significant social concern suggests the importance of kinship to the Komachi.

Kinship was a key symbol for the Komachi of their social order; it was the way they understood what it was to be Komachi. Kinship sustained its effectiveness as a metaphor because it played an active role in shaping social relations and the social order, and because the Komachi used kinship to create social bonds. But we must also recall that the single most significant Komachi property transaction, gaining access to animals, was enacted through the medium of kinship affiliation as sons inherited from their fathers. As inheritance was the means through which Komachi classes reproduced, the key metaphor of Komachi unity was also one of the primary frameworks of continuing social division. Moreover, the very act of forging kinship affiliations was often divisive. As we shall see, though all Komachi claimed that they were all kin, examination of people's kin networks showed great differences in the kinds of kinship affiliations formed by employers and shepherds. Thus kinship did not just bind people together. Like the relationship of shepherd to employer, it too had its ambiguities.

Understanding the Komachi entails understanding their system of kinship affiliation. Understanding the articulation of kinship with class and the ways kinship both reduced and reinforced the divisions of class, structured other alliances and divisions, and bound and separated individuals within and across class divisions is therefore vital for understanding the Komachi.

## Komachi Kinship: An Overview

Komachi kinship affiliation reflected and promoted both divisive and solidary forces in Komachi society. No single homogeneous kinship system joined all Komachi equally in a stable, timeless net of affiliation. Rather, Komachi kinship was a practical system, used strategically by active agents, and as a result it was a system that reflected and to a degree created the divisions and strains within Komachi society. Komachi kinship was the social framework of a society under stress. It was not a beautifully articulated web but a collection of jury-rigged lashings, simultaneously binding some parts tightly together even as it created strains elsewhere and promoted divisions that ultimately jeopardized the coherence of the whole.

Because they were members of an Islamic society and residents of the Middle East, the Komachi did not have a kinship system that was uniquely theirs. Descent, and particularly inheritance, shared the pronounced agnatic bias one finds throughout the region, though as we shall see, descent groups per se were of little importance. Kinship terminology was of the "Sudanese" type. The Komachi accepted Koranic incest prohibitions as a given: men did not marry their mothers, daughters, sisters, paternal and maternal aunts, daughters of brothers and sisters, foster mothers, foster sisters, wives' mothers, stepdaughters, and sons' wives.[1] Within the limits set by Islam, the Komachi expressed a strong preference for marriage with close kin, *qom khish*, who were generally construed to be kin no more distant than one's second cousin. At the same time, multiple marriages between sibling sets—what the Komachi and other Persian tribes called *gav ba gav* (cow for cow) marriage (Barth 1961)—were proscribed, preventing both sister exchange marriages and the marriage of brothers to sisters. Status endogamy was also strongly favored. Finally, there was a generally held feeling that a husband should be older than his wife. In the Komachi view, the dominant marriage rules were the preference for close kin and the proscription of multiple marriages. Status endogamy and the relative ages of spouses were seen as desirable and did constrain behavior, though contrary instances did occur.[2]

Of 96 marriages contracted prior to 1974 that I gathered data on, 31 (32 percent) were between close kin, with 22 of those (71 percent) between first cousins, but only one violated the prohibition of multiple marriages between sibling sets—and I would be remiss if I did not note that virtually all the dire consequences that were alleged to result from such unions did occur in that one. Though the Komachi explicitly denied any preference for marriages with patriparallel cousins, 50 percent of first-cousin marriages were father's brother's daughter marriages.[3]

In the general context of Middle Eastern kinship, Komachi kinship resembled systems such as those described for Morocco, Algeria, Tunisia, and Baluchistan,[4] where kinship affiliation was neither categorical nor given. Komachi kinship was not official, that is, not "single, immutable, defined once and for all by the norms of genealogical protocol" (Bourdieu 1977:34), but was instead complex, multifaceted, and, almost by definition, bilateral. Given the flexibility and the practical nature of

Komachi kinship, it is not terribly surprising that the Komachi were indifferent genealogists. Some Komachi, generally less important employers, could recount elaborate (and, based on comparisons, correct), bilateral genealogies showing their formal connections to more important men, and, indeed, the formal interconnectedness of all those who had connections. The genealogies that most Komachi gave, however, comprised their fathers and mothers, most of their parents' siblings, and then a list of their direct agnatic ancestors. This list/genealogy never ran more than seven generations, and frequently many fewer. In one of my favorite interviews, I asked a neighbor about his grandfather and he said, "What do I know? He's dead." Though in fact he knew a bit more than nothing about his grandfather, his attitude toward his ancestors was typical of the Komachi: ancestors were *gozasht, raft, taman-shod* (done, gone, and finished). Formal kin were just that, and they were soon forgotten.

Having said that, and given the existence of much earlier literature on Middle Eastern kinship, I think it useful to preface further discussion of Komachi kinship by noting that one thing I will not be considering in great detail are *taifes*, patronymic groups. While the Komachi considered *taifes* salient social categories—indeed, *taifes* were the central elements in their model of tribal structure—it was difficult for me to divine just what *taifes* did. Certainly *taifes* were not corporate in any meaningful sense of the word: they neither controlled property nor acted politically. *Taifes* were slightly endogamous, though it was hard to separate this from the general preference for close kin marriage, and I never heard the Komachi speak of whom one should marry in terms of *taifes*. It was probably not accidental that in common Komachi usage (reflecting broader Persian usage, at least among pastoralists) *taife* referred to both patronymic groups and tribes as wholes. Quite obviously, the Komachi felt that they shared some solidarity with other members of their *taife* (most of whom were, after all, their formal close kin). At the same time, I cannot overemphasize how strongly I feel that *taifes* did little or nothing; it therefore seems to me that they are of little use to the anthropologist seeking to understand the Komachi. At best, *taifes* conferred a regularity, an apparent order or simplicity, on tribal structure that belied its complex, nearly chaotic reality. *Taifes*, in short, exemplified formal kinship; daily life showed the practical basis of Komachi kinship.

## Kinship in Practice

### CLAIMS

Mahmoud, an unmarried man in his mid-twenties, had been Ali's shepherd for four years. During the winter of 1974–75, Mahmoud constantly complained of pains in his legs. Finally, for several days in late winter he stopped working. Ali had Mahmoud taken to a doctor and supplied with medicines. Though he resumed work, Mahmoud still hobbled about and complained of pain; occasionally he remained in camp rather than going out with the flocks. Ali and, more outspokenly, his wife, Sekine, were furious. I heard them tell other herd owners that Mahmoud was malingering. Sekine later shouted out this accusation in camp, and Mahmoud and another shepherd's wife—Mahmoud's prospective mother-in-law—responded. All parties shattered the still of the desert air with very loud, acrimonious, and long-running debates over who was or was not working for the salary he deserved, who was or was not malingering, and who was or was not being properly sympathetic and concerned about someone in pain.

On June 15, as negotiations for hiring shepherds for the coming year began, Mahmoud left Ali's camp, saying, "I will not return." On June 20 he did return but insisted that he would not work for Ali. Mahmoud's father arrived in camp late that afternoon, however, and he soon brought Mahmoud to negotiate at Ali's tent.

During negotiations, the question of Mahmoud's illness came up. Mahmoud claimed that he couldn't work because his leg hurt and that he wouldn't work unless he was certain that he could do the job as it ought to be done. Responding to Mahmoud's explicit and implicit claims, Ali and his wife replied that Mahmoud would be taken to a better doctor, so there would be—*"en sha'allah,"* if God wills—no question of his being unable to work.

They claimed that Mahmoud surely knew he was part of their *oulad,* family, and thus he must know that were he unfortunate enough to become ill, they would spare no expense or inconvenience getting him to a doctor. "Did we not," they asked, "take you to a doctor and get you drugs last year? Haven't we done for you what we would have done for one of our own children?" (For the moment let me note only that the statements in this exchange are complex representations of half-truths on both sides. This is an important point to which I shall

return later.) In any event, Mahmoud acted as though he was not mollified.

At this point, two employers from other camps dropped in on the
negotiations. Nearly the first words they uttered after the obligatory ritual greetings were, "We are all members of one tribe, we are all kin,
there are no strangers here," repeating a refrain that was by now familiar
even to me and perhaps was used nearly unconsciously by the participants. Ali picked up this rhetorical thread, confirming yet once more
that they were all one *taife* and claiming again that he had always
treated Mahmoud like one of the family. Here, Mahmoud's father, who
with the two passersby was acting as a sort of broker, interjected that
Mahmoud was literally one of the family, Ali being Mahmoud's mother's father's father's brother's son. This comment passed without
demur, though in fact Ali was at best Mahmoud's mother's father's
mother's brother's son's son's son, which is not close kin by normal
Komachi reckoning. Shortly thereafter, the discussion turned to dollars and cents, and Mahmoud ultimately agreed to return as Ali's
shepherd.

Looking analytically at the negotiations between Mahmoud and
Ali, several points emerge. First, the two sides were contending over the
nature and meaning of Mahmoud's illness. This was not simply a discussion of the etiology of disease, but class conflict between employer
and shepherd. Second, the discourse about work and illness was
couched in terms of kinship and its obligations. Put differently, the discussion was about the relationship between two people who were (at
least in the discourse) presumed to be bound by the additional, preexisting tie of kinship. In the context of the negotiations, claims of kinship
entailed for both employer and shepherd such mutually recognized obligations as behaving toward kin in a supportive, mutualistic, nonexploi-
tative way and helping them in their time of need (again, at least in discourse). It was obvious during the negotiations that the claim of kinship
was being used to bridge the gap between Mahmoud and Ali and ease
the conflict between shepherd and employer. I shall examine later the
implications of using kinship claims in this way. First, however, we
must explore the question of Komachi kinship more deeply. We may
start by noting that the negotiators, in fact, made two distinct claims
of kinship: (1) a general claim of common kinship, "we are all one,"
and (2) a specific claim that Mahmoud was one of Ali's family and particularly that he was a *close* kinsman. These were claims of a radically

different order, and they and their implications should be clearly distinguished.

## PATTERNS

Komachi could conceive themselves as all kin to one another because they used broad, flexible, and inclusive criteria to calculate affiliation. When I asked people who I knew had joined the tribe whose kin they were, I was occasionally told, quite seriously, that they were their grandchildren's kin. Their children having married someone who was more clearly Komachi, the newcomers claimed kin by both marriage and descent. Common kinship of the "we are all one" variety meant only that every tribe member had a (presumed) kinship tie with *some* other tribe member. Working from these claims of kin ties with *any* other Komachi, people traced chains of marriage and descent that linked even the most marginal Komachi to the very center of the tribe. From any one connection, the Komachi made further connections to people who were centrally Komachi. In this way all Komachi could show themselves to be undeniably Komachi. In Mahmoud's case, for example, everyone knew that Mahmoud's father had entered the tribe from outside, so that Mahmoud had no Komachi kin on his father's side. Claims for kinship with other Komachi on his mother's side were somewhat stronger, however, and with those links Mahmoud could claim kin affiliation with Ali. Ali's acceptance of the claim immediately placed Mahmoud as Komachi, for Ali was at once the richest man in the tribe, an employer, and a head of camp. As a man with 112 kin no more distant than first cousins, he was truly a man of whom it might be said, "All Komachi are his kin."

In addition to Komachi claims of general common kinship, the Komachi made specific claims to being *qom khish*, close kin. As the Komachi used the term, it had a double meaning. On the one hand, it implied formal genealogical space: no one more distant than a second cousin was really close kin. On the other hand, the term connoted a practical relationship: *qom khish* were affectively and interactionally close kin. Employers tended to have many kin, so their networks for practical *qom khish* were selected from among their formal kin. Ali, for example, had 64 first cousins, among whom were his closest friends and associates. Ali's close kin were simultaneously first cousins and brothers-in-law, nephews and sons-in-law, all of these and business partners, and so on. At the same time though, Ali had formal kin, first cousins, with whom he had no practical relationships. For shepherds, who had few kin, the situation was quite different; I shall discuss this in more detail later.

The claim that all Komachi were kin did not mean that all Komachi were, or claimed to be, descendants of a single eponymous ancestor. The Komachi believed that their tribe was formed through the intermarriage of disparate peoples. They told me that "in the beginning of olden days [roughly seven generations ago] members of three *taifes* [patronymic groups] entered the Komachi territory, and they began to marry among themselves. Since then, they have become *pichide* [intertwined], and that is how the Komachi came to exist." While this view was correct in its broad outline, it clearly oversimplified the situation. First, in addition to the three intertwined *taifes*, 34 adult Komachi were members of other *taifes*. Thus, nearly 30 percent of all *taife* members were not members of the "original" three. Second, an additional 28 men and women were members of no Komachi *taife*. Overall, just over 40 percent of the tribe's members were not members of the three major patronymic groups. The agglomerative process that made people Komachi reached more widely than the myth admitted. Indeed, if we calculate the "Komachi-ness" of male heads of household by assuming that a "native" Komachi is one whose father was born in Komachi camps, then a bit more than one-third of the tribe's members were relative newcomers. Though the tribe may have had its origin in the intertwining of three *taifes*—and that is doubtful—it clearly grew through the accretion and amalgamation of people in ones and twos as much or more than it did by combining *taifes*. Moreover, examination of important aspects of Komachi kinship affiliation shows that claims of common kinship clearly meant different things for different people.

## Class and Kin

Eighty-eight percent of all Komachi marriages were class-endogamous. Marriages between members of employer and shepherd classes were uncommon, and the frequency of such cross-class marriages seemed directly proportional to the similarity of a couple's economic circumstance. Marriages between the very top and bottom layers of Komachi society were thus very rare. What, then, linked Komachi classes? Not only did wealthy Komachi not marry poor Komachi, but there were differences between the two groups so thoroughgoing that they make the question of how the groups were linked, how people could see themselves as part of a single tribe, simultaneously problematic and vital to an understanding of the Komachi.

I have suggested that the Komachi claim that "we are all kin" masked some complexity, and so let us examine it with particular regard to employers and shepherds. Consider the distinction between kin and close kin. Members of the tribe differed radically in the numbers of formal close kin they had. Ali shared close kinship affiliation (for these purposes cut off at first cousins) with 112 other members of the tribe: he was formally close kin to at least 20 percent of the tribe's total population. Ali was the extreme case, but wealthy and important men like him did have many formal close kin. Male heads of employer households had a range of 2–64 first cousins, with a mean of 30. By contrast, shepherds did not have many formal kin, with a mean of 9 and a range of 0–39. The shepherds' lower mean is in part attributable to the fact that 9 of 22 shepherds had *no* first cousins in the tribe, itself a significant point.

The two groups differed so greatly in the number of close kin they possessed largely because employers and shepherds had very different origins and different historic relations to the Komachi tribe. Using our earlier criterion for "native" Komachi, we find that over 80 percent of Komachi employers were "native" Komachi—that is, they had fathers who were born in a Komachi camp—while nearly 60 percent of Komachi shepherds were not. As the tribe grew by accretion, the proportion of poor men to rich men who became attached was greatly skewed. There was a strong tendency for Komachi employers to be born in the tribe (and, given our earlier discussion of Komachi classes, they were most likely to be born employers as well). To the degree that Komachi society was a social body that reproduced itself sexually, employers were the reproductive organs: the historical descendents of historically Komachi antecedents. By contrast, 58 percent of the shepherds were recent arrivals, members by attachment rather than descent. It is not surprising, then, that poor Komachi, and especially incoming shepherds, ultimately staked their claim to tribal membership by asserting or demonstrating kinship ties with wealthy, important, centrally placed Komachi.

Formally speaking, the claim "we are all kin" had substantially different potential meanings for employers who had many kin and whose networks ramified broadly, and for shepherds who had nearly no close kin within the tribe. One group was, in a way, telling the truth; the other's claim was something else. I say "something else" deliberately, for I do not mean that shepherds' claims were untrue. They were a different kind of claim, one with equal validity but very different implications.

A difference in the number of kinship ties they had was not the only aspect of kinship affiliation that distinguished shepherds from employers. Rates of cousin marriages varied significantly by class. Forty-nine percent of all status endogamous employer marriages were close kin marriages, but only 21 percent of shepherd marriages were close kin marriages; 38 percent of Komachi employers married first cousins against only 6 percent of Komachi shepherds.[5] Thus, not only did employers have more kin, but they also were more likely to have some kin to whom they had dense, multiplex ties. On the other hand, shepherds had few kin and had fewer kinds of ties with the kin they did have. We may come to understand why this was true when we look at the creation of kinship affiliations in more detail.

## Alliance, Division, and the Creation of Ties

Let us begin our discussion of practical kinship by examining political alliances and showing how men recreated significant alliances among formal close kin. The practical network of Ali—who, as we have seen, had many kin—is a good starting point. Ali's closest associates in the tribe were his first cousins Asghar and Agha Hossein (his mother's sister's son and father's brother's son, respectively). In addition to being cousins, the three men also shared the following ties: Ali's wife was Asghar's oldest sister; Asghar's wife was Agha Hossein's sister; Ali's youngest sister was married to Agha Hossein's (and Asghar's wife's) youngest brother; Ali's oldest son was married to Asghar's brother's daughter; and Ali's third daughter was engaged to Agha Hossein's (and Asghar's wife's) oldest sister's son (see Figure 2). In addition, even though most of Agha Hossein's and Asghar's children were too young to be married or engaged, everyone assumed that when it came time for them to be married off, the three men would make matches among their children.

People assumed that Ali, Asghar, and Agha Hossein would make

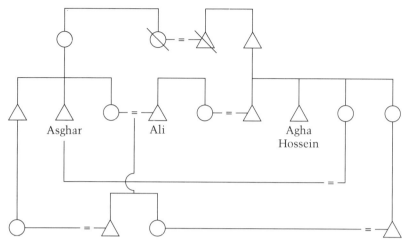

*Figure 2.*
*Kinship ties linking Ali, Asghar, and Agha Hossein.*

matches among their children because the kinship ties among the three men represented active, practical relationships in other spheres. Ali, Asghar, and Agha Hossein were all partners in a garden and motorized well in the *garmsir*. Ali and Agha Hossein camped near each other outside Jaghin during the winter; during the fall of 1974 they shared the cost of truck rental for migration, and during spring migration in 1975 the two camps migrated as a unit, never more than a few hundred yards apart. Indeed, as Agha Hossein shared his camel driver with his younger brother Mohammed, three camps migrated together. Asghar wintered some distance from Agha Hossein and Ali and did not migrate with them. On the other hand, he and Ali's oldest son were partners in a meat-buying venture during the summer of 1974, and in the summer of 1975 Asghar was a partner with Ali's son-in-law in a date-buying scheme. The close relationship among the three men was also manifest hundreds of miles away in Kerman City, where Agha Hossein's oldest son shared a room with two of Ali's sons; Asghar rented a room in the same building for his own school-age children. Not surprisingly, the men attended one another's weddings and circumcision celebrations, exchanging large gifts, and their wives assisted one another in food preparation at these events. The men visited each other frequently, and they generally supported each other in tribal political issues. For example, during 1975, when heads of camp were debating where to sink a motorized well (which they hoped the government would supply), Ali, Asghar, and Agha Hossein were unified in their position and argued as a bloc. They did so, I should add, not simply because they were friends and allies, but because they camped near one another and had a common interest in the placement of the pump. But that is precisely how the dialectic of structure and practice progresses. Linked by both the structural bonds of multiple close kin ties and the practical ties documented above, it seemed most likely that the three men would arrange marriages among their children, thereby reinforcing and re-forming the structural bonds that joined them.

As did all Komachi relations, the men's relationships had potential lines of fracture, and they did not always work together as a bloc. For example, I watched Ali try to steal away one of Agha Hossein's shepherds, and another time Ali suspected (probably correctly) that Asghar was trying to steal one of his shepherds. In Ali and Agha Hossein's joint economic ventures, Agha Hossein (who, in truth, was not terribly bright) often seemed to come out on the short end. Moreover, one can easily imagine that when the time came for the three men to try to negotiate marriages, competition might generate significant conflict among them. Nonetheless, there was solidarity among the men, and when, for example, Agha Hossein was defrauded of a considerable sum of money by an itinerant con artist, the man he turned to for advice and assistance was Ali.

Ali's relations with Agha Hossein and Asghar show how preexisting ties of kinship were reinforced through practice and created significant practical (in the sense of "useful") affiliations. Indeed, during the time I was with the Komachi, what I saw were relationships giving contemporary substance to ties that had been created by the men's fathers. A look at the tribe's genealogy shows that this re-forming of ties had been constantly happening in many ways.

Meshedi Yarbok Mohammedi was by all accounts one of the wealthiest and most important members of the first ascending generation above Ali and the other men I lived with. The marriages Yarbok made for his children between the 1940s and 1970 are noteworthy for two reasons: first, with one exception, he did not marry his children to close kin but made political marriages linking him (and his sons) to men who were nearly his political equals; and second, his children's marriages display a pattern that will help us track the interaction between rule and practice in Komachi marriage.

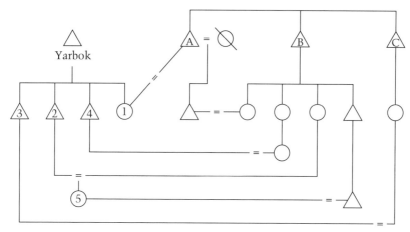

Figure 3.
*Marriages of Yarbok's children. Numbers reflect the order in which marriages occurred.*

As Figure 3 shows, Yarbok created a very dense network of kinship ties by marrying his sons and daughters to three generations of Abrahimi men and women. These marriages effectively linked Yarbok (and his children) to the politically and economically dominant men of Yarbok's generation. As wealth is inherited, these marriages also established significant links among his children and the men of their own generation who were likely to be economically (and hence presumably politically) important. Marriages made by Yarbok's children and their peers for Yarbok's grandchildren, including several negotiated in 1974 and 1975, reaffirmed the ties initially forged by Yarbok by establishing new, overlapping ties.[6] This suggests that the bonds Yarbok had created by means of his children's marriages had indeed become important, for ties that were unimportant did not get remade. A neighbor of mine whose status in the tribe had clearly fallen told me that his father's sister was Yarbok's mother. I checked and found that this was true, but the relationship carried no weight and had never been reaffirmed. In this case genealogical links were clear enough, but the relationships they created had become unimportant, and had been allowed to lapse. Practically speaking, there might as well have been no tie.

The former *katkhoda* of Shirinak made a similar set of strategic marriages for his children between the late 1930s and the mid-1960s. The *katkhoda* was not a pastoralist but had married a tribal wife, and he too married his children to the children of important Abrahimi men

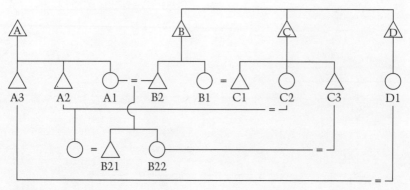

*Figure 4.*
*Marriages of the* Katkhoda's *children.*                    △ = *Katkhoda*

(see Figure 4). At this late date it seems that each side gained from the marriages. The *katkhoda* was an important local figure, the representative of the major landowners in the area and a modestly successful landowner in his own right. The marriages therefore gave the Abrahimi men excellent ties to the settled community in the area and access to its resources. Marriage of the *katkhoda*'s children into the tribe appears to have given him a means of ensuring all of them a far more comfortable economic position than might have been possible if they had had access only to shares of his agricultural holdings. The *katkhoda* was very successful in creating formal links among his children and significant tribesmen; moreover, the links he made were reinforced, so that in barely two generations the *katkhoda*'s children had become central and important members of the Komachi tribe.

Given the Komachi rule prohibiting multiple marriages between sibling sets, the pattern evident in the marriages of Yarbok's and the *katkhoda*'s children reveals that, by marrying their children to first cousins (or to a cousin and his uncle), Yarbok and the *katkhoda* were marrying their children into the closest genealogical space possible. These patterns, illustrated in Figure 5, show what I call extended and oblique (deferred exchange) marriages, respectively, and are evidence of strategic matchmaking.

Many Komachi marriages—including those arranged in accord with the rules—were political events. Extended and oblique marriages resulted from attempts to consolidate political and economic ties by

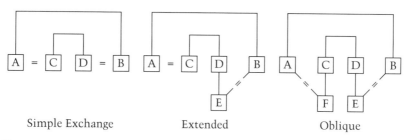

Figure 5.
*Extended, oblique, and exchange marriages.*

means of marriages that adhered to the rule prohibiting multiple marriages between sibling sets. Komachi who had significant common interests marked and reinforced their relationships through the creation of new kinship ties, and so peoples' networks of kin became dense clusters of overlapping ties—loci of practical relations—that faded out rapidly into single-stranded ties linking formal kin. Such overlapping ties were the markers of strategic decisions, past and present. Because they joined close kin, Komachi marriages created not a broad net of tribal solidarity but a series of dense nuclei bound to each other only weakly. I explore the implications of this pattern below.

The distributions of marriages between close kin, oblique marriages, and extended marriages support the view that these were political matches. As we have seen, there were important differences between the rates of close kin marriages among employers and shepherds, and the frequency of extended and oblique marriages also varied greatly with class. Like close cousin marriage, extended and oblique marriage patterns were frequent among those members of the tribe who were active in the political arena—employers—while they were uncommon among those who were not active in that arena—shepherds. Of 51 marriages between members of employer households, 28 (55 percent) were extended or oblique, while of 36 shepherd marriages only 4 (11 percent) were of that type. One may see differences in kinship affiliation between shepherds and employers as arising from two bases: shepherds' relative paucity of official kin within the tribe, and practical barriers that effectively precluded shepherds marrying politically. Shepherds by definition were of low status and did not need to be as concerned about protecting their reputation via cousin marriage. Indeed, shepherds' considerations in arranging a marriage were generally of a totally different order. One of the shepherd marriages contracted during 1975 was arranged by an employer who pressured a former shepherd in his debt into "giving" his daughter to the employer's current young shepherd. With cases like this not uncommon, shepherds were denied the ability to participate in marital politics as players other than pawns. People who have no autonomy are not free to play games of power.

Taken together, the differences between Komachi employers and shepherds in numbers of close kin, numbers of close kin marriages, and numbers of oblique and extended marriages created two groups that had radically different kinds of kinship affiliation. Because employers had many kin and married kin, their kin networks tended to be dense and multiplex, and their relationships with their closest kin were likely to be elaborate and involuted. By contrast, shepherds' kinship affiliations tended to be single-stranded and diffuse. Seen as a whole, kinship ties in the employer class resembled not a homogeneous web, but a congeries of dense clusters of relations with rather frangible official linkages among them. Shepherds, by contrast, had neither dense clusters of practical kin nor an extensive integument of official close kin. Considered as a group, shepherds evoke Marx's proverbial potatotes in a sack: units resembling one another but having few ties among them. Indeed, one is to a degree compelled to see the Komachi tribe as containing two quite distinct populations.

Given this reality, one is confronted by two major questions: How did the two Komachi classes come to have such radically different structural characteristics? And given the reality of the relationship between shepherd and employer, and with regard to both kinship affiliation and economic circumstance, what did link the groups? I have begun to answer the first question by showing that shepherds and employers had different historical relationships to the Komachi tribe, a theme I shall return to later, and by suggesting that marriages in the two classes had different political intentions. The following discussion, which focuses on the creation of ties among employers and between employers and shepherds, will add flesh to the skeletal discussion of the politics of marriage and, at the same time, clarify the nature of the links that joined rich and poor together. With regard to the latter point, one must remember that the Komachi social order was unstable and that I am therefore concerned with the development of divisions between employers as much as divisions between employers and shepherds.

## Komachi Marriage Negotiations

Komachi marriages followed a long process of public and private discussion and negotiation. Among the Komachi, as elsewhere in the Middle East, marriage negotiations cannot be understood as mere teenage matters; they were major symbolic displays that made and marked men's places in society (Bourdieu 1977; Rosen 1979; Eickelman 1976, 1981; Geertz 1979). As critical turns in the game of honor, success in negotiation transcended the importance of the immediate event. This gave negotiation its emotional charge. All remaining aspects of the process unfolded within the atmosphere of fierce competition engendered by the association of spouse selection with honor. Recalling the conflicts that arose during the negotiation of shepherd contracts, one may sense accurately that "being someone" among the Komachi involved a constant assertion of one's position and perpetual attempts to improve or maintain that position in the only meaningful arena available, that is, among one's peers. Hence among the Komachi, as is the case elsewhere in the Middle East (Bourdieu 1977; Geertz 1979), making a marriage was a socially perilous venture, and a man's inability to negotiate an advantageous marriage for his child was a major failure. Perhaps as a result of this, Komachi marriage practices permitted men to avoid failure by preserving an illusion—often a very transparent one—of independence and noncommitment until agreement was certain. No party to marriage negotiations would admit publicly that negotiations were under way or that any commitment had been made until the formal public request for the girl (*mar katkhoda*) had been made. Public disclosure occurred only after a series of preliminary negotiations that were nonbinding and, ideally, noncompromising. The process had two significant features: it permitted all interested parties, including those not directly involved in the negotiation, to make their feelings for or against a match known before a final decision had been made; and it left room for men to protect themselves from the appearance of premature commitment. Because everyone had access to the process, families could evaluate alternative choices and map strategies. At the same time, since virtually everyone in the tribe knew who was interested in whom and roughly how negotiations were proceeding, people's protection from the appearance of rejection was, in fact, often very thin. It makes sense that such protection was thin, because intertwining a man's struggle for status with his attempt to marry off his child meant that others constantly scrutinized his actions and reactions. These actions and reactions were themselves shaped by the knowledge that people analyzed and evaluated his behavior and the quality of the marriage he had arranged. Marriages among the Komachi elite helped determine both tribal structure and individual status, and so were political events at both the macro and micro levels.

I now turn to a detailed retelling of marriage negotiations during 1974 and 1975, focusing on five marriages. I have chosen to focus on these five matches for several reasons. First, as shall become apparent, none of these matches was an independent event: the making of one match constrained the others, in terms of both the flow of events and the outcome. Thus, the flow of events surrounding marriage negotiations, while complex, is part of a whole and has a coherence that a sample of one, two, or six arbitrarily chosen cases would not have. Second, the five marriages were important events because they involved the sons and daughters of the most powerful members of the tribe, nomadic and settled. And third, because they involved politically important Komachi, the marriages exemplified quite clearly the implications of marriage negotiations. In order to make the events easier to follow, I shall introduce the actors first.

Ali was the wealthiest man in the tribe. His eldest son, Akbar, was seeking a wife in 1974 and 1975.

Xosro, Ali's patriparallel cousin, the husband of Ali's sister, and a much older brother of Ali's daughter's husband, was a former head of camp who had settled in 1964 to deal in meat and carpets. His son, Xodadad, and his daughter, Xajije, were seeking and being sought as a spouse, respectively, in 1974 and 1975.

Hassan was father's brother to Ali and Xosro, and the second wealthiest man in the tribe. He was seeking a wife for Hossein, his oldest son by his second wife.

Kourosh was a recently settled head of camp. Married to Xosro's sister, his own sister was Hassan's second wife. Kourosh's father, Yarbok, had been the most important man in the tribe in his generation. Kourosh had two daughters, Kobra and Kaniz, who were married in 1974 and 1975.

Reza, also head of a camp, was married to Xosro's oldest sister. Reza sought a match for his oldest son Rostam and for his daughter Roxsare.

Malek too was the head of his own camp. He was Reza's brother;

his wife was Ali's mother's sister's daughter. He had a son, Mohammed, and three daughters to marry.

The relations among these men are illustrated in Figure 6.

## Five Marriages during 1974 and 1975

In the summer of 1974,[7] Akbar broke off his engagement to a nontribal schoolteacher and reentered the tribal marriage pool, complicating an already very complex situation. In violation of the conventional wisdom that one's wishes should be kept private, if not secret, Akbar let it be known that he wanted to marry Kourosh's daugher Kobra, whom rumor already associated with Hossein (the son of Hassan) and with another young man, Ahmad. At the same time, Akbar's mother strongly favored his marriage to her own brother's daughter, while his father, Ali, seemed to favor a match with his sister's daughter (who was also a father's father's brother's son's daughter), Xajije. However, Xajije's fa-

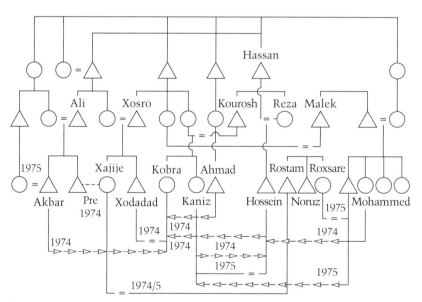

*Figure 6.*
*Kinship ties among men involved in marriage negotiations during 1974 and 1975. Arrows indicate rejected marriage proposal.*

ther, Xosro, was said to have promised his daughter to his sister's son, Rostam. Throughout August 1974 people wondered if Xajije would marry Rostam, while Ali indicated that he opposed that match. Ali argued that because many years ago he and Xosro had spoken of marrying his second son to Xajije, he still had a claim to her. Xosro acknowledged the earlier discussions but said that those arrangements had long since been abandoned (which was true), and so Ali had no claim. In mid-September Xosro let it be known that he wanted Xajije to marry Rostam, and that although he would not agree to having a wedding ceremony in 1974 he would let Xajije sign a marriage contract with Rostam. With Xosro's position public knowledge, Rostam's representatives prepared to make a public request for Xajije's hand and thereby ratify the event. Under normal circumstances Ali, the girl's mother's brother (and father's brother's son) and the wealthiest man in the tribe, should have played a major role at this event. Despite many entreaties referring to his "duty," however, he refused to attend or participate, even though Rostam's representatives indicated a willingness to compromise on either the time or place and even though they and many others begged him not to create a *taife shekaste*, a broken kin group.

After Ali refused to compromise, Rostam's representatives—who had extended themselves by making personal appeals to Ali—refused to appear at the long-planned wedding feast for Ali's second daughter and the son of another of Ali's sisters. They also openly ate a meal hosted for them by Xosro instead of the wedding meal. The conflict between the two men meant that both of Ali's sisters were inconvenienced: Xosro's wife had to prepare an enormous festive meal for guests at a time when her greatest concern was helping her sister manage her son's wedding reception, and the sister whose son was being married could no longer count on the undivided assistance of her closest kinswoman. The *taife* was indeed *shekaste*, for, as we shall see below, Ali and Xosro remained at loggerheads.

In any event, on September 18, the day following Xosro's controversial "dinner party," Ali's patron, a wealthy bazaar merchant from Kerman City, came to mediate a dispute over wild licorice roots that he wished to purchase. As it happened, I drove him to tribal territory. During the drive, he discussed affairs with his local factotum, and the major topic of their discussion was whether Xosro could still be made to give Xajije to Akbar. When Ali's patron arrived, however, Ali told him that he had no interest in who Xajije married. Moreover, after Ali's patron had settled the economic problem and had returned to Ali's quarters, Ali asked him to send for Kourosh. Ali then requested his patron's help in asking Kourosh to give Kobra to Akbar.[8]

Now it was common knowledge that several other men wanted to marry Kobra. One of these men was Ahmad, who was Kobra's father's mother's brother's son. In early September, Ahmad's mother approached Kobra's mother about a match (Ahmad's brother had told me a few days after it happened that this overture had been favorably received.) There were also rumors that Hassan's son Hossein wanted to marry Kobra. Kourosh, however, was rumored to have said that while he would not let Hossein marry Kobra, he *would* let him marry his other daughter, Kaniz. This was an interesting point and was much gossiped about, for a tentative arrangement between Kaniz and Mohammed (son of Malek) had been broken off in mid-August when Kourosh announced he would not let Kaniz migrate. Since Hossein would inherit a large flock and was not considering settling, Kourosh's treatment of Mohammed was seen as having been a ploy. Hossein, however, said that he would not settle for Kaniz and would either marry Kobra or have nothing to do with any of Kourosh's daughters.

Akbar's bid for Kobra thus occurred in an already complicated situation, and when Ali's patron suggested that Kourosh give Kobra to Akbar, Kourosh, not surprisingly, politely refused to make an immediate decision. When pressed, Kourosh asked Ali's patron to go outside with him for a private talk; they returned a few minutes later, and the question of Kobra and Akbar never again rose.

On September 20, however, Kourosh announced that he had agreed to give Kobra to Xosro's son Xodadad (a father's sister's daughter marriage). As Xodadad was attending high school in Kerman City and Kobra was an illiterate tribal girl, it was an unexpected match. Akbar was bitterly disappointed by the turn of events, and Ali was clearly embarrassed by them, for he had been caught in an exposed position and it appeared that Xosro had bested him. These events ended the wedding season of 1974.

The next events in the sequence began during the summer of 1975, and the primary actors were: Kourosh again, this time for his daughter Kaniz; Malek and his family; Reza for his daughter Roxsare; Hassan and his son Hossein; and Ali and Akbar, again.

Tentative arrangements between Malek's son, Mohammed, and Kourosh's daughter Kaniz having fallen through, Malek was again seeking a wife for Mohammed. Malek's position was difficult. He also had three daughters to marry, the older two of whom were beginning to be spoken of as "old," implying that their father had not been able to arrange suitable matches for them. Malek was trying to arrange a marriage for Mohammed that would not violate the prohibition on multiple marriages and block the marriage of one of his daughters. For example, while the marriage of Mohammed to his father's brother's daughter, Roxsare, was an excellent match (and Malek's brother, Reza, strongly favored it), it would block a marriage between Reza's son No Ruz and any of Malek's daughters. Malek's wife, therefore, was intent on looking elsewhere: she made overtures to Malek's other brother and to distant kin in a neighboring tribe. Rebuffed in both of these attempts, she too fell back on the match of Mohammed with Roxsare. Then she and Malek renewed their efforts to find possible spouses for their daughters. Two possibilities were Hassan's son Hossein, and Akbar. Both were from excellent families; both had been spurned by Kourosh the year before, and both were available.

Hossein seemed the better prospect. Although Akbar had said that he did not find his cousin attractive, his mother wanted him to marry her brother's daughter, and people assumed that unless he made a forceful display of independence, his mother, who was a very strong-willed woman, would prevail, as she ultimately did. Therefore, Malek's family concentrated their attentions on Hossein.

Kourosh had previously rejected both Mohammed (for Kaniz) and Hossein (for Kobra) as suitors, and Hossein had, in turn, spurned Kaniz. However, when Kourosh heard that Malek and Hassan were arranging marriages for their sons that would leave Kaniz unattached, he claimed that he still considered Mohammed engaged to her. Malek's family, by contrast, claimed that they had wanted Mohammed to marry Kobra, not Kaniz, and that Kourosh's attempt to substitute one daughter for another was unacceptable. Moreover, they said, whichever daughter had been involved, Kourosh had rejected their suit, so they were free to do as they pleased.

On the evening of October 5, 1975, Malek attempted to arrange simultaneously Mohammed's marriage to his father's brother's daughter, Roxsare, and a marriage between Hassan's son, Hossein, and one of his daughters. No adult voiced opposition to Mohammed's marriage. Everyone agreed that if the fathers, Reza and Malek, who were brothers, favored the match, no one had any right to oppose their wishes. Problems quickly arose over the second match, however. Hassan's family attended the meeting, but none of his wife's kin were there. Following the lead of their oldest brother, Kourosh, who let everyone know that he strongly opposed the marriage, the rest of her brothers did not attend. Malek's family wanted to conclude the match anyway; they argued that by not attending, Kourosh had forfeited his right to speak. Other tribespeople, however, strongly disagreed. Malek's wealthiest and most important kinsman, the man who should have been his strongest spokesman, said it would be "unseemly" to conclude arrangements under those circumstances and that he would not give his approval to the match while Hossein's matrilateral kin were absent.

This turn of events generated furious discussion. On the one hand, Malek and his supporters argued that the approval of kin was unnecessary. Given that both fathers approved, who had any right to challenge their decision? Moreover, they asked, was making a match without the approval of kin any more "unseemly" than the refusal of the kin to attend and make their position known? Others, while not directly addressing the question of who did or did not have a legitimate say in the marriage of a man's children, continued to hold that it was unseemly to proceed without the boy's kin. This anthropologically fascinating discussion of culturally acceptable practice was cut short, however. Reza's teenage son, No Ruz, began to call out against the proposed match between Mohammed and Roxsare, for it would prevent his marriage to Malek's youngest daughter. In his outburst, No Ruz shouted down and physically threatened several of the most prominent members of the tribe. His outburst ended any possibility of rational discourse, and Hassan and his family returned to their own camp with no arrangements having been made. The next day, as I spoke to witnesses and participants, virtually everyone agreed that the situation had been mishandled. People felt the attempt to solve a delicate matter publicly was misguided, that the match should have been arranged—and a marriage contract signed—privately and then announced as a *fait accompli*. Still, people were surprised to discover that Mohammed and Roxsare had been driven to the nearby town in the middle of the night, only a few hours after the public wrangling had broken up, to sign a marriage contract. Only the marriage of Hossein remained unresolved at that point.

On October 8, Malek's married daughter visited Hassan and damaged her sister's cause when she criticized his actions. Kourosh, meanwhile, was furious about Mohammed's marriage to Roxsare. His anger did not subside when Malek's wife said, "Kourosh is not really upset about Mohammed. All he cares about is money; if we give him one hundred tomans [about $70], he will think he has come off well." Kourosh and his brother then visited Hassan and made a concerted effort to arrange the marriage between Kaniz and Hossein. I was later told that Kourosh offered to sign a marriage agreement immediately and to let Kaniz migrate with Hossein, or to help Hossein settle if he chose. Kourosh was able to put some pressure on Hassan, and his attempt was successful.[9] On October 10, Hossein and Kaniz signed a marriage contract. Even then, Kourosh continued to castigate Mohammed and his family. The marriage negotiations of 1974 and 1975 thus ended as they had begun, in conflict. Still, Hossein, Rostam, and Akbar married their mothers' brothers' daughers, Xodadad married his father's sister's daugher, and Mohammed married his father's brother's daughter.

I found Komachi negotiations rich and exciting material to observe and work with, and they raise many points of interest. For example, all the marriages whose tortuous negotiations I describe above followed norms; hence the questions of how norms and practice were related and why events flowed as they did clearly are significant. As I have dealt with these issues elsewhere (Bradburd 1984b), I wish to stress here the dominant practical and structural effect of the marriage negotiation process. Given the rules or preferences for marriage with (formal) close kin, and given the distribution of formal kin among wealthy and important Komachi, important men often competed with one another in the race to make the best marriages for their children. Strategies abounded, and it is clear that existing relationships among men shaped their marriage strategies in many ways. Most obvious was that the general and specific tenors of the relationships determined whom one might want or not want as a kinsman. During 1974 and 1975, for example, Xosro and Ali were on opposite sides of the economic dispute mediated by Ali's patron. Although Ali had no direct interest in the economic dispute, he was closely allied with his wife's brother, who was locked in struggle with Xosro and Kourosh. Disagreement over Xajije's marriage therefore took place in an already charged atmosphere. In fact, it was not only charged, it was complicated. Ali and Xosro had once been fast friends, and a tentative arrangement had been made to marry Xajije to Ali's second son. Xosro settled, however—becoming a potential rival to Ali's wife's brother—and the relationship between the two men changed. Later, Ali sent his second son to high school in Kerman City and broke off the understanding about the boy and Xajije. But the marriage negotiations did not involve Xosro and Ali alone, and a whole constellation of relationships among men was important. Take Kourosh, for example, who ultimately married his daugher to Xodadad instead of Akbar. Kourosh, who was married to Xosro's sister, had recently settled, and for several years Kourosh, his younger brother, and Xosro were the only settled tribesmen. It is not surprising that their relationship became close.[10] Looking at the circumstances even more closely, we note that Kourosh was able to settle, and indeed found it advantageous to settle, because he had many daughters who were not directly productive in the pastoral sector but could be converted into very productive labor as carpet weavers. Kourosh's daughters were thus economically valuable. By signing a marriage contract between Kobra and Xodadad, who was young and settled, Kourosh was able to assure himself several more years of Kobra's direct and noncompensated labor.[11] He would not have had access to this labor had Kobra married Akbar or Hossein. In effect, then, the match that Kourosh and Xosro arranged marked a bond between them as allies in a dispute at the same time that it linked two men who had a close relationship (hence the alliance), re-formed affinal ties, was economically rational for Kourosh, and was a good political move for Xosro.

Again, marriage with close kin, even if it took place only to save a kinsman from embarrassment, intensified kin ties within the network of already close practical kin. Since no one helped an enemy, no matter how formally close he was, all cousin marriages affirmed a tie, and created an ever-denser node of relations. Affirmation of the tie, of course, made men closer; that closeness was marked by a tie that in turn might be made to bear a heavier practical load. Interestingly enough, fortuitous or indirectly strategic marriages with close kin had much the same result as those planned to form or reaffirm significant practical relations: they intensified relations within an already salient—if informal—group.

## Ties, Strategies, and Structure

The preceding examples highlight an important reality of Komachi kinship affiliation: it was a means of drawing people together that even as it bound people together, created divisions. As we have seen, within the limited field of potential marriage partners available to the Komachi, one man's creation of a tie often interfered with another's attempt. As more than just the match was at stake, the hostility and tension engendered when important men maneuvered for position was not always trivial or transient. As a man's main competitors included men whose children were ideal candidates for a "good match," the antagonisms that arose during one set of negotiations often helped structure attitudes and results for other negotiations, so that practice helped structure structure.

Of course, divisions were not caused simply by marriage or the hostilities of marriage negotiations. Komachi marriage patterns and negotiations show that the maintenance of political status and the creation of alliances that were politically or economically useful were the strongest determinants of the shape of Komachi kinship. Practical considerations—divisions and solidarities based on tribal political economy—motivated most matches. Kinship affiliation and political economy were intimately linked. Parallels between marriage negotiations and shepherding negotiations went far beyond their form: both sets of events created real and very significant divisions in the relations of wealthy and important men.

As a result of the pressures noted above, clusters of practical kin, the foci of significant relationships, were small, and while there were individuals who bridged them, clusters tended to be discrete. Both Yarbok and the *katkhoda* married their children to the sons and daughters of the same five brothers. That this marked the centrality and importance of the brothers is clear. But the brothers were not a solidary group and were not a bridge linking together other groups into the unified (*pichide*) tribe of Komachi official kinship. On the contrary, by the next generation there were two quite separate and opposed clusters of cousins tenuously linked by past relationships. Ali represented the focal point of one group comprising the *katkhoda*'s sons, Asghar and Akbar, Agha Hossein, his sister Shoyeste, and her husband as its core members. On the other side there was the cluster centered about Xosro and Kourosh Yarbok, which included Kazom Yarbok and Shiri Xabar, Xosro's brother. Looking at the events and ties of 1974 and 1975, one sees that Kourosh married his son to Xosro's daughter and that Kourosh, Xosro, and Kazom were all settled into the carpet and meat-brokering businesses in Shirinak. One would also discover that Kourosh and Xosro's children shared rooms in Kerman City, and that when Kourosh's oldest daughter was being sought by every potentially eligible young man, including Shoyeste's son Ahmad, Shoyeste had approached her sister, Kazom's wife, and asked her to intervene (presumably with her husband, Kourosh's brother, and perhaps her sister-in-law [and cousin]) to promote the match. When Kourosh married his daughter to the son of Xosro (his wife's brother), Shoyeste's relationship with her sister became quite cold, and Shoyeste, arranging a match between her son and Ali's daughter, very clearly allied herself with Ali, Asghar (whose wife was also Shoyeste's sister and in whose camp she and her husband lived), and her brother Agha Hossein by excluding her sister from the proceedings. The difficulties between the two groups had, as I noted earlier, some economic base, and the differences were exacerbated by marriage negotiations and a fight between Agha Hossein and his brother-in-law Kazom over musicians hired to play at two successive ceremonies. So far from making the cousins solidary, the in-marriages of Yarbok's and the *katkhoda's* children created clusters of ties that were lines along which the offspring of the five brothers became divided.[12]

We have seen that both political concerns and the structural logic of the marriage system[13] drove wealthy Komachi apart. The marriage system worked constantly to create divisions, or at least potential divisions, that helped form the lines of stress and potential fracture along which practically-based divisions grew. Practical divisions helped determine where lines of kinship affiliation would be doubled and redoubled or left to languish, creating the centers of solidarity and lines of fracture about which practical choices were made. And so the dialectic went on and on.

The impact of practice on structure and the limits of structure itself are clearly revealed in the case of Ali and Xosro, which I have discussed above. Central figures in the marriage negotiations and the economic dispute of 1974 and 1975, the two men were probably more closely linked by preexisting ties than any two other men in the tribe. Indeed, as Figure 7 suggests, the men were joined by ties that were so dense, and that involved so many people who were themselves intimately linked to both men, that open conflict was difficult to sustain; the structure of preexisting relations held Ali and Xosro together. At the same time, they were caught in conflicts of economic and political origin that *practically* made effective alliance impossible, and indeed

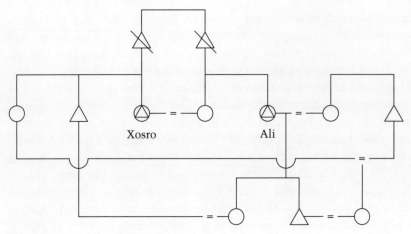

*Figure 7.*
*Kinship ties linking Ali and Xosro.*

generated constant low-level tensions. The relationship between the two men was always difficult, and occasionally substantially disrupted normal social intercourse—as when Xosro entertained guests during the wedding feast of Ali's daughter, or when Ali refused to appear at the *mar katkhoda* for Xosro's daughter. Caught in a web of structural linkage and practical antipathy, the relationship between the men had many features of an unhappy but indivisible marriage: the bonds between them could not be denied, but living within the bonded relationship was unpleasant and difficult. Their relationship was a constant series of small conflicts, petty insults, and violations of expected conduct that elicited nearly constant comment and frequent active intervention and mediation by mutually related kin, members of other tribes, and outside patrons. Presumably, the structural consequences would really occur in the next generation, when the practical antipathy between Ali and Xosro would crystallize into the absence of any marriages or other direct relations between their children. People who were second cousins would then draw formally, structurally, and practically apart. If kinship was the framework ("we are all kin") that united all Komachi and counterpoised other divisive forces, we can begin to see why the Komachi tribe was not a perdurable social entity.

## Kinship, Residence, and Relationship

In pursuing the questions of kinship and tribal unity, one must remember that the Komachi were pastoralists who dwelt in small groups distributed over a large area. Not everyone was in daily contact, but social interaction among members of the same camp was constant and intense. Examination of the significant relationships within residential groups—camps—shows that the kinship affiliations with the greatest affect did not link politically active and important men to one another but linked women either to men or to other women. Equally, examination of relations between camps shows us little that moderated preexisting relations among important men.

All Komachi dwelt in camps that were the loci of most day to day social and economic activity; they were major observable social units beyond the household. Each camp was centered about a wealthy and important man, called by the Komachi the *sar ehsham*, the head of camp (literally, "head of the retinue"). The camp's core was formed by the head and his hired shepherds (whose residential strategies were limited, as we have seen). Shepherds were rarely close kin with their employers and were never, in my observation, close agnatic kin. Households not bound to the head by contractual ties were generally bound to him through kinship, being either his close kin or linked to him through kinship ties to either his coresident kin or his hired shepherds. Camps were named for their heads; Komachi spoke, for example, of *"ehsham* Asghar" or *"ehsham* Ali." The *sar ehsham*'s tent was almost always pitched at one end—the *head* end—of the straight line of tents that made a Komachi camp. Camp heads were generally prominent in the tribe and dominant in their camps. Since camps were built about their heads, they existed as named units for as long as the head was alive or active. Camp composition changed from time to time, but changes tended to be gradual rather than rapid, and camps were semicoherent units. Directly or indirectly, most members of the camp were bound together by their ties to the head, who were thus central nodes of the social order. Indeed, two men were particularly strong and dominant heads of camp; each was so central to his group's self-perception that he remained the focal point for the group well after his death.

Before proceeding to a discussion of camps' internal structures, a brief discussion of the relations among camps and between camp and tribe is in order. In the broadest sense, no formal relationships existed among Komachi camps. *Sar ehshams* were not part of a larger, more formal political structure. *Sar ehshams* did not meet officially as a council or a body to discuss issues; no collective decision of *sar ehshams* would be in and of itself binding on any single *sar ehsham*. There was no tribal hierarchy; rather, there was a congeries of camps, each centered about its own head. Relations between camps were simply manifestations of the relationships that held between their respective heads. As a corollary to this, relations between the remaining members of different camps were equally unstructured: people's significant relationships with members of other camps did not have to be identical to their head's relationships with the other heads.

Because camps were so centered about their heads, and because relationships between heads (and camps) were not structurally regulated, factors that impinged on the relationships between heads of camp had a profound influence on tribal structure. Work by Gregory Johnson that examines some organizational limits and constraints on decision-making behavior in small groups illuminates one aspect of these relationships. Johnson's work (1982, 1983) has to do with group dynamics and the notion of "scalar stress," particularly dealing with the establishment of hierarchical structures and the relationship of the development of hierarchy to problems of information flow. Johnson argues that natural limits on individuals' abilities to process information lead to the development of regular organizational forms within human institutions. Specifically, Johnson argues that if nonhierarchically organized groups grow in size so that there are more than six "basal organizational units," stress greatly increases. This "scalar stress" can be measured in a number of ways, including frequency of dispute and "degradation of decision [making] performance." Johnson also notes, and I wish to emphasize this, that although stress begins to develop as groups exceed six basal organizational units, a variety of measures indicate that the maximum operational size for nonhierarchically organized systems appears to be roughly fourteen basal organizational units (1983:180). All things being equal, the solution to scalar stress is either the elaboration of a hierarchical structure that reduces and channels information, reducing it to a manageable flow, or the fissioning of the group into smaller units.

Basal organizational units are *the* decision-making units within a system. Because nuclear family households were all independent economic and social units, it might seem as if they should be the basic Komachi organizational unit. However, given the structure of Komachi camps and the nature of the relationships among them, it seems clear that camps were in fact the tribe's real basic organizational units. Given Johnson's argument that when a nonhierarchically organized group exceeds fourteen basal organizational units either it will break down or a hierarchy will form, it is interesting to note that while the Komachi tribe as a whole comprised eighteen camps in 1974 and 1975, several smaller groups (Meshedi Gholami's two camps and the two camps headed by Shah Mirza's sons) seemed to be in the process of splitting off. Perhaps this was a case of a nonhierarchical group with more than fourteen basal organizational units breaking apart. While Johnson's notion is hardly a sufficient explanation of the tensions and conflicts among wealthy Komachi, one can see it as a factor that might aggravate those tensions, resulting in the tribe being a conglomeration of camps rather than a more coherent body. I will return to this point later.

The absence of formal, structured relations among heads of camp also meant that practical ties helped determine the geographical distribution of camps. The case of Agha Hossein, Ali, and Asghar shows this process at work. Because Agha Hossein had a nearly paternal relationship with his much younger brother Mohammed, they shared a hired camel driver. As a result, they camped together on migration, and even camped near each other in the *garmsir*. Because Agha Hossein was very close to Ali, they camped near each other and migrated together. The camps moved as a cluster because of the personal, practical relationship of their heads to one another, not because of the positions of the camps within an overarching political or kinship system. In short, an important outcome of the freedom that heads of camp had in choosing where they would reside or migrate to was that important people who were close in practical and formal terms often dwelt near each other. As a result, nodes of relations among important men took on a geographical as well as a genealogical character. One sees these nodes, or at least their effects, when one looks at the tribe as a whole. It is immediately apparent that many parts of the tribe had greater solidarity than the whole itself. To illustrate this, let me briefly expand my discussion of the splitting off of Meshedi Gholami's camp and Shah Mirza's sons' camps.

There were roughly 115 households whose members claimed to be Komachi, and these 115 households were divided into three groups with relatively clear boundaries. First, there was what I call the main body of the tribe. This group numbered 73 households and included members of the three "original" patronymic groups, three smaller patronymic groups, and assorted individuals who dwelt in 13 camps. Members of these camps migrated together, and had summer and winter quarters that were largely contiguous, though, as we have seen, this group itself was internally divided. Meshedi Gholami's camp, numbering 13 households, had summer and winter quarters that were some distance away from those of the main body. Most residents of this camp were Gholami's close kin. The third group of 16 households in two camps was built about the late Shah Mirza's sons. These 16 households shared summer quarters with the main body of the tribe, although their camps stood at the boundary of Komachi territory. Their winter quarters, however, were some 40 miles of very rough road away. (A final camp with 4 households moved back and forth between the main body of the tribe and the two brothers' camps.) In the cases of the two smaller clusters, ties among members of the clusters themselves were far stronger and denser than their ties to the main body as a whole. Moreover, though both smaller groups were bound in certain ways to the main body, the two groups were at opposite ends of tribal territory and there were few ties between them. I take this as evidence of a growing separation. This process of tribal deconstruction seems closely linked to the ongoing creation of dense but poorly connected nuclei of close kin. Personal ties that reinforced formal relations created nodes of close kin that played a central role in the Komachi social order's structural dynamics. When a group divided, it did so along lines created by differences in the quality and quantity of ties that linked wealthy and important men.

Coresidence arose through the interplay of structured and practically based relationships among members of independent households, only some of which operated in relation to the head per se. To the extent that coresidence was practically based, that is, based on friendships, fights, economic circumstances, and the like, it was explicable but unpatterned and unpredictable. Still, patterns of coresidence suggest ways in which structure and practice were intertwined, and they generally involved permutations of relations among kin. For example, during the eighteen months I dwelt with the tribe, only four households never camped with kin. Kinship was both the key metaphor for Komachi social relationships and the practical marker of significant social relationships. Komachi lived with kin, and although kinship ties did not of themselves create the amicable—or even workable—social relations necessary for coresidence or other cooperative activities, kinship ties provided the pathways for creation of ties, the framework of other solidary relationships, and the adhesive to make those relationships fast. Kinship was more than just a metaphor.

Examination of coresidence patterns of camp members directly related to camp heads in the tribe's main body (thirteen cases overall) shows that heads lived with their married daughters (four cases), their mothers and mother's kin (three cases), and their wives' kin (three cases), but only rarely with agnatic kin (two or three cases, depending on how one wishes to count them). Closer examination shows, moreover, that two of the three cases in which the head lived with his mother and his mother's kin are better seen as cases in which the real focus of the camp—that is, the one for whom it was named—was the relatively recently deceased father of the current head. Rather than being clusters of head plus mother and mother's kin, these are more accurately described as clusters of the head plus his wife's kin. Overall, nine of thirteen heads of camp lived with their married daughters or their wife's kin.[14]

Though there were no formal rules for residence, there were nonetheless dispositions that directed choice in predictable directions. Brothers tended not to live in the same camp unless they were both living with their widowed mother. The fact that Yarbok and Darvish, both heads of camp (and both deceased by 1974), were continually remarked as having been close to each other throughout their lifetimes, combined with an absence of similar contemporary cases, led me to believe that conspicuous fraternal harmony was rare. Darvish's three sons showed a more common pattern. Nominally, the three resided in a single camp "led" by the oldest brother; in fact, however, he spent his summers living with his shepherds about a kilometer away from his brothers, on the path leading toward his wife's kin. The younger of his two brothers also moved one summer, trading places with his first cousin (Yarbok's youngest son) because of friction among the brothers. Each brother, concerned primarily with his own interests, found it difficult to live or work with a brother whose interests were not identical. Brothers, of course, did not have to compete. However, Komachi households tended to compete for scarce resources—animals, labor, or spouses for their children. Since brothers were, by definition, both the recipients of shares of a common estate and of nearly identical social status, they were natural rivals. Rivalries among brothers tended to be particularly pronounced among employers, for they were truly competing for shepherds, spouses for their children, and, in the final analysis, status. Just as brothers did not live in the same camp, coresidence of fathers and married sons was uncommon.

Because Komachi camps were centered about a single wealthy and important man, politically prominent Komachi rarely lived together. Whether we read this physical separation as a cause or effect of relationships among the Komachi elite is unimportant at this point. It *is* important that there was little in the Komachi residential pattern that brought wealthy men together, while there were forces asssociated with camp structure that helped drive them apart. The most notable of these, of course, was the need to hire shepherds. As hiring shepherds cannot be done cooperatively when men live apart, camp heads necessarily came into direct competition with each other. I have described the tension that this created.

By contrast, coresidence of closely related women was far more common. This probably occurred because both the social life and the economic activities of camps put a premium on cooperation among women. Komachi camps were the hubs of pastoral production, and all the dominant productive activities that took place there (except shearing and the actual herding done by shepherds) were women's work. The labor demands of wealthy households far exceeded their internal labor resources, and so while the women of each household were responsible for filling their household's productive needs, they accomplished this through informally organized cooperation among households. Even though much of the assistance was unidirectional, flowing from poorer households to wealthier ones, women cooperated in other ways as well. For instance, two of Ali's married daughters lived in his camp, and each gave birth to her first child in early spring of 1975. Their mother, in spite of an already enormous workload, gave her daughters much assistance; she had her youngest daughters help them with animal care, preparation of dairy products, gathering firewood, and bringing water. The married daughters, for their part, often helped their mother with tedious, though not strenuous, activities such as preparing *kashk* and milking. In another camp, the situation was somewhat reversed; there an older woman, the apparent victim of a stroke, was incapable of carrying out her tasks and was being helped by her two coresident married daughters. Even in less dramatic circumstances, there was considerable cooperation and assistance. Women worked with other women, helping one another with pastoral production and the preparation of food, especially for ceremonial meals or when a guest came; women baked bread together or shared the work of making a large pot of *ash*, a thick soup.

Komachi women preferred to live among those women with whom they worked best and most easily. Mothers and sisters were women with whom they had worked all their lives; their techniques and their habits were comfortable and familiar, and they could be counted on. Food production and child care tended to be easier in cooperation with mothers and sisters than with others. And because camps were isolated social units that were frequently miles apart, particularly during the winter peak of pastoral production when women only rarely left their home camp, the camp was the social universe for many women. Coresident women were the only females a woman saw regularly, so, not surprisingly, they wanted their neighbors to be women with whom they were completely familiar and comfortable: their mothers, daughters, and sisters. This desire may have been magnified by the pervasiveness of the conflict between employer and shepherd households. As we have seen, it was women who publicly voiced their household's position in such conflicts, and having a mother or daughter in the camp was likely to assure the presence of a staunch ally.

Komachi men probably tended to live with female kin because there were structural reasons that drove men apart (for example, concerns of inheritance, close similarities in status, and potential competition for shepherding labor) and because few forces drew them together. Kinswomen, by contrast, had fewer reasons to quarrel among themselves and more reasons to cooperate. Komachi households thus usually dwelt where their female members had kin ties. It seems possible to make an even more general argument: because Komachi men competed, their relationships often divided the tribe; women's relationships, particularly with their equals, were far more solidary.[15] As a result, women's relationships with their mothers, sisters, fathers, and brothers provided much of the practical and affective glue that held the Komachi social formation together.

With the exception of this discussion of men and women and their kinship ties, my discussion of kinship and marriage has largely concentrated on relations among men, and in particular those among wealthy and important men, because the ties and schisms between men represented the likely lines of fission and fusion that were central to the group's historical development. Nonetheless, it is useful here to turn away briefly from my central theme and discuss women and marriage—though, as we shall see, this will quickly return us to the question of labor and cooperation.

A careful reading of my discussions of marriage negotiations and shepherding negotiations will show that while men's reputations were at stake, women played major roles in the events. While men may have occasionally negotiated marriages directly with other men, women often undertook many of the preliminary contacts and the attempts to discover who would or would not accept a proposal. While the Komachi were not one of the Middle Eastern societies in which men had never seen, did not know, and could not evaluate potential spouses, women's input in the early, informal stages of negotiations was still very important.

Komachi women were not limited to clandestine roles in the early stages of negotiation. Women used their ties to one another and to men to arrange marriages. Although father's brother's daughter marriage was the most common type of cousin marriage, both mother's brother's daughter and father's sister's daughter marriage were common. The last two forms of marriage, of course, involve links between a sister and brother. In two cases that I observed closely, it was the sister's active pursuit of a match that made it come about. For example, as I noted in my discussion of Akbar's marriage to his mother's brother's daughter, his mother, Sekine, strongly favored the match and spoke out forcefully in favor of it and against other matches. While Ali did try to arrange the match that Akbar preferred, it was clear to everyone that once that match failed, Akbar would marry his mother's brother's daughter, no matter what he said to the contrary. I must stress that though this was an excellent match from the girl's family's perspective, they did nothing to promote the match but indicate that they favored it. Sekine twisted all the arms and in essence publicly established the certainty of its occurrence.

Women intervened in other marriage negotiations as well. In the case of Malek's son Mohammed, for example, I noted that his mother visited kin among the Komachi and distant kin in other tribes looking for spouses for her son and daughters. She also disparaged Kourosh's protests about Mohammed's marriage, and Mohammed's married sister unsuccessfully put pressure on Hassan. Even though her husband favored the match, I saw one woman strongly support a daughter who refused to marry an older widower. And I knew of one girl who became "crazy," *divune,* until a match was arranged with the man she wanted to marry. As with shepherd's illnesses, one might argue that becoming *divune* was a weapon of the weak. If so, it was effective. In the field of negotiating marriages, Komachi women were not shrinking violets.

The important role of women in marriage negotiations was highlighted by their role in the *mar katkhoda,* the formal request for a girl's hand. While the girl's father was the nominal host of the meeting, the final say was given to the girl's mother. Of course, when negotiations had reached this point, outright refusal of a match was unlikely. However, the timing of the marriage was completely negotiable, and at several *mar katkhodas* I heard women refuse to allow an immediate marriage or even refuse to have an engagement formally announced. The mothers based their refusal on the amount of work they had to do, claiming that they could not manage household production without the help of the daughter whose hand was being sought. This claim was never belittled, and in several cases in which the prospective husband's suit was pressed, the mother's claim was supported, first by her married daughters and then by her husband. It seemed that an insistent mother could indeed delay a marriage at this point. Thus, the burden Komachi women bore in pastoral production gained a clear, ritualized, and public recognition during the *mar katkoda,* as her husband and the men of other households were forced to publicly acknowledge and deal with her workload and her need for help.

Here the striking parallel I noted earlier between the positions of women and shepherds is again revealed. As was the case with shepherd's contract negotiations, those who worked did gain occasional ritualized public recognition of their arduous lot.

# 8

## TIES THAT BIND

Not all Komachi kin relationships involved just the wealthy and powerful. Relationships also linked the wealthy and important to less important Komachi. For example, Ali, whose ties to other important men we have considered elsewhere, also had important relationships with his sister's sons. Much poorer than Ali and not politically powerful, these men and their families were an economic asset to Ali. As noted earlier, wealthy households needed female labor and met this need by putting pressure on their neighbors. Along with shepherds' families, poor Komachi with few animals who lived in the camps of their wealthier kinsmen supplied significant amounts of female labor to wealthy households. Senne, Ali's mother's brother's daughter and sister's son's wife, was Ali's wife's most consistent helper: she helped Ali's wife milk her animals, boil and roll *kashk*, and weave tent panels. As with shepherds' wives, none of this labor was directly compensated.

Ali, in turn, was Senne's brother's patron, speaking for him in marriage negotiations and generally supporting his suit. The brother, for his part, helped Ali shear sheep and helped dig a foundation for a storehouse Ali was building in Shirinak.

Ali also married his second daughter to his sister Xanom's second son, although the man was much older than she and was very poor. In doing so, of course, Ali reforged the link he had with his own sister (see Figure 8). As that relationship was something of a burden—she was widowed, poor, and quite cranky—it was clear that Ali was not gaining or reforging a link with the politically or economically powerful. Rather, he was avoiding the discomfort his sister could (and would) have caused him and assuring himself continued access to *komak* from his sister and the unmarried members of her household. And by bankrolling his new son-in-law in minor economic ventures, such as buying and selling animals and dates, Ali was able to draw on an essentially free source of labor through which he could put his surplus income to work. Finally, even though political clientage was weakly developed among the Komachi as a whole, Ali gained clients who depended on him and thus formed a claque he could count on. It is clear that Ali benefited from the relationship, and it is equally certain that his poorer kin also benefited; they received the patronage of a wealthy and important man; they

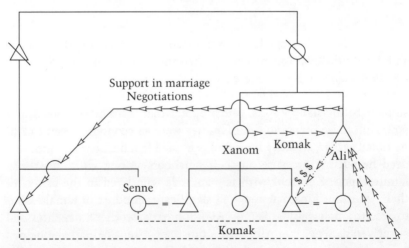

Figure 8.
Network of ties linking Ali and his sister Xanom.

were able to make an excellent marriage that shored up their shaky status and renewed ties that were likely to keep their most important source of patronage available in the foreseeable future; and they reaped the substantial economic benefits of continued close relations with a wealthy man who could and would help them economically—albeit in a self-interested way.

Because déclassé Komachi like Ali's sister's family married down as well as up, kinship ties linking them to their wealthy and important kinsmen played an important role in validating the claim that all Komachi were kin. When the poorer Komachi shepherds traced their ties to the wealthiest Komachi employers, the list of links adduced invariably included people like Ali's sister and her sons. The poorer close kin of wealthy men were mediators whose upward and downward relationships joined the very rich to the very poor. Since, as we have seen, poor shepherds and wealthy employers rarely married each other, rich men's poorer kin created the only direct linkages between otherwise separate social universes.

Mediating links persisted not just because men like Ali chose to let their sons or daughters marry poor kinfolk. These links were constantly recreated because, as we have seen, wealth was not stable. In every generation households slipped in status; their members were then forced to make marriages with their new equals. As long as wealthy Komachi did not deny that their poorer kin were kin, then the newly poor provided an additional set of links that permitted people to demonstrate—without manipulating genealogies—that all Komachi were kin.

Of course, other ties also linked the rich and the poor, and they too deserve consideration.

## Intratribal Patron-Client Relations

Komachi patron-client exchanges had a structure that is the reverse of what a general picture of patron-client ties would lead us to expect. Instead of the patron gaining political support while the client derived goods or other economic benefit, the patron extracted noncompensated, economically beneficial services from the client, often under the rubric of *komak*, while the clients received less tangible benefits from their patron.[1] Nonetheless, patron-client ties served to link the wealthy and the poor in a relationship other than that of employer-employee. Although patron-client ties benefited the wealthy more than the poor, they were still of mutual if unequal benefit. For example, employers lent shepherds the money they needed to establish their households (gaining access to female labor as a result), and employers often arranged, oversaw, and lent money for shepherd families' celebrations. Where there was a cash outlay, the employer who acted as a patron was almost always the shepherd's current employer. In more than a few cases, wealthy employers acted as *tarafs* for their current (and occasionally former) employees, advancing them money, wheat, tea, and sugar against their herd's produce. Here too, of course, employers profited.

Employers also acted as patrons during marriage negotiations and wedding and circumcision celebrations. In the case of marriage negotiations, employers spoke for their shepherds, and, as I described above, they were often able to put substantial pressure on other parties. An interesting pattern of behavior often appeared in the negotiation of marriage contracts. As I have noted, though relatively few kin ties directly linked wealthy employers and poor shepherds, wealthy Komachi did have poorer kin, and those poorer kin had direct ties to those poorer still, so that there were indirect linkages between poor shepherds and wealthy employers. Not only did wealthy Komachi not deny indirect ties to poor Komachi, they affirmed these claims by appearing as poor men's spokesmen in marriage negotiations under the explicit guise of being committed agents for one party because they were kin. Thus a patron's supportive action was often considered under the rubric of fulfilling obligations to one's kin. This helped foster the perception of the tribe as a community of kin even though direct links between the two tribal classes were generally absent. Thus, although the employer-shepherd relationship was exploitative, the claim of common kinship and its implications of mutuality and support was not a pure fiction. Employers did help shepherds and act for them in ways that validated the claim of common kinship. One could even argue, I think accurately, that the obligations of common kinship impelled employers to do things for shepherds. Claims of common kinship were not simply mystifications of the real relationship; the real relationship was ambiguous.

This ambiguity was heightened by other facets of Komachi life that also helped foster a sense of community. Rituals and celebrations and the exchanges that took place at them played a particularly important part in creating this sense of community and commonality.

## Rituals and Exchanges

At the end of the summer, the Komachi sent their herds south to winter quarters in the care of hired shepherds. When the herds went, the remaining members of the tribe were freed from the burdens of animal care. The Komachi said they were *bi kar*, without work, during this period from late summer to October. Nearly all Komachi marriage and circumcision celebrations occurred during this period, as did *rozehs*, religious meetings in which the martyrdom of Imam Hossein was recounted. Komachi weddings and circumcisions were similar; I will discuss them jointly, followed by a discussion of *rozehs*.[2]

Wedding and circumcision celebrations lasted three days. The first day was spent in preparation: at least two guest tents—one for men and one for women—were pitched; enough bread was baked to feed two to three hundred people several loaves each at two meals; formal invitations were addressed and delivered; the *parchem*, a decorated tree that was the centerpiece of the celebration, was prepared and erected; and a meal was served to those who helped with the preparations, generally the groom or boy's close kin and neighbors.

A typical invitation, preprinted in the city, read: "Ali Abrahimi invites you to celebrate the marriage of his son Hossein to Fatimeh, the daughter of Abbas Emiri, with him at his home in Shirinak at 4:00 P.M. on the 26th of September 1974. There will be music, dinner, and lunch. Fruit punch [*sharbat*] and cookies [*shirini*] will be served." Note the enumeration of the foods to be served; I will return to it later.

Early on the morning of the second day, women of the host household, their close kin, and neighbors again began baking bread. In the afternoon several animals were butchered and huge cauldrons of stew and rice were put on the fire for the evening's meal. In late afternoon the first guests began to arrive. No sooner were they in place in the appropriate guest tents[3] than they were given *davoh* (powdered sugar mixed with spices) and the first of many cups of tea. The remainder of the day was spent in dancing, drinking tea, talking, and, late at night, eating a meal that invariably comprised a soupy meat stew; a large portion of rice prepared with raisins, turmeric, and other spices; and large quantities of bread. While important guests were served first and received the best portions of meat, all guests received roughly the same quantity of food.

The third day was the high point of the ceremony. After more tea, cookies, talk, and another meal of stew, rice, and bread, the celebrant (groom or boy) was conveyed to the nearest water source, stripped, bathed, and dressed in brand-new clothing. Then he was carried back to camp. About halfway to camp, the procession stopped and the *pahnaz* (a list of pledges of young female animals promised the groom or boy by his closest kin) was written up. After the *pahnaz*, the procession proceeded to an area near the *parchem* where a throne of carpets, pillows, and blankets was constructed. The groom or boy was carried to the throne and seated there facing Mecca. Everyone gathered about, and the *fazl* (cash gifts) were presented by the guests. Initial gifts were given by the celebrant's closest kin: his parents, siblings, and grandparents. The first gifts presented were invariably the largest ones and were presented in a special manner.

Gifts were not handed to the young man on the throne but to one of the several kinsmen or friends who acted as his agents. The presenter of the gift announced, for example, "This is from his brother, Qorban Ali." Taking the gift, the agent announced, "Here is thirty-five dollars from Qorban Ali." He passed the money to the second man who often repeated the message. A third man, meanwhile, carefully recorded the transaction, writing down who gave the gift and how much was given. After the first gifts from close kin, gifts from other guests were rather less ceremoniously delivered; people leaned through the crowd and handed money to one of the collectors while announcing who the gift was from. Every gift was recorded. Individual gifts varied greatly in size. Poorer men gave as little as $1.50 while wealthy men often gave $15.00 or more. Usually, kinsmen and neighbors gave first, followed by important guests and then poorer guests with smaller gifts. When the last gifts had been given, the collectors carefully counted the cash and totaled the amounts on the list of gifts. When the figures matched, the money was wrapped and it and the list were presented to the groom. The total amount of the *fazl* varied; in 1974 and 1975 it ranged from a low of roughly $400 to just over $2000.

After the year's weddings and circumcisions were over, the Komachi sponsored and attended *rozehs*. Komachi *rozehs* were events at which the attending congregation was told a portion of the historical drama of the martyrdom of the Imam Hossein, read a sermon, and fed a meal of meat stew. Recitals of the sacred history of Shi'ite Islam, *rozehs* were quintessentially religious events, affirming for believers the nature and the reality of the sacred history and eschatology within which they dwelt.

To give a *rozeh* one had to hire a *rozehxund* from outside the tribe to lead the service, prepare a meat meal for guests, and arrange a tent for the *rozeh* itself. Hiring the *rozehxund* and killing the animal for the meal required the outlay of money by the host, who was often but not necessarily a head of camp. While the cost was borne by a single individual, *rozehs* were identified with camps as wholes. This identification with camps was constantly apparent, as men and women who lived in camps having *rozehs* but were not themselves hosts invited people to "their" *rozeh*, or told me that their *rozeh* had been better than another camp's. Members of the host's camp and their closest kin (geographically and practically) formed the primary congregation for most *rozehs*.

An examination of rituals suggests that to be Komachi was to participate in a variety of exchanges—some ritualized, others not—that linked tribespeople in bonds of mutual obligation. The quid pro quo of the celebration revealed the social as well as economic nature of these bonds. A Komachi gave a gift not only in order to receive one in return (or to pay one back), but also because he had eaten meals explicitly promised in the invitation. Food was freely given, for it was part of the celebration, a kind of communion, but food and *fazl* were not independent. To be a member of the tribe, one had to exchange food freely, give hospitality, and enter into economic transactions. To be Komachi was really to be among those who exchanged among themselves *more than with anyone else*. The transactions also suggested the underlying ethos of commonality. Social ties were maintained by balanced reciprocity. Unequal exchange implied boundaries; it is therefore important to note that exchanges between wealthy and poor were not occasions of noblesse oblige. Exchanges between wealthy and poor were equal: the poor man gave the rich man what little he could afford, and the wealthy man reciprocated by giving the poor man the same small amount he had been given or could have expected. An examination of what he had received and from whom showed the recipient of *fazl* his place in society. At the same time, the very act of giving his gift marked out for each tribesman both his own place in the society vis-à-vis other individuals and his membership in the society. Thus, through the dialectics of prestation and the transfer of food, wealth, and assistance, Komachi celebrations revealed and constructed the Komachi social order, marking individuals' places in the community and the extent of the community as well.

*Rozehs* had many of the same features as weddings and circumcisions. The distinctions of wealth, status, and gender were again marked by seating, order of eating, and performance of the role of host. Networks of close kin were revealed in the composition of the congregation. However, there was a major difference between the *rozeh* and a celebration. Celebrations were communitywide events. They were expressions of solidarity of the tribe as a whole. *Rozehs*, by contrast, had for their primary congregations residential camps. They ritually marked off the only salient social units within Komachi society larger than a nuclear family household, and identified them as moral communities. *Rozehs* made a camp a congregation, something made more than an ephemeral economic unit, and it is not far-fetched to see *rozehs* as both creating and reinforcing claims of commonality and unity between shepherds and employers. It was through the celebration of community at events such as *rozehs*, weddings, and circumcisions that members of camps developed feelings of commonality that made them able to call on each other for *komak* or appeal to common kinship in the face of conflict.

It is important to note that ceremonies were one of the main arenas in which the notion of *komak* was legitimized. We have seen that, in practice, the bulk of *komak* was transferred from poor to rich as noncompensated labor. At celebrations *komak* was omnipresent. Poor women and men helped their wealthy neighbors, but they worked next to other wealthy men and women who were also giving *komak*, generally to their close kin. Everyone who shared in the labor was fed, and everyone felt themselves to be part of an exciting event. Moreover, at a poor man's celebration, wealthy neighbors gave *komak*, lending pots and pans and helping to cook and serve. At celebrations, in short, people really did help each other selflessly, and I do not think that the help was cynically given. When at other times people claimed they were one, or that they needed *komak*, the claim was not made across an impenetrable barrier to people who had never seen any evidence of solidarity. The reality of relationship between rich and poor, as was so often the case among the Komachi, was ambiguous.

Komachi society was diffuse. Part of a larger political entity, its members spoke the same language as their neighbors, had the same customs as many of their neighbors, and, indeed, were kin with many of their neighbors. The Komachi were culturally (or ethnically) unmarked. Moreover, there was little physical coherence to the tribe: the Komachi were nomads, living in small camps dispersed over a wide territory. Because the tribe was small, all Komachi knew all other Komachi, and there was an idiom—kinship—for their unity. But the ties that bound them were essentially weak. Celebrations were the only times when all Komachi were drawn together physically, when the tribe was a body. It seems that Komachi rituals laid out the social order where it was otherwise vague. Rituals affirmed who was who, and showed how people were tied to one another. In so doing, rituals also helped create the social order they represented.[4]

People also demonstrated solidarity in less formal ways, acting as kin should act and giving support when it was needed. When Xosro fell off his motorcycle and injured himself, he feared he was dying. Word of his misfortune passed to all his close kin. His mother, brothers, sisters, children, and cousins (whom he reckoned by the dozens) gathered around him, assured him he would recover, and debated cures; one went to ask his urban patron to bring an urban doctor. In this crisis, Xosro was literally surrounded by his network of *qom khish*, a forgathering of kin that was obviously comforting to him and to those concerned for him. Significantly, Ali, whose complicated relationship with Xosro we have already discussed, was among the kin who came and stayed until it was clear that the crisis had passed. In similar situations I saw the same massing of kin, and while no adult Komachi died while I was with the tribe, I was often told that ideally people died surrounded by their kin. Again, kinship was more than a metaphor; it was a metaphor that motivated action.

This metaphor of kinship obviously received its power from kinship's place in Komachi practice, but it is important to recognize that kinship as a metaphor of solidarity acquired additional power from the values of Shi'ite Islam that permeated Komachi life. Shi'ite liturgical expression strongly stressed the value of kinship and family, at least at the local level. In nearly every momentary crisis someone would call for a *salavat* (blessing used in crisis), the refrain of which is "God bless Mohammed and *his family*" (emphasis added). It is difficult to imagine people who heard this refrain thousands, if not tens of thousands of times, not feeling that the concepts of family and kinship were important. Similarly, when the martyrdoms of Hossein and his followers at Kerbala were recounted (at *rozeh*s, on tape recordings, or on radio broadcasts), one did not hear accounts of general loss but tales of children weeping for their parents, parents for their children, and siblings for each other. The terrible pain and suffering of the martyrdoms was made manifest by stressing how the martyrs lost their kin (or their kin the martyrs). Kinship and family, and the solidarity they generated, were in a very real sense sanctified by their constant repetition in this powerful, sacred liturgy.[5]

## The Outside World and Komachi Feelings of Community

Exchanges, patronage, and appearance at crises were all practices that supported and created the perception of community, generating solidarity through the actions of the Komachi themselves. A sense of community was also created in a way by the outside world itself. Examining the Komachi as a closed system, shepherds and employers against each other under the desert sun, ignores an understanding of what it meant *in practice* to be a Komachi nomad. The Komachi were a very small tribe surrounded by and bound to the larger settled Persian society around them. Komachi views of themselves were partly autochthonous and partly constructed in response to the views (and concomitant actions) of the settled world. Komachi self-identity was shaped through social interaction, and collective identity was shaped through the cumulation of individual experiences and collective and individual reflection on it. The following anecdotes illustrate the nature of this experience.

Ali and I left our winter quarters camp for a trip to the neighboring town of Manujan. There, among other things, we met the son of the town's indigenous political leader—basically a legitimated warlord. We were invited to his house for a meal. The son was younger than I, and he deferred to me when his servants brought tea or food. I, in turn, deferred to Ali because he was my neighbor, my host, old enough to be my father, I deferred to him in camp, etc. The occasion was rather odd, a sort of poorly defined game of musical chairs, as I deferred to Ali, who was very deferential to the son, who was in turn deferential to me. But what I wish to comment on is that Ali, the wealthiest and the most important man among the Komachi, in effect bowed and scraped to the much younger son of the political leader of a small town in the middle of nowhere. Moreover, the son consistently acted toward Ali in a way that marked the latter's inferiority.

On another occasion when Ali accompanied me on a trip to see the governor of the local district, the governor spoke with me and offered me tea, while he acted as though Ali—who, after all, was one of the citizens of his district—was not there at all. Later, when I took several Komachi to a chromite mine to get them medical attention, I was taken off and given cold beer by the mining engineers and the doctor while the nomads were left to sit in the sun until the doctor got done with his social obligation. On still another occasion, wealthy former land-lords in the summer quarters came uninvited to a nomad wedding, took over a guest tent, had a special meal prepared for them, monopolized the host and head of camp, whom they treated as their servant, and left, having had a "colorful" day in the countryside. My wife and I were often asked by the occasional urban Persian visitor—in front of the Komachi we lived with—how we could stand spending time out there in the middle of nowhere with no one to talk to and nothing to do.

Komachi tribespeople, whether they were rich or poor, were treated the same way by virtually all settled Persians who had any claim to rank or status: as though they were contemptible, ignorant, unfeeling specimens of the lower orders, people who warranted no consideration and were treated with none. One important aspect of the practical experience of all Komachi, shepherd and employer alike, was the way most of the external world did not differentiate among them, seeing them only as tribespeople and pastoralists and treating them all as inferiors.[6] Claims of common kinship, or oneness, therefore represented an objective reality for the Komachi: to important elements of the outside world the Komachi *were* all one, all equally insignificant. As such, the claim of commonality had force. Differences among Komachi—which were substantial—were moderated by the commonalities they shared. Wealthy tribesmen exploited the poor, but they did it within the limits of a system that defined their relationship in moral terms: employers had obligations to shepherds who were kin. Claims that all Komachi were kin made experiential sense when they were compared with the quality of the obvious nonkin relationships that held between Komachi and the outside world, and they made all the more sense for being objectified in ritual exchanges and the patronage granted poor kinfolk. I am not suggesting that just because rich and poor Komachi helped one another as kin or participated in rituals emphasizing kinship and commonality, the ambiguity of shepherd-employer relations disappeared, nor am I suggesting that shepherds were not aware of their exploitation. I merely suggest that the claim that all Komachi were kin did not appear to be transparently false. It had objective confirmation, as did class divisions in Komachi life; as a result, ambiguity characterized much of Komachi life.

This ambiguity was nowhere better illustrated than in exchanges of food between employer and employee. Shepherds were guests at employers' *rozehs* and celebrations, where they received their shares of the ritual meal as part of the community. When employers killed sacrificial animals, shepherd families in the camp got their shares. When shepherds hosted celebrations or *rozehs* and when they made sacrifices, employers received their shares as well. These exchanges were part of the stuff from which communality was made. But, as we have seen, shepherds received other food as well. Part of their wage was food: meals eaten in the employer's household, tea, and sugar. This food was not given freely. Far from marking solidarity, this food marked a boundary. When it was eaten in the employer's tent it negated the host-guest relationship, and when it was eaten elsewhere it still remained the antithesis of freely given food. Only shepherds received food of both kinds. Perhaps this explains their role in a ceremony, the *sadeh*, that seemed almost a wry, ritualized comment on the whole exchange of food. The *sadeh* took place fifty days before *Now Ruz* (the Persian New Year), that is, at the very end of January, and was conceived as celebrating the end of winter. Members of each camp built a huge bonfire, and children from the camp collected flour from every household. The flour was given to a shepherd, who used it to bake the unleavened shepherd's bread, *komaj*. When the bread was done, it was distributed *mesle gusht*, like meat, within the camp, and everyone ate a piece. Thus, we might say that the shepherd integrated everyone into his society by giving everyone a piece of what he ate. As the *sadeh* was also a time when small children hit their parents, when the world was turned upside down, we can see that the integration that came from the shepherd's distribution of bread was not quite the same as that which came from the distribution of meat. Shepherds were the same, but they were different. All Komachi were one, but not quite.

# PART IV

# SUMMARY AND CONCLUSION

# 9

# CONTEXTS AND
# CONJUNCTIONS:
# TOWARD AN
# UNDERSTANDING
# OF THE KOMACHI

Ambiguity, paradox, and contradiction seem to characterize the Komachi social order. Understanding the social order entails recognizing its ambiguities and their sources. In earlier parts of this book I have explored the ambiguities, and now I turn to the sources. I shall start once again with the shepherd-employer relationship.

Rich and poor Komachi were linked in structured relationships in which the poor worked for the rich under conditions that maintained and reproduced their poverty even as their work helped sustain the rich (if not make them richer). The exploitative nature of the relationship remained largely unhidden. Employers attempted to extract both compensated and noncompensated labor value from their shepherds with remarkably little dissembling of their purpose. How did such a relationship arise? Why were employers so single-minded in their extraction of surplus? If employers were so greedy, why did they choose to hire shepherds at all? And what does the existence of a relationship of this type tell us about Komachi economy and society?

Poor Komachi became shepherds because they lacked sufficient animals to support their households. But relationships of people to the means of production do not just happen. People's relationships to things—including animals—are social, and are the result of complex social and historical processes. For a people such as the Komachi, who lived within a much larger cultural system, the relations of production that determined access to resources were not autochthonous. Rather, they arose through the conjunction of Islamic laws, the pressure of capitalist markets, and the realities of pastoral production.

As I have described, most Komachi gained access to breeding stock through inheritance. Komachi inheritance practices did not accord completely with formal Islamic conventions, but the broad parameters of the Komachi inheritance system were influenced by, indeed determined by, the understandings arising from Islam. Specifically, Islam enjoins partible inheritance. In principle, each son receives a full share of his father's estate while each daugher gets one-half a brother's share. One may look upon the Komachi (or other pastoralists) as less than perfect Muslims because women do not inherit regularly, because they have anticipatory inheritance, or because the number of animals given to each son is based on practical calculations of a reasonable share at a given moment rather than an absolute, formulaic distribution, but such a view clearly would be a narrow one. Each Komachi son inherited a share of his family's estate; the herd or property was divided nearly equally among the inheriting children, and it was virtually never passed on undivided. The viability of Komachi households was directly connected with this cultural understanding: family herds were constantly divided and redivided in accord with the broad outline of Islamic conceptions of partible inheritance, so that each household had to face the challenge of balancing its needs (and the future needs of all its male children) against the productivity of its herd.

But why did this have to be so? Why couldn't a young man transform his status through labor by either buying animals with his cash wages or receiving animals instead of a cash wage? We gain most insight into Komachi society if we approach a question such as this somewhat indirectly, asking first the question to which it is surely related: Why did Komachi employers seek so single-mindedly to extract surplus value from their shepherds?

The limits of upward mobility arose directly from the conditions of Komachi existence. While pastoralists' herds may have had an apparent potential for dramatic herd growth in any one year, the realities of long-term herd ownership reduced that potential equally dramatically. Over time, Komachi herds grew quite slowly. Men lived with the ever-present fear that their flocks—their families' livelihoods and their sons' futures—would be irretrievably diminished, and so they did not transfer animals freely to people other than their sons.

One must also remember that 1974 and 1975 were boom years in Iran, and nomads, including the Komachi, rode that boom. But the animal that sold for $30 to $50 in 1975 had sold for only $7 in 1970. While the costs of being a nomad had also been lower in 1970, comments such as "All shepherds are rich now" suggested that generally times had not been better in the good old days. Given the chances for good years and bad, it seems quite likely that before the boom all but the wealthiest Komachi occasionally lived in straitened circumstances, were in debt to their *tarafs*, and thus had to exploit those less fortunate than themselves to maintain their own rather precarious existence. That they continued to do so when times turned better and lamented the lost opportunity to be even more exploitative says little for them as an example of a moral economy, but it suggests much about the nature of economic systems such as that of the Komachi—specifically, that Komachi shepherd-employer relations were not some odd form of tribal political economy but were the relations of a social formation caught in the world market system and becoming capitalist.

Kermani pastoralists like the Komachi have produced commodities for the world market since the late seventeenth century. As that market was first mercantile and then capitalist, merchants who traded with people like the Komachi were always concerned with making a profit, with drawing wealth from the pastoral economy. Looking at the Komachi in 1974 and 1975, it was apparent that three hundred years of integration into the world market had had their effect. Wealthy Komachi exploited poor Komachi; merchants in Kerman exploited wealthy Komachi; and all but the wealthiest Komachi operated on margins so small that being generous with one's shepherd could mean becoming one. The means through which employers drew wealth from their shepherds itself showed the impact of capitalist expansion. Shepherds were not the pastoral equivalents of sharecroppers, nor did they work under any physical coercion. They worked because they needed to pay for the goods they had to consume; they had to meet the costs of their social reproduction. The relation of production that controlled access to male labor mandated the contractually regulated exchange of labor power for a cash wage. If this relation of production was not purely capitalist itself, it was surely inflected by capitalism, and it enabled the employer to draw surplus value from his shepherd by paying him less than his labor power was worth.

On the one hand, a description of the Komachi as a people affected by world capitalism points to a reality so obvious as to be meaningless. People who produced meat in response to the consumer demand fueled by international oil revenues were not simple tribespeople. On the other hand, the fact that they were integrated into the world market system did not make the Komachi purely capitalist, either. For one thing, the extraction of substantial surplus labor power under the rubric of *komak*, an eminently noncapitalist relation of production, demonstrates the weakness of the claim that because the Komachi were caught within the capitalist world market system, they were capitalist per se. Other circumstances also challenge the claim that the Komachi simply were part of the capitalist world system. Of these, by far the greatest problem is created by the distribution of the means of production in Komachi society. Marx saw capitalism as the bringing together of capital and "free labor" in the production process (Marx 1967). "Free labor" is that ironically labeled category whose members are neither serfs nor slaves and hence are jurally free, but who also have been completely freed (cut off) from ownership of the means of production and therefore have nothing but their labor power to sell.

Now, Komachi shepherds were indeed poor. But to be poor was not to be devoid of animal wealth. All Komachi, rich and poor, owned animals, and even the poorest Komachi could acquire one animal a year as a portion of his wage—not much, but still something. The significance of that one animal is that it shows quite clearly that while Komachi relations of production did reproduce impoverished households that had to sell their labor, they did not reproduce households that had *only* their labor to sell. Instead, Komachi relations of production ensured poor nomads access to the means of production, even if the amount was small.[1] Komachi shepherds, therefore, were more than just free laborers.

In the same vein, for employers to have been full-fledged capitalists, the major factors of production (and hence of social reproduction for employer households) should have been commodities acquired through buying and selling. However, one could not acquire, transfer, or sell the dominant means of production—animals or pasture—as commodities. Inheritance was the only regular means by which households gained significant or adequate access to animals, which were the primary means of production. And while male labor could be acquired through quasicapitalist contracts, female labor—vital to the Komachi economy—either came as *komak* or was done by wives and daughters (or, less frequently, mothers and sisters). Households acquired most female productive labor through the same kinds of relations as they did animals: relations of kinship. It is clear that kinship ties were significant relations of production for the Komachi, and that *kinship and class were not separable.* At the same time, the rules of inheritance and kinship were largely elements of an Islamic jural superstructure; thus it is equally clear that Komachi relations of production were Islamic in their basic structure and hence noncapitalist, at least originally.[2]

Equally noncapitalist were the attitudes that seem to have underlain the use and abuse of shepherding labor. Shepherds did virtually all the actual work of herding while wealthy herd owners literally bought themselves free time by their use of shepherds. By doing so, wealthy Komachi were explicitly following the general Persian and perhaps larger Middle Eastern practice of avoiding manual labor.[3] This may seem a pejorative turn of phrase or a case of negative stereotyping, but we must recognize that cultural attitudes toward work and toward the expenditure of physical effort vary. The !Kung San described by Richard Lee (1979) appear to view work as a necessary evil: it is something that one does but, all things being equal, it is not what one wants to do. Genesis 3:17–20 describes work as God's punishment, and makes it quite clear that at least some of our cultural forebears did not think that labor was in and of itself good. We perhaps need to be reminded of these less than positive views of work because in our own society work has a generally positive value. In Iran, wealth and power were used to acquire the physical labor of others. This was not simply a question of allocation of labor time; while it may indeed be more efficient for the industrialist to plan corporate strategy while the chauffeur drives his or her car, among the Komachi practice resulted from a cultural attitude toward the labor itself. The Komachi believed that wealthy men ought not to work; that was the reward of wealth and power.[4]

The Komachi saw manifestations of this attitude toward work in virtually all their dealings with nontribal Persians. Anyone with the wealth and status to have a car had a driver. People with wealth and power had retinues of agents, servants, helpers, and hangers-on.[5] While the Komachi could not meet these exalted standards, they shared the value system that fostered them. When, for example, during contract negotiations Mahmoud said, "I will never work again," everyone present interpreted it to mean that he wanted to be like his employer. People never spoke positively about how much work they did. For example, I never heard anyone boast about how quickly he was able to shear sheep. Rather, people complained about work. When shepherds threatened to leave during negotiations, employers sat about bemoaning their supposed fate and saying they would have to sell their animals. When I asked them why their sons could not do the work, they responded that it was unthinkable—not physically impossible, but *unthinkable*. Indeed, the only person I heard brag about the quality of her work was a barren woman who, having no children to talk about, spoke instead of the quality of her clarified butter and yogurt. Other women mocked her behind her back.

Wealthy Komachi used shepherds because they felt that work was demeaning. This view was reinforced by the fact that only the poor, shepherds, and women were actively engaged in the labor process. Of course this begs the question of why Persian society as a whole fostered this attitude toward work. At this juncture, however, it is the effect rather than the cause of this value that is most significant. This attitude toward labor was not only an important reason why a market for shepherding labor existed within Komachi society, but also restricted the number of potential shepherds. Members of households with marginal resource bases did not see shepherding contracts as a way to improve their problematic economic status. Shepherding was not a strategy for economic self-improvement (as it appears to be among the Yomut) because it led to a decline in social status that more than counterbalanced the marginal increase in wealth it might have brought. Rather, with work not valued, and shepherding stigmatized, one worked as a shepherd only because one absolutely could not avoid it; it was a marker of real need. When a young employer said to me, "I would never work as a shepherd, not even if I had only one animal," he was indeed saying a great deal about his society.

Given the above, it seems to some degree futile to pursue the question of just how to characterize the Komachi economy. It is clear that Komachi relations of production were not purely capitalist; it is equally clear that they were not entirely traditional, tribal, or domestic. Indeed, what emerges most vividly from an examination of Komachi economic life is a picture of various modes of production in uneasy and unstable apposition. It is less an articulation of modes of production than a bit of cultural bricolage, a system of practical solutions to numerous contextual contingencies that more or less worked and was for the moment part of a capitalist world system. It was hardly Weber's rational capitalist economy, though—indeed, it was hardly a definable kind of economy at all. That, perhaps, is the central point. The Komachi social formation, the Komachi form of production, and Komachi daily life encompassed understandings, determinants, and constraints arising from such diverse origins as the limits of raising sheep and goats in Kerman Province, strategies of heirship codified in a trade center on the west coast of Arabia 1,300 years ago, the pressures of producing commodities on the periphery of the world market, and much more. It is no wonder, then, that the Komachi did not have an economy that could be defined easily; they had instead the problem of practically integrating these forces in their daily lives. The ambiguity of shepherd-employer relations echoed the refractory reality of the forces that dominated Komachi life. Calling the Komachi "simple commodity producers," "peasants," "kulaks," or "tribespeople" masks the complexity of Komachi life more than it clarifies issues.[6]

As we have seen, though the Komachi tribe was small, it did not have a simple structure. Rather, the tribal whole was cut along many lines, dividing and redividing the community into numerous smaller, weakly linked aggregations. Members of the tribe belonged to three larger and three smaller patronymic groups; economic differences between rich and poor Komachi were structured so that the tribe comprised two classes; beyond simple apportioning of households into residential camps, camps separated into three geopolitical clusters whose members had denser and more coherent ties among themselves than with members of the other two; and, finally, within the geopolitical clusters there were nodes of close kin (*qom khish*) with dense, multiplex, load-bearing ties among their members, in contrast to the far more attenuated ties between their members and members of other similar groups.

## Structure and History

Divisions and solidarities played themselves out in tribal history as groups and individuals came and went, fused and fissioned. On a larger scale, tribes waxed and waned through their developmental cycles. The Komachi tribe grew while other tribes disappeared: tribes that had appeared on earlier lists as neighbors of the Komachi no longer existed; many Komachi claimed to be descended from tribes that no longer existed; the Komachi spoke of tribes that had broken up; and the Komachi origin myth claimed that the tribe was formed through the intermarriage of three patronymic groups with widely divergent geographical origins. Even as the tribe was growing, the social fabric was being knit and unraveled at the same time: of the roughly 115 Komachi households in 1975 (many of which were not native Komachi), about 30 appeared to be hiving off to form new groups.

Under favorable conditions—in the absence of war, famine, or other pressures for depopulation—tribes would clearly grow until they burst, first through agglomeration itself, but later because the structural logic of the system virtually demanded it. Given the labor demands of wealthy households and the relations of production governing access to labor, any population growth among the rich, whether by sexual reproduction or accretion, required a proportional expansion of the poorer households because each wealthy employer household needed labor from several poorer ones. Some of this labor came from formerly wealthy households that had become poorer, but much labor was acquired as poor households from other, poorer tribes or from the settled community became attached to the expanding core. I say "became attached" rather than "attached themselves" deliberately. While shepherds might seek employers, my observations suggested that, more commonly, competition between employers forced the least successful competitors to actively recruit labor from other tribes. Thus tribes should have grown as employers brought potential new members into the tribe.

However, Kermani tribes such as the Komachi and their neighbors were unstable social systems, formed by processes that joined together people who did not share a common ancestry. Tribes disappeared as their members broke off to join other, newer groups or as they merged with other similar groups to form a new and larger group. Given their instability and what appear to be relatively short developmental cycles, tribes remained small, rarely larger than the Komachi. Understanding the causes of this instability and the reasons these tribes divided at the points they did is central to understanding the Komachi.

We can gain some insight into this process of division if we examine the simultaneous processes of tribal division and tribal formation in the interesting example of Meshedi Gholami's camp. During the early 1950s, Meshedi Gholami, then a man in his late forties or early fifties, relocated his camp near an irrigated garden he had bought that was beyond the traditional boundary of Komachi territory. He was accompanied in this move by his sister and her husband. The two couples' children formed the core of the group. Thereafter, the members of Meshedi Gholami's camp lived apart from other Komachi in both summer and winter quarters. The distances were not tremendous, roughly 40 miles, but they were enough to limit contact during the summer and almost to preclude it in winter. While the move cut off the members of Meshedi Gholami's camp from interaction with all Komachi save their closest kin, it did bring Gholami's group into relatively close contact with members of tribes other than the Komachi, particularly in summer quarters. As a result, the composition of the group and of the kin networks of its members changed. Gholami's oldest children were all married to his siblings' children or Komachi from the main body of the tribe. His younger children, however, were married to members of the neighboring Jebel Barzi tribe. Effectively, ties to the Komachi were being attenuated, while ties with other groups were being developed.

From the perspective of the parent tribe, in this case the Komachi, the separation of new cores reduced the size of the tribe and hence was a stage in its devolution.[7] From the perspective of the colony, the long-term implications of migration and establishment of new networks is less clear. For example, after the death of Meshedi Gholami, his group might drift apart, some members returning to the main body of the Komachi and others becoming members of neighboring tribes. Its members might also increasingly intermarry with members of the Jebel Barzi or another neighboring tribe. Thus, the group that was centered about Gholami could disappear, the Komachi population either flowing into another tribe or remaining Komachi. Alternatively, the group might become the core of a new tribe as the group increased in size through reproduction, spouses marrying in, and the attraction of shepherds. Gholami's group could become a new tribe, occupying its own heartland and having its own core and its own developmental cycle. It would most likely be called the Gholami and its formation would come at the expense of the Komachi and some other tribes. Ultimately, one would expect it too to feed its members to still newer tribes. Gholami's camp was not an isolated case. The camps of Shah Mirza's children were similarly dividing off from and emerging out of the Komachi tribe, and Komachi tribal history itself clearly showed the effects of people moving in. This process of division, formation, and redivision thus appeared to be the normal developmental cycle of tribes such as the Komachi.

## Division Examined

The Komachi tribe existed as a congeries of camps. Formal relations among camps were determined by the relationships of the various heads to one another. Camps were themselves structured units, centered about the wealthy and important men who were their heads and generally composed of a cluster of his close kin and employees. Shepherds were transients: economic and social conditions (often the growth of antagonisms between them and their employers) drove them from camp to camp as they changed employers every few years. Groups of kin clustered about camp heads were more stable, and so camp cores composed of heads and their dependents tended to endure.

Camp heads were structural equals: there was no hierarchical ordering of relations among them. While it is true that heads of camp could be influenced by the desires and decisions of others, they acted with considerable independence. Indeed, conceptions of honor required men of influence to be autonomous. Heads of camp did not necessarily seek to dominate other heads in their interactions; instead they sought the more subtle goal of appearing not to have had their actions constrained. The end result of this concern with autonomy was not entirely different from that of a desire to prevail: there was little cooperation, and individuals saw their positions structurally, that is, vis-à-vis others. The significant outcome of this cultural attitude was that heads of camp tried to better their own positions, acting out of concern for their own interests rather than a concern for the interests of the tribe as a whole. As the continued existence of the tribe as a functioning body depended on the continued cooperation and consensus of camp heads, the importance of cultural understandings of honor for the Komachi tribe's long-term dynamics is hard to overestimate. In a very real sense it meant that the tribe was a collection of structural equals—heads of camps—and their individual followings. Relations among heads of camp thus determined tribal history.

Because they were nomadic pastoralists, the Komachi population tended to be thinly spread over a substantial area.[8] Other forces amplified that tendency. A dispersed population appears to have been an almost natural result of economic success, for the search for greater economic gain drove wealthy Komachi to establish themselves in areas on the margins of tribal territory in response to desires both for more and better pasture and for land for cultivation. Meshedi Gholami, for example, moved 40 miles away in response to an unusual opportunity to purchase agricultural land in an area surrounded by good, open pasture. Ali, Agha Hossein (his close friend and cousin), and Agha Hossein's younger brother Mohammed (who was married to Ali's youngest sister) moved their winter quarters from near Manujan to the outskirts of Jaghin—a distance of about 21 miles, a one-hour drive—to gain access to new, open pasture, and Ali was attempting to negotiate rights to garden land in the area. When the Komachi tribe as a whole moved from the area around Jiroft to the vicinity of Manujan in an attempt to gain more pasture, many of the wealthiest Komachi established some rights to agricultural land in Manujan, in this case irrigated orchards and the fields that surrounded them.[9]

These were not simply employers but the wealthiest men in the tribe, strong heads of camp who had several hired shepherds of their own and needed substantial extrafamilial labor to manage their dairy production. At the age of seventy, having married off many children and divided his herd at the marriage of each son, Meshedi Gholami still owned over 300 animals. Ali, with 800-odd animals, was the weathiest Komachi, and Agha Hossein, with about 375 head, had the fifth largest herd. Particularly wealthy and important men such as successful heads of camp often led out-migrations. In part this was because they felt most strongly the tensions their activities created. They were the active participants in tribal politics; they competed among themselves for spouses for their children and shepherds for their flocks; and they were the ones for whom questions of honor and status were important.

If competition among wealthy men created tensions and potential for division, economic forces favoring the movement of wealthy men to the tribe's periphery certainly amplified the destabilizing effect of those tensions. Wealthy men needed the most pasture, and because they owned more sheep they often needed the best pasture as well. Though Komachi herding strategy generally led to a dispersal of flocks over a fairly wide area, wealthy men had larger breeding flocks than others and therefore had more animals to pasture within walking distance of their camps than did poorer Komachi. In effect, then, large herd owners felt somewhat greater resource pressure than their poorer neighbors. One reason for their greater sensitivity to resource pressure was that the structure of pastoral production conjoined with Komachi relations of production made it likely that over time the rich would get richer while the poor stayed poor. Wealthy men's herds were thus far more likely to increase in size than were the holdings of poorer men. And certainly the pressures of a predatory world market system promoted competition among wealthy herd owners and led them to maximize their holding, which quite likely led, in turn, to increased competition. It is worth stressing here that resource pressure drove wealthy men to the edges of tribal territory; wealthy men were not likely to attempt to hold on to—or seize—pasture in the center of tribal territory because such pasture was likely to be more heavily grazed and thus poorer than lands near or beyond the edge of normal use.

Other factors also favored the movement of wealthy rather than poor Komachi. Traditionally, the Komachi and their neighbors did not exercise exclusive control over a contiguous territory, as larger confederations did; rather, they gained access to pasture within the tribal territory through dyadic ties with important members of the local settled community, with tribesmen giving substantial gifts to their patrons for the privilege of using pasture. Under these conditions, men with a large disposable surplus were more likely to secure access to pasture than others. There were also structural implications of wealth that promoted rich men's ability to move. Truly wealthy men owned animals enough to need several shepherds. With their animals, their shepherds' animals, and the female labor the shepherd households could supply, wealthy men could form a viable camp. The leader of such a camp would be unchallenged in decision making, and in effect could go where he wished. By contrast, poorer men needed other equals to have a viable camp. Movement of such a camp to the periphery would necessitate more agreement and cooperation than was common among the Komachi.

The movement of wealthy and important men as pioneers shaped the process of tribal development. Wealthy and important men tended to have dense networks of close kin. If several camps moved toward a new territory, it was quite likely that the heads of camp would be closely related. As we noted above, Ali, Agha Hossein, and Agha Hossein's brother Mohammed had very close attachments to one another, lived in close proximity to one another, were practically and formally closely related, and had moved together to a new winter territory some distance from the main body of the tribe. Meshedi Gholami's new tribelet was built about a core of his closest kin: his sister, her husband, and both his own and his sister's children (who were, of course, linked by marriage). Similarly, Shah Mirza's sons lived in camps in which their married sisters and their father's sister's married children formed the core.

Because new tribal cores were, in effect, built around the dense practical network of a few closely linked wealthy men, such new cores had at their inception a certain coherence. Moreover, almost by definition, wealthy and important men were not young men, and they often had children who were either married or of marriageable age. While married children were in theory economically independent, it was clear that they often found it helpful to remain close to or in their father's camp, and the wealthy household's need for vast quantities of female labor made married daughters (and, much less frequently, daughters-in-law) welcome. To the degree that married children stayed near their father, a new tribe would have a core of closely related kin: all the more so, if the closely related heads of camp had arranged marriages among their children. A new group formed by several wealthy heads of camp would thus have a structure congruent with that seen in larger tribes, that is, there would be a group of closely associated men—probably kin themselves—surrounded by dependent close kin. Normal patterns of marriage would then quickly lead to the existence of a new tribal core of wealthy pastoralists who shared a network of dense kin ties.

Wealthy core households were accompanied by a number of poorer households whose relationships to wealthy tribesmen were largely contractual and whose relationships to one another were largely accidental. It is evident that core members of the tribe woud have more kin than members of the periphery because their ancestors had moved to tribal territory and formed a new tribe with their kin. But why would shepherds not come over time to have many kin as well? And why were there radical differences in the patterns of kinship affiliation among shepherds and employers?

The structural logic of the instability that was characteristic of Kermani tribes helps explain the different patterns of kinship affiliation.

Were tribes relatively stable, marriages among peripheral members of the tribe would lead over time to an ever denser set of ties among them. Assuming the continuation of class distinctions, one would expect to find the tribe eventually composed of two classes or two economic statuses that had otherwise similar internal structures. But ancestors of current core Komachi had lived and married in close proximity for several generations, creating the dense networks of overlapping ties mentioned above, while peripheral Komachi not only moved more frequently than wealthy tribespeople did but also moved alone rather than as members of a kinship cluster. Peripheral Komachi lacked the dense matrix of kin ties possessed by members of the core. Given the processes described above and the fact that tribes were not stable, the constant dissolution and reformation of tribes promoted the periphery's lack of coherence.

Looking further at this process, we can see how practice gave force to the structural causes I have just described and so helped create tribal history. Within the ever-changing cast of characters that made up a tribe, shepherds and employers were locked in a class struggle that generated substantial conflict between them and literally drove them apart. Shepherds were joined to their employers by contractual relations that were exploitative and divisive as well as by ties of clientage that palliated but did not eliminate the tensions of the shepherd-employer relationship. Claims of common kinship had a reality beyond metaphor that did moderate conduct and conflict within the relationship. But at the same time claims of kinship highlighted the relationship's essential contradiction, and so illuminated the peculiar and ambiguous place of the shepherd in the social order.

The ties that bound shepherds and employers to one another were rather weak. Shepherds were joined to other shepherds by ties that were also diffuse, weak, and few and far between. Faced with stress and conflict and bound by the weakest of ties, when shepherds had had enough they moved from one tribe to another. They were a floating population that moved so frequently because they had few roots, and remained rootless because they moved so frequently. The distinction between core and periphery does not simply identify two groups that were not alike, but recognizes that one group had had a long association with the Komachi tribe and was in fact likely to have been its nucleus, while the other was a group only by contrast to the core, and even then only temporarily. While the tribe itself was a body that was always in flux, the two groups—core and periphery, employer and shepherd—still had radically different relationships to the tribe in history.

If we imagine the processes of wealthy men moving out and shepherds moving around taking place within many tribes at once, we can see that new tribelets or cores that hived off from their parent tribes would come into closer contact with each other (that is, with other tribelets at their common boundaries) than with members of the tribes they left behind. Marriages among members of these cores led them to become intertwined (*pichide*) and formed new tribes composed of core segments from diverse origins integrated (at least initially) by marriage. A periphery of poor tribespeople, many of whom were shepherds, were attached to this core by contract, clientage, and broad calculation of kin. Thus, a new tribe would start and grow. But friction would develop between wealthy men, who would form alliances with only a few of their closest kin. They would move out to the tribe's boundary, and the process would begin again, with shepherds moving in and out and around all the while.

While friction among important men exacerbated tribal instability, saying that men disagreed hardly explains tribal history. Examining relations among men in conjunction with social structure, however, allows us to see how the divisive tendencies of each complemented the other's in a way such that practice and structure jointly had a significant effect. Two rules dominated the Komachi marriage system: the preference for marriage with close cousins and the prohibition on multiple marriages between sibling sets. The structural implications of the two rules are interesting. Preferential marriage with close kin, if carried on systematically, will lead to a concentration of marriage ties within a cluster of close kin, a concomitant involution of the in-marrying group, and the emergence of lines of fission and division between involuted in-marrying groups.[10] Multiple marriages between sibling sets (simple exchange, or *gav ba gav*, marriages) create a very tight bond between two families but exclude all other families from the relationship. The Komachi prohibition of such marriages thus forced people to create a more diversified network of ties. However, men could marry off their children in what I have labeled oblique and extended marriages (for example, marrying three sisters to men whose fathers are brothers) and still create restricted (though not as tightly) networks of kin. Assuming a preference for close kin marriage but a prohibition on exchange marriage, one would expect wealthy Komachi to marry off their children in a fashion that created dense knots of kinship affiliation. However, because families were large, it was unlikely that a man would be able to marry his children into one close genealogical space. Thus, following the rules and preferences would lead to a collection of groups of people who were linked to each other by dense networks of ties, but each group would be linked to other groups by fewer, weaker ties. In effect, following the rules exactly would produce nearly the same result that followed from practice, except that clusters of kin would be defined genealogically rather than politically, as they appear to have been.

What is of central significance here is the notion that the logic of the Komachi marriage system led to a society that was constantly in the process of dividing against itself. The wealthy families that formed the tribe's core were driven apart by the logic of the marriage system as well as by the practical forces I have isolated above. Indeed, the two pressures were mutually reinforcing. Practical considerations created conflict and alliance; alliance was marked by the creation or recreation of significant ties with close kin; allies were selected from among close kin; and alliances were marked by marriage. The system turned in on itself, and practice and structure combined to generate dense clusters of kin that stood apart from other similar clusters and so formed the natural lines along which tribes ultimately divided. Momentum for this division came from many sources.

Relations among wealthy and important Komachi were not completely solidary. The underlying structures of kinship affiliation—the identification of close kin and the creation and recreation of ties with them through marriage—resonated with, channeled, and to some degree amplified practical divisions, even as those divisions shaped networks of kinship affiliation. Thus structural and practical lines of fracture coincided. But it was the conjunction of these structural and practical conditions with the mobility required by a pastoral mode of production that permitted division to take place, for it is difficult to imagine how kinship structure and practical antagonisms would generate communal fission if, for example, the Komachi had raised rice in paddies rather than sheep and goats on the open range. In effect, one must speak of the structures of kinship affiliation and the structures of pastoralism conjoining with practical considerations to generate division.

One ought not see conflict among employers as something that just happened to occur. I have suggested throughout this work that while shepherds and employers were not perfect analogues of the proletariat and bourgeoisie, the distinctions between them were the distinctions of class, and the conflict between them was class conflict. Conflict between shepherds and employers arose because the structured relationship between them was exploitative, and the daily experience of that exploitation generated hostilities and tensions between shepherds and employers, between shepherds and employers' wives, and, not, least, between employers' wives and shepherds' wives. This conflict was reduced to some degree by the movement of shepherds from employer to employer, by the catharsis of contract negotiations, and by the claim of common kinship. While claims of common kinship and actions that marked commonality (of a sort) could sometimes moderate the conflict between employer and employee, at other times the very juxtaposition of the exploitative shepherd-employer relationship with the solidary bonds of alleged common kinship made the exploitation more egregious. Similarly, employers' wives' insatiable demands for labor under the rubric of *komak* grated on the wives of shepherds not simply because they involved labor, but because of the way those demands blurred categories and created dissonance. When the tensions became too great, shepherds moved. But movement of shepherds promoted competition among employers as they sought to hold their current employees or replace them with new ones. Moreover, the nature of Komachi shepherd-employer relations made the job of shepherd so onerous that only those who *had* to be shepherds were. Cultural attitudes toward work made Komachi employers loath to care for their animals themselves, and led them to treat shepherds in a way that made being a shepherd most unattractive. As those who could avoid working as shepherds did so, the very structure of shepherd-employer relations led to a restriction on the number of shepherds that heightened the potential for competition among employers. In effect, class conflict between Komachi employers and shepherds was damped at the real cost of class solidarity among employers. Tensions arising among employers over competition for shepherds and their wives' labor played themselves out through the marriage system and became amplified until eventually real fissures appeared in the social order. Simultaneously, antagonisms that arose as men strove to make marriages for their children created the kind of disharmony that led them to compete among themselves for shepherds, in the marketing of sheep, or over where a tribal well should be placed. Each of these antagonisms created disturbances in other relationships. Structured by the logic of the kinship system even as they helped to create the actual lines of that structure, these conjoined antagonisms ultimately dissolved tribes such as the Komachi.

We have so far a picture of conjunctions within conjunctions within conjunctions. But even this last set of conjunctions was embedded as well. Not only did pastoralism give the Komachi the potential to move, but the Komachi also lived within historical circumstances that enabled them to realize that potential. One precondition for division was the ability of pastoralists such as the Komachi to move to pastures on or beyond the borders of their initial territory. For this to happen, there had to be land for expansion.[11] As we have seen, this condition held in Kerman Province for much of the nineteenth and twentieth centuries, and quite probably for a substantial period of time before that. Of course, room for growth was itself historically contingent, becoming available via a series of depopulations—the last clearly caused by transformations in agricultural production as Persia became more integrated into the world market—and ceasing to be available during my own period of contact with the Komachi as explosive postwar population growth, the expansion of motorized irrigation of cash crops, and government rangeland policies placed real limits on the quality and quantity of pasture available.

There are other Persian tribes, such as the Bakhtiari, the Basseri, and the Qashqa'i, that had hundreds of thousands of members and long histories. How was it that they existed in apparent stability while tribes such as the Komachi did not? How could they be large, while tribes like the Komachi divided before they could grow to such sizes? Examining the larger tribes, we find that they were divided into many smaller units (see particularly R. Tapper 1979b for a discussion of these units). To a very substantial degree, their unity was political and was engendered (and sometimes forcibly maintained) by an internal political hierarchy. These hierarchically structured tribes (known as tribal confederations) were statelike political organizations. Within confederations, surplus was often extracted from "commoner" tribespeople by a ruling elite of khans, *il-khans*, *il-begis*, and so on. Even where confederations existed, however, one finds little evidence of either an elaborate bureaucracy or a stable hierarchical structure. The degree to which individuals were free to change residential affiliation varied from society to society (and probably over time within societies as well). Mobility was clearly associated with access to pasture, and thus with a household's economic viability. Freedom to move was probably directly related to political independence and inversely related to the degree of political centralization of particular tribal polities. The need for mobility as a whole probably contributed to the lack of fixed hierarchy. Mobility traditionally put even tribal confederations on the margins of state control. While this often worked to the benefit of tribes—for example, permitting members of the tribe to avoid taxation and conscription—strong, centralizing states invariably attempted to incorporate tribes more effectively into the larger body politic. Pressures on tribes during these periods were generally severe, often leading to substantial (and occasionally disastrous) dislocations of tribal life. Over the long run, Southwest Asian tribal and state power have generally been inversely related, and one finds a slow but constant cycle of alternating ascendancy.

Given mobility, the absence of a coherent bureaucracy, and the cyclical nature of tribe-state relations, even the largest and most powerful tribal confederations were not stable, clearly bounded social systems. Frequently waxing and waning in size and power, drawing in members from other tribes or from the settled community as they expanded and sloughing members off as they contracted, most Persian tribes had composite memberships of diverse origins; they were thus more political structures, artifacts of incomplete state control, than they were ethnic groups, or groups based on common language or common descent (though these were often seen as salient boundary markers). Indeed, even though they were larger and their processes perhaps harder to track, most Persian tribes seem rather like greatly expanded versions of the Komachi. Political centralization provided a unifying force somewhat stronger than Komachi kinship, and their greater size made the movement in or out of small groups relatively inconsequential, but it seems quite clear that larger tribes were only marginally more stable than smaller ones, that large tribal sections and confederacies too came and went (Barth 1961).[12]

In any event, tribes such as the Komachi had no hierarchy and no politically based unity. The question now becomes, why did the small southern Kermani tribes not join together to form the large tribes and confederacies for which Persia is so famous? Two arguments are commonly put forth to account for variation in tribal political structure in Iran: ecological determinism and state impact. Ecological arguments stress the availability of agricultural resources or differences in carrying capacity and hence in population density (Barth 1960; Salzman 1967,

1979). The essence of this view is that only where population density is high enough to warrant regulation of access to resources will political hierarchies—the agencies that will regulate that access—form. The second argument proposes that tribal hierarchies tend to form not as a result of internal conditions, but rather due to pressures from an external state or statelike system (Garthwaite 1984; Irons 1979; Burnham 1979). These are not, of course, mutually exclusive hypotheses.

As Kermani tribes have been encapsulated within a larger state for all of their recent history, one might be tempted to assume that their apparent absence of hierarchy was more reasonably attributable to low population density than to state presence. Indeed, Kerman was depopulated during the nineteenth century and its tribes had growing room well into'the twentieth century. Unfortunately, equally good evidence suggests that the rest of Persia also suffered population loss during the mid- to late nineteenth century and that tribes were the largest population losers (Gilbar 1976).[13] Given the nature of our historical information, it is unlikely that we can identify definitively the reason why significant political hierarchies failed to develop among tribes in south Kerman. However, the combination of the following circumstances seems germane: (1) very low rainfall; (2) poor pasturage; (3) relatively low population density; (4) open (if poor) range available for population expansion; (5a) a geographical location at the extreme margin of Persian society, (5b) few major population centers or significant trade routes in areas controlled or frequented by tribes, and therefore (5c) marginal and irregular state presence in the region.

For whatever reason, many of the tribes in Kerman and virtually all the tribes in the Komachi region were not politically unified under a single leader. Instead, as they reached a size of 70 to 100 households, they began to split apart. Johnson's work, as noted above, suggests why this occurred. Komachi camps averaged six households per camp. Assuming that figure held for other tribes in the region, a tribe of 70 to 100 households would have had 11 to 16 camps (or basal organizational units). Kermani tribes thus broke down at just the point at which hierarchies would have had to form if they were to remain stable.

In effect, then, one can see tribal instability arising through the conjunction of numerous structures and contexts, including those of human information processing, the dynamics of animal populations, the regional marriage system, Islamic notions of property and inheritance, the requirements of nomadic pastoralism, and the historical impact of world capitalism (in many spheres). Ranged against these forces one finds notions of solidarity growing out of shared experience, exchange, claims of common kinship, and the antipathy of the outside world. To the degree that the Komachi saw themselves as a community, that there was solidarity among them, or that they derived support and comfort from their fellows, we can say that claims of common kinship did work, that peoples' perceptions of the social whole helped it remain one. Ultimately, however, the center cannot hold and things fall apart.

# 10

## CONCLUSION

The preceding study examines the nature of class divisions and kinship affiliation among the Komachi, describing the historical context in which the former arise, exploring the ambiguous and tension-laden manner in which kinship and class articulate, and demonstrating the way in which the structure and tenor of Komachi social relationships within and across the lines drawn by class divisions and kinship ties contribute to the Komachi social formation's structural instability. In so doing, the study not only describes the Komachi but also points to questions that could be asked about other Iranian pastoral communities, greatly increasing our understanding of their nature; provides insight into the nature of unstable and unbounded societies; and suggests some implications the presumption of instability has for ethnography. Finally, the open and refractory nature of the Komachi social order shows particularly well the power of the historical materialist approach outlined in the introduction. I will address these points in order.

## The Komachi Case and the Study of Iranian Pastoralists

Historical evidence from Kerman shows that by the beginning of the eighteenth century the region's pastoralists were producing commodities for international markets. While Kerman's pastoralists may have been particularly early entrants into the market, by the mid-nineteenth century many pastoralists were producing materials that found their way to national or international markets. Thus, assumptions that Iran's pastoralists have been engaged until recently in some form of subsistence production, that until recently they have been little affected by the pressures of the world market, or that their structured economic inequalities are recent phenomena all seem out of place. These assumptions are sustained far more by the paucity of attempts to trace the history of pastoralists' relations to the market than by hard evidence. Indeed, while pastoralism shaped Komachi society in many significant ways, it did not cause the Komachi to have a relationship to the market that was fundamentally different from that of settled agriculturalists (see Asad 1978). To a striking degree, the Komachi were *pastoral peasants*; careful examination of other Iranian pastoralists' economic relationships to the settled world would show that the same was true of many of them. Much of what we know about the impact of capitalism on rural societies elsewhere in the world seems directly applicable to Iran's pastoral economies, though in the case of Iranian pastoralists little attempt has been made to use this knowledge.

The Komachi case also suggests that, perhaps as a result of the early work of Barth (1961) and Irons (1975), we have approached the study of pastoral economies in Iran with upside-down expectations. Specifically, my discussion of wealth in pastoral economies points out that the cumulative effect of random changes in herd size due to good and bad years and good and bad luck is not an equalization of wealth (cf. Black-Michaud 1972:621; Barfield 1981:125) but, absent redistributive mechanisms, an ever-increasing economic differentiation.

In an early study of pastoralists, Barth argued that animals were capital and had the potential for increase. However, he argued that leveling mechanisms and other forces led to an equalization of wealth among the Basseri (1964). Among the Komachi, animals can and do increase in number over time, but without leveling mechanisms, division of a wealthy pastoral household's animals among a number of heirs is unlikely to make those heirs poorer than their parents. Actually, it was easier for moderately wealthy Komachi to pass their economic status on to their heirs than it was for agriculturalists, whose nonreproducing property had to be divided into smaller shares—hence the *katkhoda's* decision to marry his nontribal children to Komachi pastoralists (discussed in Chapter 7). In sum, without leveling mechanisms, herd growth may promote the reproduction of economic differentiation.

Finally, evidence from studies of other pastoral communities (e.g. Bates 1973; Barfield 1981; Black-Michaud 1972, 1986) and of nonpastoral societies elsewhere shows that linkage to the capitalist world market further promotes economic differentiation. One conclusion of this study is, therefore, that all things being equal, we should expect pastoral economies such as those in Iran to show evidence of significant and stable economic differentiation. Cases of leveling, where they are found, are what must be explained.

If economic differentiation is not abnormal, then effective description and categorization of pastoral economies not only must show that wealthy and poor pastoralists have more or fewer animals per household or per capita but must carefully document the details of the social relations of production that determine access to the means of production, generally animals and pasture, and the goods that are produced. Where different groups within a society have different kinds of access to the means of production, or where one group extracts wealth from another—as was clearly the case among the Basseri, the Lur, the Qashqa'i, the Bakhtiari, and the Central Asian Arabs, as well as the Komachi (Barth 1961; Black-Michaud 1972, 1986: Beck 1980, 1986; Brooks 1983; Garthwaite 1983; Barfield 1981)—then recognizing that the problem is not simply one of differences in wealth but of differences in class will greatly increase understanding of these societies and their histories.[1]

For example, while one need not accept Marx and Engels's dictum that "the history of all hitherto existing society is the history of class struggles" (Marx and Engels in Turner 1978:473), the history of the Komachi social formation was shaped by class conflicts. Since many commonly described patterns of behavior among Iranian pastoralists— shepherds changing employers or temporarily ceasing to work, shepherds killing and eating employers' animals, employers extracting noncompensated labor from shepherds and their families, and poor people settling or changing their tribe—are known to be characteristic of class conflict elsewhere,[2] our understanding of the history of pastoral groups in general would be greatly increased by explicit exploration of the role of class and class conflict within them.

## The Implication of Instability

While the instability of the Komachi social formation is particularly striking, many of the features related to or characteristic of Komachi instability—including movement of people into and out of a community, systems of making marriages and reckoning kinship that isolate individuals and groups of individuals as they link them, the presence of class relationships and class conflict, the relatively easy movement of people and the means of production, and relatively dispersed residential patterns—seem to be present in other Iranian pastoral communities as well. The evidence from pastoral Iran strongly supports Wolf's contention that the referents for analytic constructs such as societies and cultures are not stable and enduring units, but rather are open, unbounded, and impermanent ones (1982).

If groups are unbounded and unstable, complex and labile, then their cultures *can* be things "of shreds and patches." As a result, effective understanding of culture and society come not from classifying and reifying them into unitary things that imply some hidden integration of the refractory forces with which their members live, but by approaching them in exactly the opposite fashion, by believing that they are disintegrated. Ambiguities, contradictions, tensions, conflict, and systemic collapse are therefore not problems to be explained or explained away, but are the markers that highlight the tracks and trails of conjunctions and disjunctions that can be identified through historical and social analysis. They are the starting point for understanding the social entities anthropologists study, because we cannot understand the entities unless we accept their essentially unbounded and unstable nature.

If social entities like the Komachi have come about through the intersection of many structures, at least since the rise of capitalism, then one needs some notion of how these structures intersect. The relationship of the capitalist market to other economic and cultural systems is often described as one of *articulation,* as in "articulation of modes of production". But *articulation* and *conjunction,* which are terms often used to describe the relations among different noneconomic structures, both suggest tidiness, the neat dovetailing of disparate pieces. The Komachi case suggests that there is no simple articulation or conjunction. Instead, there seems to be a collision of many forces leading to the creation of a shatter zone filled with unclear paths, ambiguous relations, uncertain choices, conflict, and tension (see, e.g., Sahlins 1981, 1985).

The choices that people make in particular cases are largely practical; like Levi-Strauss's *bricoleur*, a person seeks to solve problems with what he or she has on hand. Some views, categories, and practices become dominant and highly salient to a society's members and to observers such as anthropologists because they are generally practicable. Other views, categories, and practices that are held, employed and engaged in by those with power enough to successfully make them dominate the "public transcript" also become highly salient. But option and inconsistency, and hence ambiguity and tension, abound. Among Kerman's pastoralists, the tribes, the named social entities we would normally call societies, come apart. Wolf argues that this is a general process and that when faced with cumulative conflict, kinship-ordered societies split apart. In the splitting, changes occur so that these systems do not simply replicate themselves (1982:95–96). There is no reason to doubt that this is true. But in Kerman, *tribes come together too.* The case of the Komachi and other Kermani pastoralists suggests that it is easier for people to abandon their homeland, their tribe, and their society than to overcome conflicts and tensions through the creation of new views, categories, or practices. Succinctly put, among Kerman's pastoralists society is abandoned before culture. This does not preclude culture change, of course, but it does suggest that what people willingly change may be ranked. I suspect that the abandonment of society before culture is the general hierarchy of response wherever territory is open or leaders lack the means of coercion to keep people in their place.

Wolf's work shows that it is impossible to understand societies that are open, refractory, and unstable without effective reference to their larger social and historical contexts, to the structures that have collided. Anthropologists cannot narrowly study "their people." But the Komachi case also suggests that in studying context and history, care must be taken not to abandon living people and what they say and do. The peculiar strength of anthropology as a discipline is that anthropologists do actually get to see the relationship of practice, structure, and history unfold, albeit in a small way, and can ask living people who are making history what they are doing and why. Seeing them and listening to them, anthropologists are introduced to the conflicts and ambiguities that make ethnography interesting and that ultimately reveal how society and culture are produced, reproduced, and transformed. People should not disappear just because the history they are making is not grand.

Our ordinary analytic vocabulary makes it quite difficult to write simply about open and unstable systems. Even when put in quotation marks, terms such as *society* and *culture* imply perduring entities. Worse, simply writing of "the Komachi" or any other named group carries the same implication. How does one write about the economic history of the Komachi that occurred before the Komachi became a tribe? To write about "the economic history of the Komachi" simply has the wrong implication, as does "the economic prehistory of the Komachi." To say that one is writing about "the history of pastoralists in Kerman who preceded the Komachi, might have become Komachi, but were clearly not the Komachi qua Komachi" is more than cumbersome, but the claim that one is writing "the history of Kerman's pastoralists" is false. I have used circumlocutions (and I hope they are neither cumbersome nor unclear), but they do not solve the problem.

## Determined in the Last Instance?

What does the Komachi case suggest about Marx and Engels's complex historical materialism, in which the economic is determinate only in the last instance? Does the analysis of complex, open, unbounded, and unstable social systems that arise from the conjunction of many structures force modifications of Marxist theory so great that it loses its explanatory power? Alternatively, is a historical materialism that stresses complexity, the interplay of structures, and the efficacy of human agency so commonsensical and so descriptive, that its usefulness as a theoretical framework is vitiated?

Engels does not simply argue for complex explanation. He argues that "the ultimately determining element in history is the production and reproduction of real life" (Engels in Turner 1978:760). Among the Komachi, the production and reproduction of real life centered about raising goats and sheep, about pastoralism, so it does seem that Komachi life was "determined by the production and reproduction of real life." But is this argument perhaps merely an artifact of classifying peoples according to their technologies as pastoralists, hunters and gatherers, or swidden agriculturalists?

Pastoralism is not simply the basis for Komachi self-identification or anthropological categorization. A number of very important features of Komachi life—including, for example, nomadism, residence in small dispersed settlements, living at the geographical and social margins of settled Iranian society, means of production which can increase in quantity over time, and so on, all of which entail other aspects of Komachi life—follow from their being pastoralists. In fact, much of Komachi history seems contingent on their being pastoralists. But suppose the features clustered around pastoralism were not really the salient features of Komachi life. Then those features of Komachi life that distinguished them from other Iranian pastoralists would become salient, and the efficacy of part of Marx and Engels's formulation could be tested by seeing if those features were economically determined. It is clear that those features do not include being Muslim, nor conveying property roughly within the framework of Islamic law, nor being Shi'ite, nor marrying close kin. What distinguished the Komachi was the social formation's small size, its absence of political hierarchy, the dramatic instability of its social order, the dominant role of hired labor in its productive process, the relationship between hired shepherds and their employers, a prohibition on exchange marriages, and a long history of producing animal fibers for export trade.

Small size, instability and lack of hierarchy are closely and dialectically related and their complex determinants have been discussed in detail above. Many of those determinants, including marriage preferences and the logic of kinship affiliation, were shared by other Iranian pastoralists. Relatively unique determinants included very limited quantities of pasture and water, low population and population density, absence of major trade routes, a position at the extreme margins of the Persian state, and inter- and intra-class conflict arising from a particularly exploitative economic relationship between hired shepherds and employers—essentially economic determinants.[3] Factoring out what is common to other pastoralists, except for the marriage rule that prohibits exchange marriage, the unique features of the Komachi social order appear to be either economic conditions—for example, the use of hired shepherds, the nature of relations between shepherds and employers, and long-term market relations—or largely determined by economic conditions—for example, size, instability, and lack of hierarchy, What is unique about the Komachi social order is thus economically determined, and historical materialism permits the effective isolation of those economic determinants; it is not overwhelmed by complexity but helps sort through the complexity of social orders such as that of the Komachi.

Though what is unique about the Komachi social order is economically determined, the whole of the Komachi social order is economically determined *only in the last instance*; that is, other factors also play a part in its shaping. Full understanding of social orders such as that of the Komachi thus requires not simply an understanding of their economic determinants but of the whole host of conjoined forces and the ways they shape and are shaped by the actions of living people. Far from losing explanatory power, a historical materialism that stresses complexity, the interplay of structures, and human agency succeeds by driving us to find out how society works in particular cases.

The Komachi case supports the notion of a commonsensical historical materialism and suggests that if recognizing a society's complexity precludes simple explanation, it does not make explanation impossible

# Appendix: Selected Economic Census Data

| Household | No. of Members | No. of Consumers[a] | Years Household Had Been Established | Status[b] | No. of Animals Inherited | No. of Animals in Herd, 1975 | Annualized Growth Rate of Herd (%)[c] |
|---|---|---|---|---|---|---|---|
| 1 | 5 | 3.5 | 9 | E | 110 | 150 | 3.5 |
| 2 | 8 | 7.0 | 23 | S | 70 | 60 | -0.6 |
| 3 | 7 | 6.0 | 26 | S | 20 | 90 | 5.9 |
| 4 | 3 | 3.0 | >40 | F | f | 100 | d |
| 5 | 9 | 7.0 | 9 | S | 20 | 50 | 11.0 |
| 6 | 1 | 1.0 | >50 | W | f | 10 | d |
| 7 | 9 | 7.0 | 9 | F | e | 170 | e |
| 8 | 6 | 4.0 | 12 | S | 15 | 60 | 12.2 |
| 9 | 8 | 8.0 | >40 | I | f | 80 | d |
| 10 | 4 | 3.5 | 8 | F | f | 105 | f |
| 11 | 7 | 5.5 | 16 | F | 33 | 70 | 4.8 |
| 12 | 5 | 3.5 | 7 | E | 110 | 200 | 8.9 |
| 13 | 1 | 1.0 | >50 | W | f | 10 | d |
| 14 | 8 | 6.0 | 16 | E | 95 | 180 | 4.0 |
| 15 | 7 | 6.0 | 29 | S | 40 | 30 | -0.1 |
| 16 | 6 | 6.0 | 35 | S | 90 | 200 | 2.3 |
| 17 | 5 | 3.5 | 7 | S | 10 | 20 | 10.4 |
| 18 | 11 | 9.0 | 22 | E | 90 | 375 | 6.7 |
| 19 | 3 | 2.5 | 2 | E/F | g | 160 | g |
| 20 | 10 | 8.0 | 30 | E | 140 | 840 | 5.9 |
| 21 | 3 | 2.5 | 3 | E | 120 | 100 | -5.9 |
| 22 | 6 | 6.0 | 23 | S | 5 | 60 | 11.4 |
| 23 | 7 | 6.5 | 10 | S | e | 130 | e |
| 24 | 2 | 2.0 | 15 | I | 60 | 20 | h |
| 25 | 3 | 2.5 | 1 | F | 30 | 30 | 0 |
| 26 | 5 | 5.0 | 22 | S | 50 | 60 | 0.8 |
| 27 | 4 | 4.0 | >40 | W/S | f | 60 | d |
| 28 | 8 | 6.0 | 29 | I | 50 | 50 | 0 |
| 29 | 9 | 7.0 | 17 | E | 90 | 390 | 9.0 |
| 30 | 2 | 2.0 | >12 | E | e | 135 | d |
| 31 | 7 | 4.5 | 11 | S | 70 | 40 | -4.9 |
| 32 | 2 | 2.0 | >35 | W/F | f | 100 | — |
| 33 | 5 | 3.5 | 5 | S | 10 | 60 | 45.0 |
| 34 | 9 | 5.0 | 10 | S/F | 50 | 70 | 3.4 |
| 35 | 11 | 9.0 | 20 | F | 100 | 110 | 0.4 |
| 36 | 10 | 9.5 | 27 | E | 330 | 705 | 2.8 |
| 37 | 2 | 2.0 | >30 | W/S | f | 30 | — |
| 38 | 7 | 6.0 | >30 | W/S | f | 60 | — |
| 39 | 8 | 5.5 | 15 | F | 30 | 70 | 5.8 |
| 40 | 8 | 5.5 | 14 | E | 80 | 400 | 12.0 |
| 41 | 10 | 8.5 | 27 | S | 70 | 60 | -0.5 |
| 42 | 11 | 8.0 | 17 | E | 130 | 300 | 5.0 |

*Continued*

| Household | No. of Members | No. of Consumers[a] | Years Household Has Been Established | Status[b] | No. of Animals Inherited | No. of Animals in Herd, 1975 | Annualized Growth Rate of Herd (%)[c] |
|---|---|---|---|---|---|---|---|
| 43 | 6 | 4.0 | 10 | E | 180 | 180 | 0 |
| 44 | 3 | 3.0 | >40 | W/E | f | 250 | d |
| 45 | 1 | 1.0 | — | U | 0 | 10 | — |
| 46 | 10 | 8.0 | 21 | E | 48 | 240 | 7.9 |
| 47 | 7 | 5.0 | 14 | F | 140 | 120 | -0.1 |
| 48 | 5 | 5.0 | >25 | W/I | f | 130 | — |
| 49 | 3 | 2.5 | 6 | F | 60 | 80 | 4.9 |
| 50 | 2 | 2.0 | >25 | W | f | 20 | — |
| 51 | 8 | 8.0 | 31 | E | 50 | 240 | 5.1 |
| 52 | 5 | 3.5 | 10 | E | 145 | 200 | 3.2 |
| 53 | 6 | 5.0 | 16 | E | 150 | 250 | 3.2 |
| 54 | 9 | 7.0 | 17 | E | 220 | 180 | -1.0 |
| 55 | 8 | 6.0 | 16 | S | 20 | 20 | 0 |
| 56 | 8 | 5.0 | 12 | E | 120 | 180 | 3.4 |
| 57 | 5 | 5.0 | 35 | S | 100 | 70 | -1.0 |
| 58 | 1 | 1.0 | >45 | W | f | 40 | d |
| 59 | 5 | 3.5 | 9 | I | 35 | 50 | 4.0 |
| 60 | 5 | 3.5 | 9 | E | 87 | 125 | 4.1 |
| 61 | 5 | 5.0 | >40 | W | f | 120 | d |
| 62 | 9 | 7.0 | 17 | S | 25 | 90 | 7.8 |
| 63 | 3 | 2.5 | 1 | F | 60 | 70 | 15.0 |
| 64 | 9 | 7.5 | 21 | S | 80 | 50 | -2.2 |
| 65 | 6 | 4.5 | 2 | E | 130 | 140 | 3.7 |
| 66 | 5 | 5.0 | 35 | IN | 75 | 25 | -3.0 |
| 67 | 3 | 2.5 | 5 | S | 30 | 30 | 0 |
| 68 | 3 | 2.5 | 2 | S | 30 | 25 | -8.7 |
| 69 | 4 | 3.5 | 18 | IN | 80 | 100 | 2.8 |
| 70 | 5 | 5.0 | 29 | IN | 45 | 60 | 0.9 |
| 71 | 6 | 6.0 | 33 | IN | 30 | 70 | 2.6 |
| 72 | 5 | 3.5 | 6 | IN | 150 | 50 | -16.7 |
| 73 | 7 | 5.0 | 13 | IN | 25 | 140 | 14.0 |

[a] Adults and children over age 13 count as one full consumer; children 12 and under count as one-half of one consumer.

[b] E = current employer; S = head of household or son now a shepherd; F = former shepherd; W = widow; I = currently independent, neither hiring nor supplying labor; N = currently independent, head had never been a shepherd; U = unmarried woman living alone.

[c] Derived by subtracting the number of animals inherited from the number of animals owned in 1975 and calculating the average rate of increase per year. See Bradburd 1982 for an elaboration of this statistic.

[d] Household had devolved inheritance, so herd growth rate incalculable.

[e] Household formed through marriage with widow/widower who had herds from previous marriage.

[f] No data on inheritance available.

[g] No inheritance was involved; herd was gained by working as a shepherd.

[h] Household has no children; all but a minimum subsistence herd was sold off.

# NOTES

## Introduction

1. As will be evident throughout the text, my understanding of class struggle has been greatly influenced by James Scott's (1985, 1986, 1987) concern with the more quotidian aspects of class strife.

2. I am not, of course, the only one to notice or comment on the use of hired shepherds among Southwest Asian pastoralists. While Barth's seminal work *Nomads of South Persia* (1961) in effect denied the importance of hired shepherds among the Basseri, Bates (1973) did briefly discuss the use of hired shepherds among the Yörük, and Irons (1972, 1975) not only argued that the relationship of labor to herd size was an important determinant of wealth among the Yomut but specifically addressed the implication of the Yomut's lucrative shepherding contracts for their household economy. Black-Michaud's early piece on the Lur (1972) suggested that the relationship of shepherd to employer might be "oppressive" and could be one of structured inequality. Black-Michaud's later doctoral dissertation and book (Black-

Michaud 1976, 1986) expanded on this theme. R. Tapper's description of the Shahsevan (1979a) briefly explored the economic relationship of hired shepherd and employer, and Beck's works on the Qashqa'i (1980, 1986) and Barfield's work on the Central Asian Arabs of Afghanistan (1981) greatly increased the information available on shepherd-employer relationships in the plateau regions of Southwest Asia. This work differs from those works by focusing more sharply on the question of hired shepherds, particularly by exploring in far greater detail the historical basis, lived experience, and structural implications of the shepherd-employer relationship. In doing so, I believe this work fills a real gap in the current literature on Southwest Asian pastoral societies in general and on the shepherd-employer relationship in those societies in particular.

3. In the text that follows I will write of structures or contexts with a very deliberate emphasis on the plural. One aspect of this conjunction of structures is captured in the notion of articulation of modes of production, which I used in an earlier discussion of the Komachi economy (Bradburd 1980). There I argued that the Komachi economy as it existed in 1974–75 reflected the impact of an expanding world capitalist market system on a "traditional" economy. However, I would now argue that the "traditional" economy itself was a conjunction of several structures, the most important of which were the structure of pastoral production in Kerman Province, the structure of Islamic property relations (which, given their source, become immediately elided with concerns with structures of kinship), and those structures that constituted the relations of production controlling access to land and fixed resources in Kerman Province. Thus the notion of articulation itself becomes problematic. A similar deconstruction might be applied to other structures of the Komachi social order, including notions of kinship and tribe.

4. Recognizing full well that there are real differences between as well as similarities in the theoretical positions of the authors in question, the following is a very brief enumeration of what I see as central, largely agreed-upon, and substantially correct assumptions of theorists concerned with structure and practice. What Bourdieu calls habitus seems close to what Sahlins calls structure (and occasionally culture) and what Thompson calls experience. For Bourdieu, habitus is "systems of durable, transposable *dispositions*, structured structures predisposed to function as structuring structures, that is as principles of the generation and structuring of practices" (1977:72). Habitus is itself the product of history, "a past which survives in the present and tends to perpetuate itself into the future by making itself present in practices structured according to its principles" (1977:82). For Sahlins, "history is throughout grounded in structure, the systematic ordering of contingent circumstances" (1985:144). Thus, "people act upon circumstances according to their own cultural presuppositions, the socially given categories of persons and things" (1981:67) and "culture is precisely the organization of the current situation in terms of the past" (1985:155). That these contexts shape, limit, and constrain what people do is obvious, but we must also remember that they

enable human endeavor; in a word, they *structure* it. Giddens (1984) presents an extended discussion of this point. Ortner (1984) and Karp (1986) present extremely cogent, critical evaluations of Sahlins, Bourdieu, and Giddens, highlighting similarities and differences in their works. Moore (1987) presents interesting insights both on the relationship of practice and structure and on the problems of doing an anthropology concerned with process.

   5. A synthesis of a theory of practice with political economy seems to me to have great merit and a kind of natural logic. Bourdieu (1977:78) notes that one accounts for practice by understanding the conditions within which "habitus is operating." A great portion of these conditions seems to lie within the conventional domain of political economy. At the same time, perhaps the weakest area of analysis within political economy is the question of just how and why people do and think what they do. Practice theory tends to open the black boxes of "false consciousness," "mystification," and "hegemony" by forcing us to consider what these things mean with regard to real, living people in particular circumstances. The relationship of this kind of work to E. P. Thompson's kind of historical materialism (1963, 1978) is obvious but worth stressing.

   With regard to practice and context, Bourdieu argues that

> practices cannot be directly deduced either from the objective conditions, defined as the instantaneous sum of the stimuli which may appear to have directly triggered them, or from the conditions which produced the durable principle of their production. These practices can be accounted for only by relating the *objective* structure defining the social conditions of the production of the habitus which engendered them to the conditions in which this habitus is operating, that is to the *conjuncture* which, short of a radical transformation, represents a particular state of this structure. (1977:78)

Beyond the aesthetics of his translated prose, I have little difficulty with Bourdieu's theoretical formulations; however, I feel that Bourdieu fails to provide adequate specification of the context with which habitus is conjoined. My overt linkage of political economy with practice theory, and the elaboration of context in this work, are thus an attempt to practice what Bourdieu preaches.

## Chapter 1

   1. Railroad construction throughout Iran as a whole had been delayed by political rivalries between Britain and Russia during the nineteenth and early twentieth centuries.

   2. I document this in Chapter 3. I raise the point here as it seems quite an important factor in the development of tribal systems in the Kerman region.

   3. In the past, opium was an important crop in the region. I discuss the significance of this below.

4. As do the Komachi, Lori and Lur herd Kashmir goats; these animals give *kork* (cashmere), but not hair for the manufacture of tents.

5. Traditionally, control over water for irrigation granted its possessor de jure rights over land for agriculture (i.e., there were not two separate sets of rights), and these conjoint rights in turn granted the possessor shares of access to nonarable regions surrounding the village (see Lambton 1953). In effect, access to pasture and water are often linked, particularly in regions near agricultural villages (i.e., the bulk of the Komachi summer quarters pasture and a good portion of the winter quarters pasture).

## Chapter 2

1. Note that rural consumption figures show virtually no rise at all during that period, increasing from $125 per capita in 1965 to $153 per capita in 1975. While these rural consumption figures are not of direct concern here, they do show that even poor Komachi were living reasonably well by rural Iranian standards during 1974 and 1975.

2. Figures from the Iran Statistical Centre confirm the view that their position in an isolated market gave the Komachi an economic boost. During 1972–73 lamb or mutton in Kerman cost an average of 115 rials per kilogram, over 20 percent more than the 95 rials of the national average. The figure for goat meat is 114 rials/kilo for Kerman, 33 percent above the national average of 86 rials/kilo. Figures for other commodities display the same pattern: in Kerman clarified butter (*roghan*) brought 240 rials/kilo, cheese 110 rials/kilo, wool 149 rials/kilo, and goat hair 58 rials/kilo while the national figures are 225, 77, 92, and 41 rials respectively. Kerman's figures also are higher than those of neighboring Fars Province (home of many large tribes), where *roghan* brought 224 rials/kilo, wool 127, and goat hair 48 (Iran Statistical Centre 1973–74:256). The price of wool in Kerman of 149 rials/kilo (roughly 97¢/pound) for 1972–73 was a few cents per pound lower than what the Komachi received in 1975, when the price of wool was at its lowest, and was substantially below the peak price of $1.88/pound the Komachi received during 1974. Note that all of these prices were higher than the U.S average price during that period, 59¢/pound (U.S. Dept. of Agriculture 1975:17).

## Chapter 3

1. I want to stress that in attempting this historical contextualization I am *not* presenting a history of the Komachi. As I noted above, the Komachi are a very small tribe and even within the rather restricted theater of Kerman Province they are historically insignificant and largely unrecorded. Moreover, as I also pointed out above, one of the particularly interesting aspects of the

social system of the Komachi and their neighbors is that they are ephemeral. As it does little good to trace the nonhistory of an ephemeral group, my description of Kerman's history does not try to show the Komachi as they were; rather, it tries to set out the kinds of political, economic, demographic, and ecological pressures on groups like the Komachi (or on those pastoralists whose descendants ultimately came to be members of the tribe now known as Komachi). In short, the historical context I set out aims at outlining the parameters and pressures affecting pastoralists in Kerman and showing the way the general trends in the region's history have influenced them.

2. Indeed, the portion of his journey that took him from the shores of the Persian Gulf into the interior of Iran passed through the same interconnected riverbeds and washes that the Komachi use during the first stage of their migration from winter to summer quarters.

3. This remains true today. In their winter quarters, the Komachi meet Baluchis and "Arabs" whose language and culture differs considerably from the "Persians," i.e., those who, like the Komachi, are native speakers of Persian, consider themselves culturally Persian, and live on the Iranian plateau.

4. British trade in Kerman represented the opposite side of another British venture in long-distance trade: the North American fur trade. Beaver, the dominant target of this trade, were not sought for their fur per se but for the downlike underfur that was felted for fashionable headgear (see Wolf 1982). As the seventeenth and eighteenth centuries wore on, beaver became more difficult to obtain. Efforts were then made to find alternative fibers for felting. One of the more successful substitutes proved to be cashmere. British, French, and Dutch interests made serious attempts to gain some portion of, or indeed to dominate, the cashmere trade. Clearly, large-scale exports of cashmere also must have had a profound effect on domestic use, though there is little information available on this.

5. There are, in fact, two varieties of goat in Kerman. Pastoralists and highland dwellers raise Kashmir goats, medium-sized, light-colored goats with both long, coarse hair and the fine underhair that is valued as *kork*. In the lowlands and the south of the province, the dominant goat raised by those who did not migrate annually to the highlands was small, black-haired, and downless. Few pastoralists near the Komachi raise these animals, although they are vital to the pastoral adaptation as the source of the black hair from which tents are woven. The fact that people in Kerman raise two varieties of goat, one of which does not produce *kork*, is important, for all figures on goat populations in Kerman must be reduced if one wants to extrapolate to numbers of *kork*-producing goats. Kermani goats produce no more than 17.5–26.5 ounces of fleece a year (English 1966). The Komachi felt that a good goat in a good year gave 17.5 ounces of *kork*. Stöber notes that Afshar nomads in Kerman reported *kork* yields of 1–14 ounces (1978:88), while Dillon's informants told him goats gave from 1 to 8 ounces of *kork* (1976:234). This range is probably attributable less to the inaccuracy of the various informants than to the real potential for great variation in production. Given the range of figures, I

have chosen to assume that a mythical average goat will produce 10.5 ounces of *kork* per year and to calculate herd figures on that base.

Willem Floor, who has examined aspects of Dutch trade and Dutch presence in the Persian Gulf during this period (Floor 1984, 1986), has suggested to me that during the first half of the eighteenth century Dutch trade in cashmere wool quite likely equaled and perhaps exceeded British trade (personal communication). This would, of course, double the amount of wool and hence the number of animals involved in export trade; hence my belief that the figure of 208,000 goats is conservative.

One can gain some idea of what this figure represents in terms of a goat population for the region from a comparison with the Iran Statistical Centre's 1971–72 and 1972-73 goat herd figures for Kerman, which are 696,000 and 657,000 goats respectively (Iran Statistical Yearbook 1973–74:246). Bearing in mind that these figures include both Kashmir goats and black-haired goats, the effect of an export trade requiring a productive herd of at least 200,000 seems obvious.

6. Kermani shawls were large (10–11 feet by 5 feet), elaborate weavings. They are of interest to us here for they too were made of cashmere from Kermani goats (Curzon 1966; Dillon 1976; English 1966; Lorimer 1908; Stober 1978; Abbott 1851; and Issawi 1971 all discuss various aspects of the shawl trade).

7. As with so many questions about Persian local economies in the nineteenth century, it is necessary to extrapolate values. In 1850, K.E. Abbott, an agent for British commercial interests, reported that Kerman City had over 2200 looms for shawls and that there were an additional 300 looms in surrounding villages. He further noted that the value of the shawls produced (presumably for export, given the nature and form of his report) was £52,000 per year (Issawi 1971). Jacob Polak, a German physician who wrote extensively on Persian handicrafts, was in the region at roughly the same time; his information on the value of individual shawls, and the duration of the weaving process, permits the conversion of Abbott's figures into estimates of the number of shawls produced. Shawls of two qualitites were produced in Kerman: "good quality shawls," which sold at 20–30 ducats (roughly £9-13) and "fine quality shawls, a quality similar to European cashmere cloth costing 5-6 ducats [i.e. about £2.5]" (Polak quoted in Issawi 1971). Given that a "good quality shawl" took between a year and fifteen months to produce (Dillon 1976:274) and assuming that the bulk of shawls exported were good quality (as they must have been to be directly competitive with Kashmir shawls), then £52,000 of shawls would be roughly equivalent to 5000 shawls at £10 apiece.

One cannot discount the importance of internal trade in shawls. J. P. Ferrier, in his diary of a trip through Persia in 1845, makes note of the shawl trade: "There is also a large sale of articles manufactured in the Province of Meshed. . . . [including] shawls of a Kashmir pattern, called in Persian

*meshedi*. These are held in greater estimation than those of Kerman"
(1856:124-5). Henry Layard (1887:3) gives us one view of how the shawls were
used in Persia: "The Matamet's spacious double pavilion was lined with cashmere shawls, and furnished with the finest carpets and silk hangings." Fully
half the £10,000 worth of shawls British consul Percy Sykes records as "exported" from Kerman for 1894 was going to other portions of Persia for use
there (Government of Great Britain 1896). We may safely assume that the
trade in shawls was substantially larger than that for export trade alone. At
this point, I can make no more acurate estimate of the proportion of production that was for external or internal use. I presume, however, that the figure
of 5,000 shawls per year that I use in the text is very conservative.

   8. Percy Sykes (the British consul in Kerman) estimated there were 3000
looms producing £60,000 worth of shawls at the end of the century (Sykes
1902:200). Sykes also noted that the shawl trade appeared to be in decline. I
would be remiss if I did not note that I find Sykes's numbers difficult to inter-
pret. Though he values total production at £60,000, he shows exports of only
£10,000. Perhaps the rest was purchased for local consumption.
   Parenthetically, the decline in exports represents another shift in European
fashion. The development of the jacquard loom, which permitted European
mass production of Kashmir-type (paisley) shawls, killed the market for real
shawls, as the latter lost their cachet.

   9. It is difficult to estimate the extent of Kerman's participation in the
wool trade. Writing of Persia as a whole, Gilbar notes that the general increase in carpet production let pastoralists to increase their herds, and he also
suggests that there was also an 18-fold increase in the value of raw wool exports. But his figures, which show exports increasing from virtually nil in the
1850s to £18,000 in 1889, £60,000 in 1902, and £270,000 in 1906–07 (Gilbar
1978:360), point to problems for pastoralists. Unless Kerman gained a great
share of this trade, the value of the wool trade to the pastoralists of the region
must have remained minor compared with the booms in the shawl and carpet
trades that preceded and followed it.

   10. Komachi sheep averaged an annual production of just over 2.2
pounds of wool per ewe. Paul English reports average wool production per animal to have been 3.3 pounds (1966:131), while Georg Stober reports that
sheep among the Afshar of Kerman generally produced between 1.1 and 2.2
pounds, with exceptional animals producing as much as 6.6 pounds (1978:88).
Given these figures, I will assume that the average Kerman sheep produces
about 2.2 pounds of raw wool per year. The Iran Statistical Yearbook reports a
total sheep population in the province of 1.7 million head for 1966 (Iran Statistical Centre 1966–67). This figure, however, must be suspect, as their figures for 1972 and 1973–74 claim total sheep populations of only 391,000 head
and 430,000 head respectively, a figure that is almost certainly too low (Iran
Statistical Centre 1972–73, 1973–74).

   11. For example, in 1894 wool was exported for 5.3d/lb while cashmere

brought roughly 7d, about 25% more. In 1851, white cashmere traded for about 5.8d/lb and brown cashmere 3.4d/lb, while sheep's wool traded for about 2.3d/lb (Abbott 1983:110).

12. For example, the British consul's report for May 1927—a peak period in the carpet trade—hints at short supply and pressure on prices. "The Russian oil [kerosene] agent started buying wool on behalf of the Russians. . . . The carpet dealers are said to be alarmed at this, because all the wool in the province, which is of limited quantity, had hither to been used for carpet manufacture, and imported yarn is very nearly double the price of domestic yarn" (Government of Great Britain 1942:3). Two years earlier, the trade report noted that "the carpet industry . . . consumes far more than all the available wool grown in the Province" (Government of Great Britain 1942). Turning to cashmere wool, still exported from Kerman in the late 1930s, one finds evidence in British consular diaries of increasing exports (£5700 in 1938, £10,100 in 1939) and increasingly short supplies: "Instructions have been received in the Governorate to discourage the slaughter of goats as the hair of these animals is a valuable export commodity. All goat hair available in this district is exported to Germany. The inhabitants are to be encouraged to eat more beef instead of goat flesh" (Feb. 1939, 27). Prices also were on the increase: "the price of goat hair has suddenly jumped from 24 rials to 46 rials" (Dec. 1938, §250) (Government of Great Britain 1939).

13. One of the causes of pastoralists falling into debt lies in the fluctuation of the value of their produce (see Bates 1971; Bates and Lees 1977 for discussions of this). Variations in climate, drought, and disease also have an impact (see below). A combination of bad years in a bad market is likely to put even the wealthiest herdowner into debt.

14. In part, this abandonment of the city itself reflects a longer trend. Dillon notes that

> while the number of looms [in the Kerman region] has nearly tripled from 1937 to 1966, the number of looms in Kerman City fell from 1,745 to 1,100 in the same period. The expansion of the carpet industry, then, has been a rural phenomena. . . . The carpet contractors have discovered that they could find a generally adequate labor force in the villages at wage rates significantly lower than those required to maintain urban weavers. (1976:299)

15. For discussions of rates of interest on trade between pastoralists and settled peoples in Iran see Barth 1961; Kielstra 1973:110 and Holmes 1974:311.

16. All of these authors' works show evidence of substantial research on the issue, including the examination and comparison of figures drawn from numerous nineteenth and twentieth century accounts. Given previously mentioned caveats about the data, these works appear to present the best overall figures for Iran's population during the period in question.

17. Clearly, the forces which later pressed on nomads as the price of bread rose had the same kind of effect when the supply of grain was disrupted for other reasons.

18. This decline was, of course, not entirely voluntary; *vide* Reza Shah's forced settlement schemes during the 1930s.

## *Chapter* 4

1. As the preceding discussion of herding practice may have indicated, herding of mixed stock complicates the organization of labor in households and camps.

2. I have calculated the average annual yield of an animal as follows. Female sheep yielded roughly $11.00 per year in wool and dairy products; female goats, roughly $7.00 per year in *kork* and dairy products. An average male goat sold for meat would bring about $22.00 (a weighted average including sales of both adults and kids), and a similar average male sheep would bring about $30.00. Discounting for the moment the meat value of female animals sold at the end of their breeding careers, we may assume that each year each ewe or nanny produced a cash return for meat equal to one-half the value of the corresponding male animal, i.e., roughly $11.00 per nanny or $15.00 per ewe. The average yield of a ewe in one year was thus $26.00, and the average yield of a nanny was $18.00. Given that the Komachi owned roughly two goats for every sheep, the average yield of a single female animal would be $21.00 per year (i.e., two goats at $18.00 each per year plus one sheep at $26.00 per year, all divided by three). As productive female animals comprise approximately 50 percent of all Komachi animal holdings for any herd owner, the annual yield of a genderless "average" animal was one-half the value of the female animals' produce plus the value of the wool or *kork* of the male animals (about $2.50 per animal). Adding as well $1.00 for the meat from female animals (which must be discounted for a yearly value by including the likelihood of loss or death over the animal's breeding life, etc.), the total yield of the "average" Komachi animal becomes $14.00.

3. For the purpose of this analysis, I have assumed that all adult men and women and all children over thirteen are full consumers; children twelve and under count as one-half of one consumer.

4. Note that the animal had to be properly killed, because in accordance with Islamic injunctions the Komachi did not eat improperly slaughtered meat. If an animal died before it could be properly killed, its body was dragged out of camp and left for carrion. People lamented the waste, but I never saw or heard of anyone eating meat obtained under those circumstances.

5. Interestingly, as some of the times when animals were killed were related to the ritual calendar or to predictable proximity to major shrines (as on migration), there were periods in which camps were filled with meat, meat was eaten at nearly every meal, and households were actually exchanging meat from sacrificial animals that they had all killed.

6. Work here means physical labor. Obviously, it was not the case that

wealthy Komachi men did no work; however, within the limits of their economic order they did as little as they could.

7. As I argue below, I believe that this relationship between labor and herd size is itself dubious.

## Chapter 5

1. It is important to note here that the wealthiest Komachi did not simply own animals; they also owned irrigated land in both summer and winter quarters. The crops grown on this land included wheat, barley, various legumes, and citrus fruit and melons in the *garmsir*. As the Komachi worked as primary producers on none of this land, all land subject to land reform regulations had been divided with the Komachi's sharecroppers. Since the divisions were recent and not fully completed, most Komachi preferred not to talk openly about their agricutural holdings, though all complained about what they had lost due to land reform. Reading between the lines of their very indirect answers, few Komachi seem to have prospered greatly from their agricultural holdings. Rather, the holdings provided them with a supplement in cash and kind to their primary income from their herds. The statement from one landowner that "I don't get my breakfasts from my land" seemed to be a not inaccurate description of agriculture's post–land reform contribution to the Komachi economy. Certainly no wealthy Komachi had any illusions about settling and becoming agriculturalists (cf. Barth 1961). Nonetheless, ownership of conjoined land and water rights assured the nomads access to water for their animals and to some pasturage around villages. For these reasons the Komachi had made, and continued to make, great efforts to own land.

2. I have excluded the households of widows with no co-resident children from the sample, hence the quartiles of 16 rather than 18 households. The widows, all in their late 60s or older, maintained semi-independent households by living in camp with a married child. Thus, though they lived in their own tents, and were often quite independent in many economic matters, neither their needs or costs made them comparable with other households.

3. While the Komachi were far less stratified than the major pastoral confederation of western Iran, where members of the tribal elite owned thousands of animals as well as vast estates, it is perhaps worth mentioning that the distribution of wealth and of resources among the Komachi resembled that in the Malay village of Sedaka that James Scott has recently used to exemplify rural class conflict (Scott 1985).

4. In fact, for the Yörük and the Komachi, inheritance and age of household combined predict respectively 35 and 40 percent of the variation in household wealth.

5. As I noted earlier, given the division of labor, widows were able to maintain independent households, but widowers with no daughters either had to remarry or move in with a married son or daughter. In practice, most men

predeceased their wives, and few men lived to see all their children married off.

6. This figure is only an estimate. I derive it as follows. In 1975, a good year, roughly 3,800 kids and lambs were born to the Komachi flocks. In 1974, a bad but not disastrous year, just over 1,000 animals were born. On the other hand, animal sales in both 1975 and 1974 were nearly identical: 1132 and 1200 respectively. Komachi could maintain a substantial sales level during bad years because they held fairly large numbers of adult male animals in their flocks. A 75 percent reduction in newborn animals thus reduced not the bad year's sales but the potential sales of the subsequent years. Assuming that the Komachi made up some of that loss in each of the next three years, a bad year caused a 25 percent drop in the sale of meat, and unrecapturable 60 to 75 percent drop in dairy production (which could be mitigated some-what by shifts in Komachi consumption), and some increase in fodder and water costs. Based on 1974–75 prices, this would cost the Komachi about $36,000 in revenue and perhaps an additional $4,000 in fodder and water. That is a decline of about 37 percent over the revenues of a good year. It is quite clear that two or more bad years in a row would magnify the effect of the loss dramatically. While it is difficult to make simple comparisons, Irons (1975:179-180) gives figures for the Yomut showing a roughly 65 percent de-cline in both cash and total income from a good year to a bad year (2250 to 770 tomans). Given this, my figure for the Komachi may well be conservative.

7. One early response to this economic pressure was entrepreneurship. Married employers of no great fortune often sought to improve their incomes by buying and selling animals bought from other tribes, fruits and vegetables bought in the *garmsir*, or other goods. The Komachi called this type of activ-ity *momale*. While the rewards of this wheeling and dealing were occasionally great, Komachi losses nearly equaled if not outweighed gains. No venture, no matter how successful, solved the problem of a lack of animals, which were the real capital needed to create and recreate independence. To some degree, this downward spiral parallels the one Barth (1961) describes for the Basseri, though among the Komachi it ends in shepherding, not settlement. In both cases the impoverishment occurs from the conjunction of the lack of an ade-quate breeding flock with the ever-increasing costs of a growing and maturing household.

8. The following discussions present models of the economic develop-mental cycle of Komachi shepherd and employer households. As with all models of this type, the data do not represent any single household. Rather, the model presents the broad outlines of a complex reality; my intention is only to show the kinds of forces operating on shepherd households, the kinds of predictable crises they will face, and the likely long-term trajectories that shepherd and employer households will follow. To do this, I have chosen to build my model about mean figures: mean inheritance, mean growth rate for herds, mean figures for household demographic structure, mean yield per ani-mal, and mean income for shepherding. I stress again that the use of such data oversimplifies the complexity of the process with which I am concerned;

it presents a sketch, not a detailed portrait, of Komachi economic reality.

9. Neither employers nor shepherds marry young, but shepherds marry later then employers. It is my impression—the sample is far too small to have any statistical significance—that the Komachi shepherds most likely to achieve ultimate economic success are those who have living fathers and still work for a number of years (perhaps as many as twenty) before they marry. Then, combining the herd they have accumulated through working and the inheritance they receive from their father, they may well have animals enough to be independent through the remainder of their lives. Given that their fathers also married at an average age of 36, there is little likelihood that more than a very few sons of shepherds will enjoy this happy concatenation of events. The late marriage of shepherds is both a reflection of and a factor in their manner of social reproduction.

10. As with many other things, it is difficult to speak of an average herd. It generally seems the case that poorer men have a larger proportion of breeding stock in their herds than do wealthy men. One result of this is that poorer households have a higher average rate of long-term herd growth than do wealthy ones. While this might appear a good thing, in fact it reflects the reality that poor households produce little or no surplus and thus cannot afford to leave male animals—in effect, cash on the hoof—unsold. The relatively large number of male animals that wealthy herd owners retain enables them to gain a greater absolute return on their meat production (bigger animals equals more meat equals more money) and provides them a cushion against bad years, an ambulatory surplus that can be sold off when the need arises.

11. The preceding discussion points to a reality of Komachi (and probably, in general, Southwest Asian pastoral) life that is worth noting. Pastoral economies like that of the Komachi operate quite near the practical limits of social reproduction. Their continued existence as people balanced between some form of traditional economy and a much more clearly determinate form of capitalist production is very precarious, and is probably tilting against pastoralism per se.

## Chapter 6

1. Indeed, the Komachi often spoke of important tribespeople as heavy (*sangin*), a trope that successfully caught both realities of wealth and power.

2. In fact, the ambiguities are even greater. Given the kind of distribution of wealth I have described above, it would seem that three classes of Komachi households exist: those with animals enough to hire labor—employers, or *arbabs*; those that supplied labor—shepherds, or *chupans*; and those that did neither—I call them independent households, for whom the Komachi also used the term *arbab*. But even though my field data showed measurable differences in the economic circumstances of independent households versus the

households of employers and shepherds, it seems more reasonable to think of the category "independent household" as a null set. Careful examination of the households in this category showed that most were either young households likely to become employer or shepherd households as they passed through their full developmental cycles, or they were the households of older persons, former employers and former shepherds who, for radically different reasons, were living modest lives in their old ages. More than two-thirds of all independent household had been established less than fifteen years or more than thirty years, two-thirds had no more than 3.5 consumers, and fully one-third had two consumers or less, generally a husband and wife or a widow. Thus while Komachi society seen synchronically seemed divided into three classes (employers, shepherds, and independents), diachronically and practically only two significant categories remained: employers and shepherds. At bottom the tribe was composed of wealthy herd owners whose herds not only produced a substantial surplus but also reproduced a breeding flock that permitted the establishment of new employer households, and smallholders whose herds were insufficient to both support the members of the household and permit children to receive an inheritance that would assure their economic future. These are clearly two quite different categories, which the Komachi terms *arbab* and *chupan* obscure.

3. In their discussions of practice theory, both Ortner and Karp take it, or Bourdieu at least, to task for seeing actors as motivated by "what is materially and politically useful for them within the context of their cultural and historical situations" (Ortner 1984:151) or like "small-scale entrepreneurs, struggling to acquire" (Karp 1986:133). While I would not wish to argue that these are the forces that motivate action everywhere, I think the Komachi ethnography makes it abundantly clear that among them, too, these are indeed the primary motivating forces. Put another way, I find that Bourdieu's description of what the people of Kabylia seem to be doing very evocative of the Komachi. People elsewhere may have other motivations, but for the Komachi economic domination was generally so intertwined with domination in general that they appear inseparable. See Lambton 1953 for a discussion of the traditional relationship between wealth and power in Persia. For another view of both *komak* and the way in which wealth was converted into power and then into more wealth see Black-Michuad's discussion of the Lur of Western Iran (1972,1986). I have discussed the relationship between wealth and power, and its effect on local-level Persian politics, in an earlier piece (Bradburd 1983).

4. Indeed, I often wondered if the melodramatic flow of events around Qadam's hiring had not been orchestrated by his wife just to that end. If indeed she did set a trap, then Ali and his wife blundered into it with a most satisfying hue and cry.

5. As most shepherds could not afford not to work, they had to judge who would be their best employer in the coming year. Perhaps shepherds weighed their decisions, asking how bad it had been, how likely it was that

another man would be a better employer, how much beyond salary the new employer offered as a patron, how near or far kin would be. But in speaking with shepherds I never got a completely clear explanation of why they did or did not move. Here I suspect one finds oneself deeply in the throes of Bourdieu's habitus: Unconscious dispositions based on a lifetime of experience lead a man to move or stay at any one time. In practice, though, the shepherds seem to have moved every four or five years. In effect, when they or their kin had had enough, when the antagonisms were too great to hide, they moved. And it seems clear that after having spent some time working for an employer the shepherd was less likely to be mollified by the negotiating process than he was previously, and therefore was more likely to switch employers. In the game of promises, the current employer was at a disadvantage. A shepherd may have believed that he would get better treatment from a new employer—indeed, a potential new employer was likely to listen patiently to a shepherd's complaint and swear that nothing like that had ever happened in his camp, so that the shepherd could almost deny the reality of his experience— but the belief that his current employer would change was far harder to sustain.

## Chapter 7

1. Koranic prohibitions are never mentioned in common discourse, but implicitly (and obviously) define the pool of potential spouses. The Komachi take these proscriptions as a given, and only the appearance of someone as out of place as an anthropologist creates speculation that these proscriptions are not natural and universal.

2. In fact, status endogamy has a Koranic base and is common throughout the Middle East.

3. While 50 percent of all first cousin marriages contracted prior to 1974 were father's brother's daughter marriages, as against 22 percent mother's brother's daughter marriages, 5 of the 9 first cousin marriages contracted during 1974 and 1975 were mother's brother's daughter marriages. Overall, 42 percent of all cousin marriages were father's brother's daughter marriages and 32 percent were mother's brother's daughter marriages. Since many examinations of cousin marriage in the Middle East have samples only marginally larger than that from the Komachi, one well might be concerned about the real strengths of the preferences those studies suggest. For the sake of comparison, let me note that Barth (1961:35) reports that 29 percent of Basseri marriages were cousin marriages (6.7 percent of which are between agnatic cousins); Bates (1973:66) notes that 44.5 percent of Yoruk marriages were with close kin (that is, within two generation, ascending or descending): 35.6 percent were with true first cousins, and 20 percent were with patriparallel cousins; Tapper (1979) reports that of 89 Shahsevan marriages, 24 (27 percent)

were with first cousins, of which 8 were father's brother's daughter marriages and 11 were mother's brother's daughter marriages.

4. In particular, Lawrence Rosen (1979), Hildred Geertz (1979), and Pierre Bourdieu (1977) describe systems very similar to that of the Komachi. Nancy Tapper has also presented detailed descriptions of how peasants, townspeople, and tribespeople get married that very effectively describe the kind of system one sees among the Komachi (1981; Tapper and Tapper 1982). While I see affiliation as somewhat less negotiable than Rosen does, my analysis has been informed by these works.

5. The difference in the distribution of close kin marriages among employers and employees is statistically significant: $x^2 = 10.15$, $p < .01$.

6. The following discussion should make it clear that the formation or re-formation of ties was hardly a mechanical process made inevitable by pre-existing structures.

7. Late summer and early fall, the period in which the Komachi arrange marriages, was a time of intense social activity. Fantastic amounts of information and disinformation circulated within the tribe. There was both a bonanza of information and an insurmountable logistic tangle. Often several groups met at once, and people circulated all kinds of rumors; the sources and rate of information flow were staggering. My wife and I concentrated all our energies on collecting information during this period. Essentially, we visited and revisited everyone who was involved in marriage negotiations. We checked, to the degree possible, the validity of rumors we heard, and we attempted to find out where they had begun and who had heard them. As constant visitors to and from the tents of people arranging marriages, we too were told rumors that we were supposed to pass on, and we were told what we hoped were peoples' real positions, which we were asked not to pass on. In my recounting of the events, "X said" means that my wife or I heard X say it. Otherwise, we too heard it on the grapevine. As I mentioned, where possible we checked the validity of rumors, but for obvious reasons some were essentially impossible to check. I am not certain that it is important just how true it is that X or Y said what they were reported to have said. What is more important is that their purported words became public, for that became the context within which action had to be taken and events played out.

8. In effect, Ali was asking his patron to put pressure on Kourosh. As Ali's patron was involved in many economic ventures in the region, he certainly might have put pressure on Kourosh had he wished to.

9. Kourosh was Hassan's wife's brother. He also was able to mobilize others to support his case, notably his younger brother, who was a business partner with Hassan, and Kourosh's wife's sister, who was married to Hassan's oldest son (by his first wife). Kourosh also had some moral claim on Hassan, for Kourosh's father had given Kourosh's sister to Hassan as a second wife for no bride price, "as freely given as a sacrifice." Because Hassan was then a widower and Kourosh's father was the most important man in the

tribe, this was an extraordinary act. Despite all that, several people claimed Kourosh arranged the match by blackmailing Hassan, threatening to give Kaniz to a widower interested in marrying Hassan's older unmarried daughter and thereby blocking her last chance at a respectable marriage.

10. Among other things, their settling meant that they spent the winter months together, isolated from all other tribesmen.

Given Barth's (1961) discussion of Basseri settlement, I think, that it might be useful to briefly discuss Komachi settlement here. As of 1975, very few Komachi had settled. Those who had were almost all relatively wealthy Komachi with many daughters and few sons. Using their daughters and the children of villagers as laborers, they ran carpet workshops capitalized by *tarafs*, in Qaryeit-al-Arab. In 1975, one recently married son of a poorer employer also settled to run a carpet workshop. As I noted above, poorer employers' sons generally were on a downward economic trajectory. This young man's settling clearly was an attempt to maintain status in the face of economic difficulty. It was too early to tell whether this was the beginning of a trend.

11. That is, until the marriage ceremony Kobra would live in Kourosh's house and would continue to work for him as a daughter, without pay. As Kourosh was really an overseer, who drew costs plus a share of the profit on a carpet, in fact he collected Kobra's salary in cash for himself.

12. These kinds of divisions may help explain why *taife* had ideological, not practical, significance.

13. I use the word "possessed" advisedly, for, as with so many other aspects of the Komachi social order, the marriage system was not autochthonous but part of the culture of the larger Islamic / Middle Eastern world of which they were part.

14. These patterns are at once less different and more complicated than they seem. From the point of view of the head, the cluster that forms about him is composed of his daughters; from the vantage point of his sons-in-law, the cluster is their wife's kin (father, sisters, etc.), and from a more removed vantage point, two married daughters living in their father's camp are coresident sisters. As H. Geertz (1979) has noted for Moroccan families, in cases like this where ties overlap, the key to coresidence may well be buried in personal history; it may therefore be misleading to simply draw "rules" inductively from observed residence patterns.

15. This is not to say that women did not disagree with each other, or that they lived lives of blissful peace. Women, as did all Komachi, looked first to the interests of the nuclear family household, and they very actively sought to protect them. However, very few disputes *among equals* seemed to arise from what I will call women's issues, for want of a better term. Certainly, Komachi men had no stereotype of women as creating problems (as, for example, Tapper [1979] reports for the Shahsevan). Women's disputes with their kin tended to be continuations of disputes in the male world rather than conflicts exclusive to women's circles.

# Chapter 8

1. I present a more complete discussion of Komachi patron- client relations and an examination of patronage in Persia as a whole in an earlier article (Bradburd 1983).

2. Given the focus of this work, I will not present a full account or analysis of Komachi rituals; the interested reader should consult Bradburd 1984a.

3. At all celebrations there were tents for men and women. At most larger celebrations employers and other guests of high status occupied one tent while men of lower status, shepherds and others, had their own tent.

4. Let me stress, however, that if Komachi rituals were important in social construction and representation, I see it as no more than a latent function. Komachi tribespeople—embedded in a society in which, as recent history has shown, religion was an enormously powerful force, and living within a larger society that presented them with rituals and a sacred ethos that made them meaningful—were confronted by their rituals as objective realities. Participation in them was part of being Persian, being Shi'ite, and being Komachi. Whatever their latent function, the Komachi appeared to have the rituals they did (and this appears to hold for other Persian pastoral groups as well) because they were members of a larger society that supplied them with ritual as it supplied them with language, national identity, or religious dogma.

In this regard, I would like to make one additional comment. It should be apparent that Komachi society was not a seamlessly functioning whole. Rather, it lacked coherence in some ways and appeared to lack stability as a social entity. I have often wondered if the apparent lack of integration was not supported by the externality of the Komachi Shi'ite theodicy. That is, because it was not particular to them, but was drawn from a world religion, the Komachi theodicy did not have to account for the particulars of their life by explaining the particulars; it merely embedded them in a larger system of meaning. Ambiguity was sustainable at the local level because order was taken care of at a distant, cosmic remove. If the Komachi had not been members of a "big" tradition, if their system of belief had been specific to their circumstances, I wonder if the discontinuities of their lives would have been harder to sustain.

5. This grounding of kinship in sacred history and sacred history in kinship is by no means limited to the Komachi. Michael Fischer (1980:173ff.) discusses this as a general feature of popular Shi'ite Islam, and Robert Dillon (1976) describes the relationship of kinship to ritual in a Kermani agricultural village.

6. What carried a stigma here was being a pastoralist. These attitudes did not therefore hold between Komachi and other nomadic pastoralists, and so the contempt of the settled world did not prevent members of the tribe from joining other tribes. Far from it: the hostility of the settled world made the Komachi feel a real commonality with other tribes, a kind of commonality that was at best neutral with regard to movement from one tribe to another.

## *Chapter* 9

1. In this regard it is useful to recall that, in effect, membership in the tribe or in a camp theoretically assured all Komachi free access to pasture. While I have noted above that restrictions on access to animals somewhat mitigated the reality of this freedom, employers did not force poor Komachi to become free laborer shepherds by denying them access to land. In sum, we do not see here the functional equivalent of enclosures in "primitive accumulation" (Marx 1967).

2. Note that in these Islamically based understandings property is seen as being divisible, transferable, and salable. Thus, while the encroachment of the world market system may have led to quite significant changes in the nature of the Komachi economy—including perhaps the transformation of labor power into a commodity—it did not lead to the breakdown of a "traditional" economy based on communal property or a lineage mode of production. Rather, one might say that the Komachi, and by extension most Islamic societies, were in a way preadapted for certain kinds of capitalist relations of production, and certainly for looking upon animals (the primary means of production) as private and disposable property.

3. In what is perhaps an extreme illustration of this point, one day a very wealthy nontribal woman visited our Komachi camp. Later the woman walked away into the bush to relieve herself, with a female servant walking some paces behind carrying a ewer (*aftabe*) for cleansing oneself. As they walked off, our hostess commented, "See, she's so rich she doesn't even have to wipe her own ass."

4. An understanding of the positive valuation of work one sees in our society might be found by reading Weber and reversing the causal arrow between the Protestant ethic and the rise of capitalism. Works by Thompson (1967) and Gutman (1973) have pointed out eloquently the profound transformation in the social value of labor that the rise of capitalism entails, while work by medievalists such as Le Goff has amply demonstrated the more ambiguous value of labor in the Middle Ages (1980:71–86, 121). With regards to circumstances in Persia (and without entering into the details of the important and quite serious debates on how to effectively categorize the nature of traditional Persian society—as, for instance, representing a feudal or an Asiatic mode of production [see Katouzian 1973, 1978, 1981; Abrahamian 1974, 1975]), it seems quite clear that the attitude toward labor prevailing among the Komachi and the society that surrounded them was at base precapitalist and representative of attitudes toward labor in a tributary mode of production. That is, in a system in which surplus was extracted from agricultural workers through essentially political means (including the threat of physical violence) rather than through the purchase of labor power, there is little impetus for the valorization of labor itself. Indeed, there is little reason for the worker to value labor or to seek to work with great efficiency, for the surplus that he or she produces is an invitation to predation. On the other hand, from

the point of view of the overlord, as long as the surplus is being produced, it matters little how well or how efficiently it is being produced. This is so because all the overlord seeks is an absolute quantity of surplus rather than a proportion of what emerges from the labor process. In short, the cultural attitudes towards labor that I have described for the Komachi may, in the final analysis, be explained by reference to material conditions.

5. This returns us to a point I made in my discussion of the general characteristics of pastoral economies, where I noted the claim that hired shepherds were less dependable than members of one's own household and that hiring them would lead to a declining rate of herd growth. Still, one finds virtually everywhere that wealthy herd owners hire shepherds—that is, laborers who may care less and work less carefully. This says something about pastoralists' perceptions of the relationship of drudgery to desired yield and of the value of their labor versus a maximization of yield. Indeed, it seems that Barth's (1961, 1964) description of the falling rate of profit among wealthy herd owners may be a classic description of people finding the drudgery of labor not worth the reward, magnified by a culturally based devaluation of labor. Whatever else they are, these attitudes toward work and profit are *not* captialist.

6. For an early discussion of the problem of articulation of modes of production see Foster-Carter (1978); see Friedmann (1978, 1980) for a discussion of simple commodity production. See Roseberry 1983 and Scott 1985 for extremely cogent discussions of shifts in local systems of production under the influence of world historical change. Wolf's work (1982) in this area is, of course, seminal.

7. We should note that the tribe is losing members of its core rather than its periphery.

8. Southwest Asian pastoralism almost everywhere entails extensive use of an environment that provides only scarce, scattered, and seasonally variable resources. As a result, while pastoral populations as a whole have at times been quite numerous (comprising perhaps 35 percent of the population of nineteenth century Iran), the primary residential groups of all Southwest Asian pastoralist societies are small—usually no larger than twenty households, and often substantially smaller—and generally they are dispersed over a wide territory. For most Southwest Asian pastoralists, maintenance of a herd also requires a pattern of annual migrations covering a substantial distance. Mobility is an important aspect of pastoral adaptation, and settlement, forced or otherwise, is generally incompatible with the maintenance of substantial herds.

9. We must recall here that land was important not simply for the agricultural products and income that it produced but because it gave nomads both water rights and access to pasture in a given area. Ownership of land ratified and regularized the nomads' relationship to a particular area and its resources so that they were no longer just interlopers.

10. Close kin marriage has structural effects similar to those of patri-

parallel cousin marriage, which is of course only a special type of close kin marriage (see particularly Murphy and Kasden 1959; Kasden and Murphy 1967; and Boon and Schneider 1974 for discussions of the structural implications of patriparallel cousin marriage).

11. This expansion was probably spurred by population growth, but population pressure per se was certainly not the only force; at the very least, desire for previously unused pasture and for agricultural land were factors as well. I should add that Kelly (1985) presents a detailed discussion of this issue with regard to the Nuer and Dinka, and argues strongly against population pressure as the "cause" of Nuer expansion.

12. In point of fact, it is not only the Komachi or Persian tribes in general that are unstable and that show evidence of being built by agglomeration and disappearing from view as their members mysteriously slip away to become part of something else. Any casual look at human history or prehistory suggests that this process of becoming and unbecoming was universal. Not only do we occasionally tend to forget that structure and history are not distinct, we often seem to forget that social bodies, the ones we examine and the ones in which we dwell, are ephemeral. I am quite convinced that the process I describe for the Komachi does not at all make them unique. What makes them unique is that their lack of continuity, their instability as I have called it, was absolutely manifest. Chagnon's work on the Yanomamo (1977) and Watson's on the Tairora (1970) are interesting examples of the effectiveness of studies that do *not* presume that social systems are particularly stable.

13. Ironically, this appears to have been a major period of confederacy building.

## Chapter 10

1. For example, because he did not think through his discovery that the Lurs he categorized as members of the "upper stratum" owned the means of production while those he categorized as "lower stratum" did not, Black-Michaud failed to see that the Lurs did indeed have classes (1986:114ff.). Among other things, this limited his ability to account effectively for historical transformations in Lur society.

2. Following Scott (1985, 1986, 1987), Adas (1986), and others, I here assume that class conflict or class struggle in the countryside involves many forms of resistance that fall short of full-fledged rebellion. The sources cited above contain particularly well developed theoretical discussions of this extended view of class conflict and particularly rich examples of this kind of class conflict.

3. For pastoralists such as the Komachi, naturally occurring pasture and water are raw materials consumed by animals in the production process and are part of the production process. Population and population density are themselves determined by the direct relationships of animals to pasture and

water and of people to animals, the latter, of course, mediated by exchange rates in the market. Trade routes are also essentially an economic resource; state presence, while not purely economic, shapes the productive process in many ways.

# REFERENCES CITED

Abbot, K. E.
  1983          *Cities and Trade: Consul Abbott on the Economy and Society of Iran* 1847–1866. Edited by A. Amanat. London: Ithaca Press.

Abrahamian, E.
  1974          Oriental Despotism in Qajar Iran. *International Journal of Middle Eastern Studies* 5(1):3–31.
  1975          European Feudalism and Middle Eastern Despotisms. *Science and Society* 39:129–56

Adas, M.
  1986          From Footdragging to Flight: The Evasive History of Peasant Avoidance Protest in South and Southeast Asia. *Journal of Peasant Studies* 13(2):64–86.

Altorki, S.
  1986          *Women in Saudi Arabia*. New York: Columbia University Press.

Amouzgar, J.
1977          *Iran: An Economic Profile.* Washington: The Middle East Insti-
              tute.

Asad, T.
1978          Equality in Nomadic Social Systems. *Critique of Anthropology*
              3(11):57–65.

Avery, P.W. and J.B. Simmons
1974          Persia on a Cross of Silver 1880–1890. *Middle Eastern Studies*
              19(3):259–86.

Banani, A.
1961          *The Modernization of Iran, 1921–1941.* Stanford: Stanford Uni-
              versity Press.

Barth, F.
1960          Nomadism in the Mountain and Plateau Areas of Southwest
              Asia, In *Problems of the Arid Zone.* Paris: UNESCO.
1961          *Nomads of South Persia.* Boston: Little, Brown.
1964          Capital, Investment, and the Social Structure of a Pastoral
              Nomad Group in South Persia. In *Capital, Saving, and Credit
              in Peasant Societies,* edited by R. Firth and B.S. Yamey. Chi-
              cago: Aldine.

Barfield, T.
1981          *The Central Asian Arabs of Afghanistan.* Austin: University
              of Texas Press.

Barthold, W.
1984 [1903]   *An Historical Geography of Iran.* Translated by S. Soucek.
              Princeton: Princeton University Press.

Bates, D.
1971          The Role of the State in Peasant Nomad Mutualism. *Anthropo-
              logical Quarterly* 44:109–31.
1973          *Nomads and Farmers: A Study of the Yörük of Southeastern
              Turkey.* Ann Arbor: University of Michigan Museum of An-
              thropology.

Bates, D. and S. Lees
1977          The Role of Exchange in Productive Specialization. *American
              Anthropologist* 79:824–41.

Beck, L. and N. Keddie
1978          *Women in the Muslim World.* Cambridge: Harvard University
              Press.

Beck, L.
1980          Herdowners and Hired Shepherds: The Qashqa'i of Iran. *Ethnology* 19(3):327–51.
1986          *The Qashqa'i of Iran*. New Haven: Yale University Press.

Bharier, J.
1968          A Note on the Population of Iran, 1900–1966. *Population Studies* 22(2):273–79.
1971          *Economic Development in Iran, 1900–1970*. Oxford: Oxford University Press.
1972          The Growth of Towns and Villages in Iran. *Middle Eastern Studies* 8(1):51–61.

Black-Michaud, J.
1972          Tyranny as a Strategy for Survival in an "Egalitarian" Society. *Man*. (n.s.) 7:614–34.
1976          The Economics of Oppression: Ecology and Stratification in an Iranian Society. Ph.D. dissertation, School of Oriental and African Studies, University of London.
1986          *Sheep into Land*. Cambridge: Cambridge University Press.

Boon, J. and D. Schneider
1974          Kinship vis-a-vis Myth: Contrasts in Levi-Strauss' Approach to Cross-Cultural Comparison. *American Anthropologist* 76:799–817.

Bourdieu, P.
1977          *Outline of a Theory of Practice*. Cambridge: Cambridge University Press.

Bradburd, D.
1980          Never Give a Shepherd an Even Break: Class and Labor among the Komachi of Kerman Iran. *American Ethnologist* 7(4): 603–20.
1982          Volatility of Animal Wealth among Southwest Asian Pastoralists. *Human Ecology* 10(1):85–106.
1983          National Conditions and Local Level Political Structures: Patronage in Pre-revolutionary Iran. *American Ethnologist* 10(1):23–40.
1984a         Ritual and Southwest Asian Pastoralists: The Implications of the Komachi Case. *Journal of Anthropological Research* 40(3):380–93.
1984b         The Rules and the Game: The Practice of Komachi Marriage. *American Ethnologist* 11(4):738–53.
1989          Producing their Fates: Why Poor Basseri Settled but Poor Komachi and Yomut Did Not. *American Ethnologist* 16(3): 502–17.

British East India Company
    1727              Factory Records, Bandar Abbas [The Gombroon Diary]. India
                      Office Records Library (London): G/29/3.

Burnham, P.
    1979              Spatial Mobility and Political Centralization in Pastoral Socie-
                      ties. In *Pastoral Production and Society*, edited by Equipe
                      Ecologie et Anthropologie des Sociétés Pastorales. Cambridge:
                      Cambridge University Press.

Busse, H. trans.
    1972              *History of Persia under Qajar Rule*. New York: Columbia Uni-
                      versity Press.

Chagnon, N.
    1977              *Yanomamo*. New York: Holt, Rinehart and Winston.

Chayanov, A. V.
    1966              *The Theory of Peasant Economy*. Edited by D. Thorner, B.
                      Kerblay, and R.E.F. Smith. Homewood, IL: Richard D. Irwin.

Curzon, G. N.
    1966              *Persia and the Persian Question*. 2 vols. New York: Barnes and
                      Noble.

Dahl, G.
    1979              Ecology and Equality: The Boran Case. In *Pastoral Production
                      and Society*, edited by Equipe Ecologie et Anthropologie des
                      Sociétés Pastorales. Cambridge: Cambridge University Press.

Dillon, R.
    1976              Carpet Capitalization and Craft Involution in Kerman, Iran.
                      Ph.D. dissertation, Department of Anthropology, Columbia
                      University.

Eickelman, D.
    1976              *Moroccan Islam*. Austin: The University of Texas Press.
    1981              *The Middle East: An Anthropological Approach*. Englewood
                      Cliffs, NJ: Prentice Hall.

English, P. W.
    1966              *City and Village in Iran*. Madison: University of Wisconsin
                      Press.

Ferrier, J.P.
    1856              *Caravan Journeys and Wanderings in Persia, Afganistan, Turki-
                      stan, and Beloochistan*. Translated by W. Jessie; edited by H.
                      D. Seymour. London: John Murray.

Fischer, M. M. J.
1980        *Iran from Religious Dispute to Revolution.* Cambridge: Har-
            vard University Press.

Floor, W.
1984        The Bahrain Project of 1754. *Persica* XI:129–48.
1986        The Dutch East India Companies' Trade with Sind in the 17th
            and 18th Centuries. *Moyen Orient et Ocean Indien XVIe–XIXe
            s.* 3:111–44.

Foster-Carter, A.
1978        The Modes of Production Controversy. *New Left Review*
            107:47–78.

Friedmann, H.
1978        Simple Commodity Production and Wage Labour in the Amer-
            ican Plains. *Journal of Peasant Studies* 6(1):71–100.
1980        Household Production and the National Economy: Concepts
            for the Analysis of Agrarian Formations. *Journal of Peasant
            Studies* 7(2):158–84.

Fryer, J.
1909, 1912,  *A New Account of East India and Persia, Being Nine Years
1915         Travels, 1672–1681,* vols. 19, 20, 39. Edited by Wm. Crooke.
             London: Hakluyt Society, Second Series.

Garthwaite, G.
1983        *Khans and Shahs.* Cambridge: Cambridge University Press.

Geertz, H.
1979        The Meaning of Kinship Ties. In *Meaning and Order in Moroc-
            can Society,* edited by C. Geertz, H. Geertz, and L. Rosen.
            Cambridge: Cambridge University Press.

Giddens, A.
1984        *The Constitution of Society.* Los Angeles: University of Cali-
            fornia Press.

Gilbar, G.
1976        Demographic Developments in Late Qajar Persia, 1870–1906.
            *Asian and African Studies* 11(2):125–56.
1978        Persian Agriculture in the Late Qajar Period. *Asian and African
            Studies* 12(3):312–65.
1979        The Persian Economy in the Mid-19th Century. *Die Welt des
            Islams* XIX:177–211.

Goldsmid,F.etal.
1876        *Eastern Persia: An Account of the Persian Boundary Commis-*

*sion*, 1870, 71, 72, vol. 1. *The Geography and Narratives*. London: Macmillan.

Graham, R.
1979        *Iran: The Illusion of Power*. New York: St. Martin's Press.

Great Britain (government)
1896        General and Commercial Report on the Consular Districts of Kerman and Persian Beluchistan. Government of Great Britain, Accounts and Papers, Report on Trade for 1894–5, Number 1671, 1896. Public Records Office (London).
1912        Report on Trade of the Consular District of Kerman. India Office Records Library, London.
1939        Kerman: Consular Diaries 1931–1939. India Office Records Library (London).
1942        Persia: Kerman Economic and Trade 1924–1942. India Office Records Library (London): L/P&S/12/3444.

Gutman, H.
1977        *Work, Culture and Society in Industrializing America*. New York: Random House.

Halliday, F.
1979        *Iran: Dictatorship and Development*. Harmondsworth: Penguin.

Holmes, J.
1974        Credit in Iranian Villages. *Man* (n.s.) 9(3):311.

Hooglund, E.
1982        *Land and Revolution in Iran, 1960–1980*. Austin: University of Texas Press.

Iran Statistical Centre
1966–67        *Statistical Yearbook*. Tehran.
1970–71        *Statistical Yearbook*. Tehran.
1972–73        *Statistical Yearbook*. Tehran.
1973–74        *Statistical Yearbook*. Tehran.

Irons, W.
1975        *The Yomut Turkmen: A Study of Social Organization Among a Central Asian Turkic-Speaking Population*. Ann Arbor: University of Michigan Museum of Anthropology.
1979        Political Stratification among Pastoral Nomads. In *Pastoral Production and Society*, edited by Equipe Ecologie et Anthropologie des Sociétés Pastorales. Cambridge: Cambridge University Press.

Issawi, C.
1971            *The Economic History of Iran*. Chicago: University of Chicago
                Press.

Johnson, G.
1982            Organizational Structure and Scalar Stress. In *Theory and
                Explanation in Archaeology*, edited by C. Renfrew, M. J.
                Rowlands, and B. A. Segraves. London and New York: Aca-
                demic Press.
1983            Decision Making Organization and Pastoral Nomad Camp
                Size. *Human Ecology* 11(2):175–200.

Karp, I.
1986            Agency and Social Theory: A Review of Anthony Giddens.
                *American Ethnologist* 13(1):131–37.

Kasden, L. and R. Murphy
1967            Agnation and Endogamy: Some Further Considerations. *South-
                western Journal of Anthropology* 23:1–14.

Katouzian, M. A. H.
1973            Land Reform in Iran: A Case Study in the Political Economy
                of Social Engineering. *Journal of Peasant Studies* 1:220–39.
1978            Oil versus Agriculture: A Case of Dual Resource Depletion.
                *Journal of Peasant Studies* 5:347–69.
1981            *The Political Economy of Modern Iran*. New York: New York
                University Press.

Keddie, N.
1972            Stratification, Social Control and Capitalism in Iranian Vil-
                lages Before and After Land Reform. In *Rural Politics and So-
                cial Change in the Middle East*, edited by I. Harik and R.
                Antoun. Bloomington: Indiana University Press.
1978            Class Structure and Political Power in Iran Since 1796. *Iranian
                Studies* 11:305–30.

Kelly, R.
1985            *The Nuer Conquest*. Ann Arbor: University of Michigan Press.

Kielstra, N. O.
1973            Credit Facilities in Iranian Villages. *Man* (n.s.) 8:110–11.

Lambton, A. K. S.
1953            *Landlord and Peasant in Persia*. London: Oxford University
                Press.

Layard, H.
1887         *Early Travels through Persia, Susiana, and Babylonia,* vol. 2.
             New York: Longmans Green.

Lee, R.
1979         *The !Kung San.* Cambridge: Cambridge University Press.

Le Goff, J.
1980         *Time, Work and Culture in the Middle Ages.* Translated by A.
             Goldhammer. Chicago: University of Chicago Press.

Loeffler, R.
1976         Recent Economic Changes in Boir Ahmad: Regional Growth
             Without Development. *Iranian Studies* 9(4):266–87.

Lorimer, D. H. L.
1908         A Report on Pusht-i-Kuh. Typescript, copy in author's posses-
             sion.

Mansfield, E.
1962         Entry, Gibrat's Law and the Growth of Firms. *American Eco-
             nomic Review* 52:1031–34.

Marx, K.
1967         *Capital,* vol. 1. Translated by S. Moore and E. Aveling. New
             York: International Publishers.

Murphy, R. and L. Kasden
1959         The Structure of Parallel Cousin Marriage. *American Anthro-
             pologist* 61:17–29.

Nelson, C.
1974         Public and Private Politics: Women in the Middle Eastern
             World. *American Ethnologist* 1(3):551–63.

Noshirvani, V. F.
1981         The Beginnings of Commercialized Agriculture in Iran. In *The
             Islamic Middle East 700–1900,* edited by A.L. Udovitch,
             Princeton: Darwin Press.

Ortner, S.
1984         Theory in Anthropology Since the Sixties. *Comparative Stud-
             ies in Society and History* 26:126–66.

Pabot, H.
1967         *Report of the Government of Iran: Pasture Development and
             Range Improvement through Botanical and Ecological Stud-
             ies.* Rome: United Nations Food and Agriculture Organization.

Parvin, M. and A. Zamani
1979        Political Economy of Growth and Destruction: A Statistical In-
            terpretation of the Iranian Case. *Iranian Studies* 12:43–78.

Paydarfar, A.
1974        *Social Change in a Southern Province of Iran.* Chapel Hill, NC:
            Institute for Research in Social Science.

Polo, M.
1926        *The Travels of Marco Polo.* Edited by Manuel Komroff. New
            York: Garden City Publishing.

Roseberry, W.
1983        *Coffee and Capitalism in the Venezuelan Andes.* Austin: Uni-
            versity of Texas Press.

Rosen, L.
1979        Social Identity and Points of Attachment: Approaches to Social
            Organization. In *Meaning and Order in Moroccan Society,* ed-
            ited by C. Geertz, H. Geertz, and L. Rosen. Cambridge: Cam-
            bridge University Press.

Sahlins, M.
1963        Poor Man, Rich Man, Big Man, Chief: Political Types in Mela-
            nesia and Polynesia. *Comparative Studies in Society and His-
            tory* 5(3):285–303.
1976        *Culture and Practical Reason.* Chicago: University of Chicago
            Press.
1981        *Historical Metaphors and Mythical Realities.* Ann Arbor: Uni-
            versity of Michigan Press.
1985        *Islands of History.* Chicago: University of Chicago Press.

Salmanzadeh, C.
1980        *Agricultural Change and Rural Society in Southern Iran.* Cam-
            bridge: Middle East and North African Studies Press.

Salzman, P. C.
1967        Political Organization Among Nomadic Peoples. *Proceedings
            of the American Philosophical Society* 111(2):115–31.
1979        Inequality and Oppression in Nomadic Society. In *Pastoral
            Production and Society,* edited by Equipe Ecologie et
            Anthropologie des Sociétés Pastorales. Cambridge: Cambridge
            University Press.

Scherer, F. M.
1970        *Industrial Market Structure and Economic Performance.* Chi-
            cago: Rand McNally.

Scott, J.
1976            *The Moral Economy of the Peasant.* New Haven: Yale University Press.
1985            *Weapons of the Weak.* New Haven: Yale University Press.
1986            Everyday Forms of Peasant Resistance. *Journal of Peasant Studies* 13(2):5–35.
1987            Resistance Without Protest and Without Organization. *Comparative Studies in Society and History* 29(3):417–52.

Smith, C.
1984            Local History in Global Context: Social and Economic Transitions in Western Guatemala. *Comparative Studies in Society and History* 26(2):193–228.

Spooner, B.
1973            *The Cultural Ecology of Pastoral Nomads.* Addison-Wesley Module in Anthropology Number 45. Reading, MA: Addison-Wesley.

Stöber, G.
1978            *Die Afshar Nomadismus im Raum Kerman.* Marburg: Geographischen Institutes der Universität Marburg.

Sykes, P. M.
1902            *Ten Thousand Miles in Persia.* London: John Murray.

Tapper, N.
1981            Direct Exchange and Brideprice: Alternative Forms in a Complex Marriage System. *Man* (n.s.) 16:387–407.

Tapper, N. and R. Tapper
1982            Marriage Preferences and Ethnic Relations among Durrani Pashtuns of Afgan Turkestan. *Folk* 24:157–77.

Tapper, R.
1979a           *Pasture and Politics.* London: Academic Press.
1979b           The Organization of Nomadic Communities in Pastoral Societies of the Middle East. In *Pastoral Production and Society,* edited by Equipe Ecologie et Anthropologie des Sociétés Pastorales. Cambridge: Cambridge University Press.

Thompson, E. P.
1967            Time, Work-Discipline, and Industrial Capitalism. *Past and Present* 38:56–97.
1978            *The Poverty of Theory and Other Essays.* New York: Monthly Review Press.

Tucker, R. ed.
1978            The Marx-Engels Reader. New York: W. W. Norton.

U.S. Department of Agriculture, Economic Research Division

1975          *Cotton and Wool Situation*. Washington, D.C.: Government
             Printing Office.

Wallerstein, I.

1974          *The Modern World System: Capitalist Agriculture and the Ori-
             gins of the European World Economy in the Sixteenth Century.*
             New York: Academic Press.

Watson, J. B.

1970          Society as Organized Flow: the Tairora Case. *Southwestern
             Journal of Anthropology* 26(2):107–24.

Wolf, E.

1982          *Europe and the People Without History*. Berkeley: University
             of California Press.

# INDEX

Smithsonian Series in Ethnographic Inquiry

*Ivan Karp and William L. Merrill, Series Editors*

Ethnography as fieldwork, analysis, and literary form is the distinguishing feature of modern anthropology. Guided by the assumption that anthropological theory and ethnography are inextricably linked, this series is devoted to exploring the ethnographic enterprise.

## ADVISORY BOARD

Richard Bauman (*Indiana University*), Gerald Berreman (*University of California, Berkeley*), James Boon (*Princeton University*), Stephen Gudeman (*University of Minnesota*), Shirley Lindenbaum (*New School for Social Research*), George Marcus (*Rice University*), David Parkin (*University of London*), Roy Rappaport (*University of Michigan*), Renato Rosaldo (*Stanford University*), Annette Weiner (*New York University*), Norman Whitten (*University of Illinois*), and Eric Wolf (*City University of New York*).